Cali

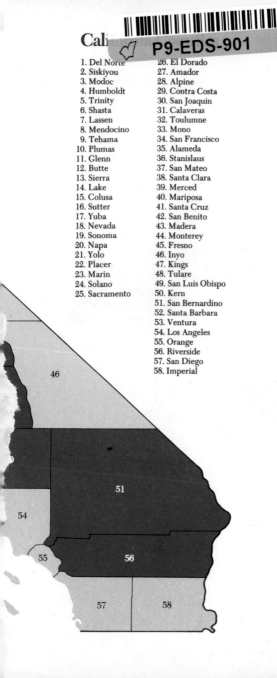

1. Del Norte
2. Siskiyou
3. Modoc
4. Humboldt
5. Trinity
6. Shasta
7. Lassen
8. Mendocino
9. Tehama
10. Plumas
11. Glenn
12. Butte
13. Sierra
14. Lake
15. Colusa
16. Sutter
17. Yuba
18. Nevada
19. Sonoma
20. Napa
21. Yolo
22. Placer
23. Marin
24. Solano
25. Sacramento

26. El Dorado
27. Amador
28. Alpine
29. Contra Costa
30. San Joaquin
31. Calaveras
32. Toulumne
33. Mono
34. San Francisco
35. Alameda
36. Stanislaus
37. San Mateo
38. Santa Clara
39. Merced
40. Mariposa
41. Santa Cruz
42. San Benito
43. Madera
44. Monterey
45. Fresno
46. Inyo
47. Kings
48. Tulare
49. San Luis Obispo
50. Kern
51. San Bernardino
52. Santa Barbara
53. Ventura
54. Los Angeles
55. Orange
56. Riverside
57. San Diego
58. Imperial

eurs' Handbook
fornia Wines

The wine ratings and descriptions in this boo[k] based substantially on evaluations that appear in *C[on]noisseurs' Guide to California Wine*, the leading pu[b]lication covering the California wine scene. The sym[]bols and their meanings are as follows:

- ✿✿✿ An exceptional wine, worth a special search.
- ✿✿ A distinctive wine, likely to be memorable.
- ✿ A fine example of a given type or style.
- ♛ A wine of average quality. The accompanying tasting note provides further description.
- ♂ Below average. A wine to avoid.
- ∮ A wine regarded as a "best buy," based on price and quality.

The Connoisseurs' Handbook
of California Wines

by Charles E. Olken and Earl G. Singer

Editors of *Connoisseurs' Guide to California Wine*

and Norman S. Roby

ALFRED A. KNOPF   NEW YORK

1981

Library of Congress Cataloging in Publication Data
Olken, Charles E.
The connoisseurs' handbook of California wines.
1. Wine and wine making—California.   I. Singer, Earl G.,
joint author. II. Roby, Norman, joint author. III. Title.
TP557.043   1980   641.2′22′09794   79-3476
ISBN 0-394-73973-6

Manufactured in the United States of America
Published November 17, 1980
Second Printing, February 1981

A NOTE ABOUT THE AUTHORS

Charles E. Olken and Earl G. Singer publish *Connoisseurs'
Guide to California Wine,* the foremost newsletter covering
the California wine scene. Norman S. Roby is Associate
Editor of *Vintage* magazine and a well-known wine writer.
All three men live in the San Francisco area.

Composition by The Haddon Craftsmen, Inc.,
Scranton, Pennsylvania
Printing and binding by Kingsport Press, Inc.,
Kingsport, Tennessee
Maps by Jean-Paul Tremblay
End paper chart by James Paul Faris
Design by Lazin and Katalan with Betty Anderson

Contents

California Wine Regions

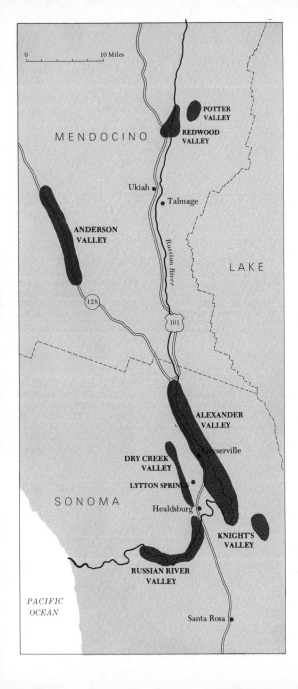

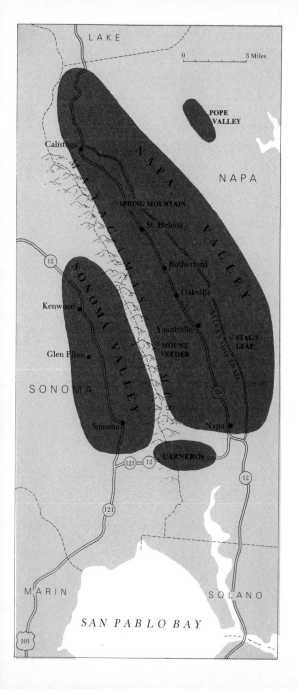

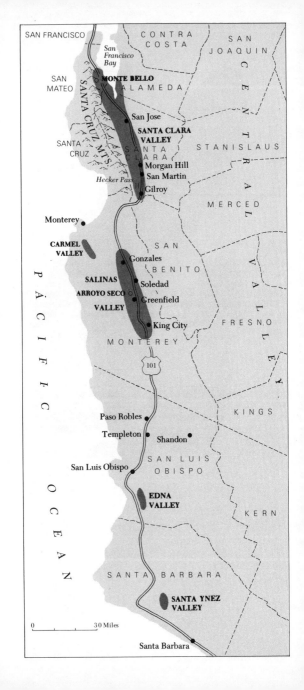

Introduction

In the early 1970s Baron Philippe de Rothschild, proprietor of Château Mouton-Rothschild, was quoted as saying: "California wines are like Coca-Cola—they all taste the same." By 1980 the Baron, like so many of his fellow Europeans, had apparently changed his mind. He came to America to announce a partnership with winery owner Robert Mondavi to produce wine in the Napa Valley.

The Baron is not the first Frenchman—and presumably not the last—to eat crow with his California Cabernet Sauvignon. California now stands center stage in the world theater of wine. Along with highly deserved recognition has come incredible growth—in vineyard acreage, in the amount of wine produced, in the number of wineries and places where grapes are grown. Where once the California wine scene was tranquil and relatively uncomplicated, there is now a veritable maze of names and styles, of "who's" and "where's" as difficult to sort out as anything Europe has to offer—and yet as rewarding.

Connoisseurs' Handbook of California Wines goes straight to the heart of the problem posed by this growth, presenting a comprehensive, concise, and authoritative survey of the wine scene as it exists today. Here are the grape and wine types, the regions large and small, the wineries and their wines, the terms used by winemakers and winelovers. Each producer, each area, each variety receives its own entry and is discussed in depth. A quick cross-check from winery to wine type to vintage can thus yield a complete picture of almost every important wine produced in California.

Nor is the information confined to California. Though California remains preeminent, grape growing and wine production are expanding in other parts of the country as well. Therefore, substantial portions of this book are devoted to the wineries and wines of the Pacific Northwest, the Midwest, the Northeast, and the Southeast. In short, all the major wine regions of the United States and Canada are included.

An American wine is usually identified by either the name of the primary grape type (such as Chenin Blanc) used in making it, or by a more generalized name (such as red table wine) if it is a blend. The first section of the *Connoisseurs' Handbook* deals with the 101 most popular grape and wine types whose names appear on labels in America. GRAPE AND WINE VARIETIES includes virtually all the wine names and grapes likely to appear on labels, omitting only the grape varieties grown experimentally, those used for blending, and those not used to make wine. Included are everything from the leading varietals of California (Cabernet Sauvignon, Chardonnay, Zinfandel) to the most prominent varietals of the East (Seyval Blanc, Baco Noir), to generic names for blends (burgundy, white table wine) and specific wine types (champagne, rosé). In general, any name that turns up on more than one U.S. bottle label will be found here.

The name on the label is only the beginning, however, when it comes to understanding the wine. Especially for the better wines, it is important to find out about the quality of the fruit from which the wine is made—and this quality is frequently dependent on weather during a particular growing season. No winery ever made exciting wine from poor-quality grapes. The second section, entitled CALIFORNIA VINTAGES, contains a detailed analysis of the year-by-year differences in grape and wine quality caused by annual variations in climatic conditions. It focuses on the five wines most amenable to this sort of critical analysis in California: Cabernet Sauvignon, Chardonnay, Pinot Noir, North Coast Zinfandel, and Amador County Zinfandel. These are the wines whose aging characteristics and general quality levels vary the most according to vintage and can be most reasonably described on a vintage basis. The judgments expressed here necessarily apply more directly to wines from Napa, Sonoma, and Mendocino counties than to wines from the

Central Coast or from other still-developing areas where annual data on success or failure is still insufficient to identify distinct vintage patterns. Nevertheless, it is fair to say that the vast majority of wines produced in America that benefit from aging are covered by this discussion of California vintages. The information in this chapter is summarized in a convenient chart form inside the back cover.

The third section is WINE GEOGRAPHY. In compiling the information for it we were reminded of the old real-estate adage that the three most important determinants of success are "location, location, and location." In addition to a good grape variety and good weather, a good location is essential if one is to have a chance at making a fine wine. Unfortunately the helter-skelter growth of the California wine industry during the past decade has frequently led to the planting of high-priced varietals in the wrong places. This comprehensive guide to the areas where grapes are grown spells out in detail the characteristics and quality of the resulting wines. Regions as large as the Willamette Valley or Sonoma County are defined and discussed; so are smaller concentrations, such as Rutherford in the Napa Valley. This section also covers the main locations of California wineries.

Section Four, WINERIES AND WINES IN CALIFORNIA, in many ways represents the heart of the *Connoisseurs' Handbook*. Contained here is a comprehensive listing of California wineries and the wines they make, plus entries on trademarks and secondary labels—more than 300 in all. Each principal entry offers information about the history of the winery, its production and capacity, quality performance, special strengths and interests. Wines representative of its ability and achievement are described using specific tasting terms and given a quality rating. Where appropriate, general price levels are indicated, and wines we consider to be *Best Buys* are specially noted.

In Section Five, WINERIES AND WINES OUTSIDE CALIFORNIA, the *Connoisseurs' Handbook* covers the hundreds of producers in the Pacific Northwest and the rest of the country who are dedicated to making table wines. Treatment is similar to that in Section Four. Omitted are manufacturers of kosher wines, flavored wines, and specialty items whose only relationship to the subject of this book is that their products have been made from grapes.

3

The sixth section, WINE LANGUAGE, is a compendium of wine terminology and descriptions. Included here are terms and phrases appearing on labels, along with clear explanations of their customary usage and true meanings—for example the difference between "produced and bottled by" (a legally controlled expression meaning what it says) and "vinted by" (an uncontrolled phrase totally lacking in definition). This chapter also provides for the sensory terms most often used in describing the appearance, smell, taste, and feel of wine, lending consistency to their use in the wine discussions in Sections Four and Five. We have done this with care but also with the humble awareness that in matters of taste no judgment is final. One person's "complex, elegant, mouth-filling dinner wine" may well be someone else's "unassuming little Zinfandel."

TOURING, the final section, is dedicated to the proposition that nothing beats a first-hand visit to the vineyard and winery. This is a personal, opinionated chapter and probably does a better job of explaining our love affair with California wine than anything else in the book.

Our intention throughout the *Connoisseurs' Handbook* is to provide useful information in a crisp cross-reference format. Each section approaches the California—or American—wine scene from a different angle; yet employed in combination they become a complete guide to wines of the United States, making sense out of the sometimes dizzying array of wines, wineries, places, and words. We hope this book leads to a greater understanding of American wines—and even more, to the greater enjoyment of them.

Much of the material in this book is based upon research and tastings conducted by *Connoisseurs' Guide to California Wine*, edited and published six times a year by Charles Olken and Earl Singer and distributed only by subscription. A one-year subscription is $20. The *Guide* reviews up to 1,500 wines, mostly vintage-dated varietals, each year. Readers of the *Handbook* interested in subscribing to *Connoisseurs' Guide* may receive a free copy of the latest issue by writing to *Connoisseurs' Guide to California Wine*, P.O. Box 11120, San Francisco, California 94101.

Grape and Wine

Varieties

ALEATICO Red muscat-flavored vinifera grape sparsely grown in California (200 acres). Rarely seen as a varietal.

ALICANTE BOUSCHET Thick-skinned red vinifera variety popular with home winemakers. Offered by 1 winery; 5,200 acres in California.

ALIGOTÉ White vinifera grape of little distinction. All but phased out of production in France and California. A few Eastern wineries have recently offered it as a varietal.

ANGELICA A sweet, fortified wine traditionally produced from Mission grapes. Its name is reportedly derived from Ciudad de (City of) Los Angeles. Produced today primarily as a sacramental wine.

AURORA (or Aurore) Soft, fragrant, simple wines are generally produced from this French hybrid, which is often used as a base for champagnes. 34 U.S. wineries produce a varietal.

BACO NOIR Very popular red French hybrid generally producing rather thin, fruity wines in most Northern states, but achieving a fuller, more mellow character in the Mid-Atlantic vineyards. At its best the variety offers vinous, slightly herbaceous qualities. 34 wineries offer it as a varietal.

BARBERA Red vinifera grape offered primarily as light-bodied, fruity, average-quality wine. Although most of the volume is in jug wine, a few producers offer limited quantities of Barbera in a traditional, robust style, high in acid and tannin and deeply colored in its youth. With bottle age it becomes softer and better balanced. 20,000 acres in California, of which 99% are in the Central Valley. Constitutes 12% of the total production of California red wine. Produced as a varietal by 34 wineries.

BLANC DE BLANCS Literally, "white from whites." This term applies both to sparkling wines and to table wines made from white grapes. A few (but certainly not all) champagnes called Blanc de Blancs have substantial amounts of Chardonnay in their makeup.

BLANC DE NOIR Literally interpreted, the term denotes white wine made from black-skinned grapes and applies to either champagne or still wines. It is seen increasingly on California table wines, partly due to the surplus of red wine grapes. In actuality, the color ranges from onion-skin to pink and sometimes even to light red. Since it lacks official definition, the phrase is often used as a prettier way to label lighter-hued rosés.

BURGER Pleasant, light, neutral wine used only for blending. Once the most widely planted white vinifera in California; now only 1,800 acres remain in production.

BURGUNDY Widely used generic name, invariably referring to inexpensive red wine blends unless specified as something else—such as White Burgundy or Sparkling Burgundy. Recently a few wineries have dropped the name in favor of Red Table Wine. Most California Burgundies are soft, slightly to medium sweet, and aimed at a broad market.

CABERNET FRANC An important red vinifera grape in France. Ignored until recently in the United States. Interest is now increasing in using the grape for blending with Cabernet Sauvignon and Merlot, its traditional use in Bordeaux. Still less than 200 acres in California. Few separately identified varietal bottlings have been offered to date.

CABERNET SAUVIGNON The most successful red vinifera grape in California, often yielding wines of world-class beauty and depth. In the best locations in Napa and Sonoma counties and the Santa Cruz Mountains, it develops ripe, almost black-currant concentration that is mixed occasionally with minty, weedy, herbaceous, and even vegetative overtones. Although frequently astringent when young, such wines soften gradually in the bottle (10–15 years for the biggest) until their full flavor shows through. These are the most expensive and highly sought-after red wines of California.

The tradition of making high-quality Cabernets without

blending has given way in recent years to blending experiments designed to emulate French practices with the grape. Today, many are blended with the Bordeaux varieties (Merlot, Cabernet Franc, Malbec, and Petit Verdot). In the medium price range, usually meant for earlier consumption, Cabernet wines are typically medium-bodied, only moderately tannic, and distinctively but less intensively flavored than the expensive top grade. In good vintages these wines can offer outstanding value. A few wineries offer rosé and Blanc de Noir from Cabernet, and some are delightful. However, the occasional jug wine bearing the varietal name is Cabernet in name only.

The generally high quality of Cabernet wines is reflected in the rapid expansion of plantings: 24,000 acres, up from 615 in 1960. 221 wineries produce Cabernet, including 15 in the Pacific Northwest and 20 east of the Rockies.

CARIGNANE Red vinifera grape yielding well-balanced but ordinary, dull wines. Used primarily in California jug wines. As recently as 1969, Carignane composed over 30% of the total red wine crush (versus 17% in 1979). 12 California wineries produce Carignane as a varietal wine from 27,000 acres.

CARLOS Bronze muscadine cross released in 1970 by North Carolina Agriculture Experiment Station. Made as a varietal by wineries in North Carolina and Mississippi.

CARNELIAN Recently released (1972) red vinifera grape developed at the University of California, Davis. Its complex heritage includes Grenache, Carignane, and Cabernet Sauvignon. Most of the 2,800 acres in California are in the Central Valley, where the grape is expected to produce balanced wines with good color and body. However, no winery has yet made Carnelian a substantial part of its regular line.

CASCADE NOIR An early-ripening red French hybrid used for rosé and red table wine by a dozen Eastern wineries.

CATAWBA Red, white, and pink sweet wines with labrusca grapey flavors and aromas are produced from this popular, purplish-red native American hybrid. Made in some 42 wineries, mainly Eastern, but including 1 in Oregon and 1 in New Mexico.

CAYUGA WHITE 2 wineries make wine from this white hybrid, developed by the New York Geneva Experiment Station.

CHABLIS Broadly used generic name for white table wine. A few wineries continue to use it on dry, crisp offerings that follow the style of wines from the Chablis region of France in some small way. Most, however, use it for inexpensive, slightly to quite sweet offerings blended primarily to sell in the jug wine market. One winery offers 5 Chablis (known in the trade as the Chablis quintet) that are identified by various colors and precious stones.

CHAMBOURCIN A relatively recent red French hybrid popular in France. Made as a varietal by 8 U.S. wineries. It yields light, simple red wines that have noticeable herbaceous qualities at their best.

CHAMPAGNE Synonymous with sparkling wine in the United States. The term applies to any wine whose carbon dioxide bubbles are derived naturally during a second fermentation in a closed container. Thus, if artificially carbonated, it cannot be called champagne. There are 3 ways to produce champagne: the *méthode champenoise,* the transfer method, and the bulk process.

CHANCELLOR NOIR Very agreeable dark red wine is produced from this French hybrid (which in France is the most popular of all the hybrids). 21 producers in the Eastern United States.

CHARBONO An all but unheard-of red vinifera grape yielding dark-colored, usually full-bodied, tart, and tannic wines in the hands of the 2 or 3 producers who choose to offer it. For the most part, the wine's heaviness has not been accompanied by exceptional flavor. Less than 100 acres in California.

CHARDONNAY (also known as Pinot Chardonnay) White vinifera grape producing superb dry wines throughout the United States. Also widely grown in France in the Burgundy, Chablis, and Champagne regions. The character is fruity, sometimes appley, with good depth and intensity. Before being bottled, the wine is often aged in small oak barrels; this process increases its complexity. In the vineyard, yields are fairly low and the grapes command high prices.

America's leading Chardonnays come from choice vineyards in Napa and Sonoma counties and to a lesser extent from isolated pockets in Santa Clara and Monterey counties. These wines, ranked among the best in the world, share a fat, rich style, full of fruit and possessing complex oak and ripe apple qualities, often with leafy or spicy dimensions. In fairly cool grape-growing areas, such as Carneros, the Anderson Valley, and the bulk of California's Central Coast, and in diverse vineyard regions from Oregon to New York, Chardonnay wines are perhaps a bit less complex. Nevertheless, they seem to produce the best-tasting dry white wines that those regions have to offer. 194 wineries, mostly in California, offer Chardonnay. National acreage is 17,500, 16,000 in California, up from 300 two decades ago. 60% of the acreage is in Napa, Sonoma, and Monterey counties.

CHELOIS French hybrid that makes a fruity, dry red wine. Best when produced in a hearty style and aged 3 or 4 years. Produced by 24 U.S. wineries in the Northeast and Midwest.

CHENIN BLANC Popular white vinifera grape yielding fresh, fruity wine when grown in North and Central Coast vineyards. Delightful Chenin Blancs have flavors often compared to melons, pears, and peaches. Most are finished slightly sweet to medium sweet and are intended for early consumption. Dry-styled Chenin Blancs come mostly from smaller Napa and Sonoma producers, who often age their wines in small oak barrels. About 70% of California's 28,000 acres are in the Central Valley. Most of it shows up in wines from high-volume producers under a California appellation and is generally less expensive and less appealing than coastal-grown wines. 99 wineries offer Chenin Blanc, 94 of them in California.

CHIANTI A generic name borrowed from the popular Italian red wine and used by a few California producers for their heaviest, coarsest red jug wines. Usually overly sweet when offered by the largest producers.

CLARET A once popular generic name now used sparingly for red wines of no specific personality. By contrast, in international usage claret refers to the red wines of Bordeaux.

CONCORD Labrusca, grapey-tasting, usually sweet-finished wine comes from this native American hybrid, which is also the base for most grape juices, jellies, and candies. About 40 Eastern and Midwestern wineries produce it as a varietal wine. Concord is also the main grape in most kosher wines.

CYNTHIANA (also known as Norton) Grown commercially in Arkansas and Missouri, this red native hybrid is made into wine by 7 U.S. producers.

DE CHAUNAC An early-ripening, vigorous French hybrid yielding fruity, balanced red wines. 36 U.S. producers.

DELAWARE This native American hybrid grape is usually grown to produce sparkling wines and relatively dry, pleasantly fruity, white wines with a mild labrusca grapiness. 30 U.S. wineries produce it as a varietal.

DIAMOND Fairly aromatic, relatively dry, spicy-fruity wines with labrusca grapiness are produced from this white native American hybrid. 3 U.S. wineries offer it as a varietal.

DUTCHESS White native American hybrid producing fairly neutral, fruity, and relatively sweet wine with muted labrusca grapiness. 15 U.S. wineries.

EARLY BURGUNDY A dark-colored, medium-bodied wine without distinctive varietal character is made from this red vinifera grape. Usually used for blending. 700 acres in California. Occasionally seen as a varietal.

EMERALD RIESLING White vinifera grape developed by the University of California, Davis, by crossing Johannisberg Riesling with Muscadelle. Although available for the last two decades, only 2,700 acres have been planted, mainly in the Central Valley. About 10 wineries offer it as a varietal, usually in a light-bodied, slightly sweet style.

FINO A type of Spanish sherry, deriving its unique sharp, yeasty character from the development of a crusty, surface yeast called *flor*. In the United States almost all *fino* sherries derive their character from cultures of *flor* yeast introduced by the winemaker into the wine rather than from surface growths.

FLORA This white vinifera grape was developed by the University of California, Davis, by crossing Gewurztraminer with Semillon. It yields pleasant, flowery wines with a trace of spiciness and is used mainly for blending, often into Gewurztraminer. 400 bearing acres in California; 4 producers.

FOCH (or Maréchal Foch) Deep-colored, hearty red wine has been made from this early-ripening red French hybrid. Some winemakers are now moving toward producing lighter reds, reflecting the variety's Gamay origins. 32 U.S. wineries, primarily in the Northeast, offer Foch as a varietal.

FOLLE BLANCHE Light, vinous, tart wine without distinctive varietal character is produced from this white vinifera grape. The traditional variety for cognac. 350 bearing acres in California.

FRANKEN RIESLING An infrequently used alternative name for the Sylvaner variety.

FRENCH COLOMBARD (also known as Colombard) Prolific, high-acid grape used primarily in generic jug wine and as the base for some inexpensive champagnes. It is second only to Zinfandel in total acreage planted and, because of high yields, constitutes 45% of California's white wine grape crush. It generally has a fruity, vaguely weedy character that is easily submerged in blending. However, a few North Coast producers have managed to make interesting varietals with simple but pleasant fruitiness in both dry and sweet styles. The 36,000 acres in California are mainly in the Central Valley. 43 wineries offer it as a varietal.

FUMÉ BLANC Popular marketing name used for Sauvignon Blancs—usually dry-finished. The trend was started by the Robert Mondavi Winery in the late 1960s to signify a change to the fruity, crisp style of Sauvignon Blanc that now dominates the market.

GAMAY The seemingly more correct identification of the grape known popularly in California as Napa Gamay.

GAMAY BEAUJOLAIS Until the 1970s the red vinifera grape variety traditionally identified as Gamay Beaujolais was thought by California viticulturalists to be the true grape of France's Beaujolais region. Then it was reidentified as one of many versions (or clones) of Pinot Noir. It is a productive vine that requires cool growing conditions and can produce either a light- or medium-bodied red wine, depending on vineyard management and winemaking choices. Because of historical usage, the vines planted as Gamay Beaujolais have been allowed to retain the name if the proprietor prefers. Another grape, the Napa Gamay, is now thought to be from Beaujolais and may also be labeled as Gamay Beaujolais.

There are 50 U.S. wineries, mostly in California, producing wine under this name. There are 4,300 acres of the traditional Gamay Beaujolais (Pinot Noir) in California; 5,300 acres of Napa Gamay.

GEWURZTRAMINER Delicate to intensely spicy wines can be produced from this white vinifera grape. The wine is usually finished in a slightly sweet to medium sweet style to counter the grape's tendency toward bitterness, but dry versions have also shown quite well. Occasionally, the varietal grape will also be offered in a very sweet, late harvest style when the grapes are concentrated by *Botrytis*.

The key to capturing Gewurztraminer varietal character lies in choosing the right moment for picking. Harvested before maturity, the grapes produce wines with a delicate, floral character somewhat akin to Johannisberg Riesling. But for the winemaker with the patience to wait for the peak of ripeness, Gewurztraminer becomes intensely and distinctively spicy while still retaining much of its floral charm.

The grape's popularity has grown steadily during the last decade, and it is now offered by 86 wineries (including 13 in the Pacific Northwest and 11 east of the Rockies). There are 3,400 acres in California.

GOLDEN CHASSELAS Medium-bodied, dry to slightly sweet table wine of limited varietal character made from Palomino grapes. (Not related to Chasselas grape of Switzerland and Germany.) 4 U.S. producers.

GREEN HUNGARIAN A wine of simple vinous character is produced from this white vinifera. The 13 California producers have each created and popularized their own versions through generous blending with more distinctive varietals. These versions vary from dry to sweet. None are distinctive, interesting wines, and we suspect that the wine's appeal is related as much to habit and an interesting name as to quality considerations. 300 bearing acres in California.

GRENACHE Almost entirely blended into generic rosé and red jug wines, in which it often is identified by its distinctive orange cast and the sweet, somewhat strawberrylike aroma that it contributes. 30 West Coast wineries offer varietal rosé and a few offer Grenache red table wines. Almost 17,500 acres are in California, and 300 acres are planted in Washington.

GREY RIESLING Popular, modestly priced, simple-tasting white vinifera wine produced from the grape known as Chauché Gris in France, not a member of the Riesling family. The widest-selling Grey Rieslings are offered in a dry, medium-acid style with light fruity flavor and no oak-barrel aging. They seem well suited for meals, especially seafood, and have become mainstays on wine lists. Since the grape has very muted flavors on its own, the better Grey Rieslings on the market are usually blended with a little Sylvaner or Chenin Blanc to uplift their character. A few slightly sweet and medium sweet versions are offered. About 20 wineries offer Grey Riesling, mostly in California. 2,300 acres in California.

GRIGNOLINO In its few versions, this red varietal wine has a light, spicy-fruity flavor and an orange hue. 5 California producers and 100 acres.

ICE WINE Called Eiswein in Germany, it is produced from grapes in which the juice (water) has frozen on the vine. Thus, if pressed when still frozen, the must has a high concentration of sugar. The wines are usually very sweet, but the balance and quality vary. Ice wine is rarely made.

JOHANNISBERG RIESLING (also known as White Riesling in the United States and simply as Riesling in Germany) A white wine of distinctive varietal character, which is made in every style from bone dry to very sweet dessert wine. The typical character is fruity and delicate with a variety of floral to fresh apple and apricot scents, depending on where it is grown. In the 1960s most California wineries produced this white vinifera in a dry, relatively austere, high-alcohol style, sometimes with a hint of oak, usually at the expense of the grape's subtle charms. The trend beginning in the 1970s, spurred by consumer demand and improved technology, has been to stress the grape's more delicate qualities and to finish the wine in a slightly sweet to medium sweet style. Another recent trend has been to allow the grapes to be attacked by *Botrytis cinerea*, the result being a luscious sweet wine. 145 producers of Johannisberg Riesling (14 in the Northwest and 22 east of the Rockies); 9,600 acres in California.

KLEINBERGER RIESLING A light, fruity white wine is produced occasionally under this name by 1 winery. The grape may be a minor German variety.

LANDOT A red French hybrid that produces a light, fruity style of wine with faint labrusca notes. 4 Eastern producers.

LEON MILLOT A very early ripening red French hybrid similar to Foch. Produced by 6 Eastern wineries.

MALBEC Red vinifera. Important as a blending grape in California prior to Prohibition. There is some interest today in its revival for use in blending with Cabernet, based on the grape's use in Bordeaux. 130 bearing acres in California.

MALVASIA BIANCA A somewhat perfumed table wine, usually finished medium sweet to sweet, is made from this white vinifera grape. 8 California wineries produce the varietal from 800 bearing acres.

MERLOT Medium red color and an herbaceous quality somewhat similar to Cabernet Sauvignon are characteristic of many wines made from this red vinifera. The tannins are commonly softer, the texture suppler, and the aroma a bit sweeter and more forward than Cabernet. The variety is a grape of major importance in Bordeaux and in many wine-producing districts, but interest in California was generated only when the Cabernet boom of the 1970s began. Its role as a blending grape to round out and add complexity to Cabernet is probably as important as its potential as a separate wine, although 49 U.S. wineries now offer it as a varietal (including 8 Northwest wineries and 4 east of the Rockies). There are 2,800 acres in California (up from 2 acres in 1968) and 130 in Washington.

MISSION Sweet white dessert wines are the traditional product from this red vinifera, which the mission padres introduced to California during the 1770s. Low acidity and weak color are two of the marks against it for table wine. However, it is still planted in 20 California counties with 4,400 acres bearing; 5 wineries produce a varietal Mission.

MOSCATO (Moscato Amabile, Moscato d'Oro, Moscato Spumante) Italian spelling for muscat and name given to wines from muscat grapes by some California wineries. Usually in sweet style, they range from table wines to fortified wines and sparkling wines.

MOSCATO DI CANELLI Italian name for Muscat Blanc used by a number of wineries for their varietal wines.

MOSELLE Generic name used by a few U.S. wineries for medium sweet white wines. The name is borrowed from a German wine district noted for its delicate, floral wines.

MÜLLER-THURGAU White vinifera grape developed in Germany by crossing two strains of Johannisberg Riesling. The result is a grape that ripens with even less summer heat than Johannisberg Riesling and still exhibits much of its floral character. Müller-Thurgau has become the most widely planted grape in Germany and is being planted in northern vineyards from Oregon to the East Coast. A few experimental plots exist in California, but there is not enough commercial acreage to be recorded.

MUSCADINE Common name for an American species native to the Southern states, of which the best-known variety is Scuppernong. 10 wineries offer Scuppernong or muscadine varietals, mostly as sweet white wines.

MUSCAT BLANC (also known as Moscato di Canelli and Muscat Frontignan) Light wine with strong muscatty, spicy aromas and distinctive flavors are produced from this white vinifera. Some producers have offered Muscat Blanc in a dry, crisp style, but most often it is finished slightly sweet to medium sweet and is suited to after-dinner use with fresh fruits. A few fortified wines. 1,200 acres in California; 18 producers.

MUSCAT FRONTIGNAN French name for Muscat Blanc used by some California wineries, primarily for sweet, fortified dessert wines.

MUSCAT OF ALEXANDRIA Aromatic, somewhat spicy table wines generally less interesting than Muscat Blanc are produced from this white vinifera, which is grown primarily for raisins and table fruit. Produced by 9 U.S. wineries (6 in California); 10,500 acres bearing in California.

MUSCAT OTTONEL A French hybrid with characteristics somewhat similar to Muscat Blanc. Planted in small quantities in Oregon and New York because it tends to ripen well in cool climates.

NAPA GAMAY Red vinifera grape long regarded as a poor Gamay relative in California vineyards, but recently gaining stature when identified (tentatively and possibly incorrectly) as the major Gamay grape of France's Beaujolais region. Amid the current confusion this grape is allowed to be called Gamay Beaujolais on labels and now commands a higher price per ton at harvest than the grape previously called Gamay Beaujolais. (See entries for Gamay and Gamay Beaujolais for more information on these interrelated wine names.) Napa Gamay yields fruity but simple wines that can be supple when produced in a light style, but are coarse and tannic when made heavier. Napa Gamay also yields rosés with good fruit and bright pink/ever so slightly orange color. 5,300 acres; 34 wineries offer a varietal.

NEBBIOLO This grape, responsible for the fine red wines from Italy's Piedmont region (Barolo, Gattinara, Barbaresco), was unfortunately dismissed decades ago in California because test plots yielded lightly colored, thin wines. New plantings in the early 1970s increased the bearing acreage to approximately 500, mostly in the hot Central Valley flatlands where the result will probably be lightly colored, thin wines. This grape deserves a better chance.

NIAGARA The most popular of the white native hybrids. The wines possess a strong grapey labrusca flavor. Used in both relatively dry and sweet wines by 33 wineries centered in the East and Midwest.

NOBLE A recent muscadine cross, used to produce red wine by 3 Southern wineries.

PALOMINO (also known as Golden Chasselas) White vinifera grape used almost exclusively for sherry thanks to its natural tendency to produce high sugar and low acid and to oxidize easily. As recently as 1968, Palomino was the most widely planted of all white wine varieties in California. However, total acreage has steadily declined as a result of a public shift in taste from domestic sherry to table wines. There are now 4,000 acres in California.

PEDRO XIMÉNES White vinifera grape yielding intensely sweet, molasses candy–flavored wines. Important as a blending grape for cream sherries. There are 200 acres standing in California.

PETIT VERDOT Lightly grown grape used primarily for blending with Cabernet Sauvignon. A few stands of the grape exist, but not enough to be recorded.

PETITE SIRAH Long used in California as the backbone for blended North Coast burgundies, this red vinifera variety slowly came into its own during the early 1970s. Although there is some confusion over the grape's heritage (some say it is the minor French variety Duriff), most viticulturalists now agree that the grape is not the Syrah variety grown extensively in the Rhone region of France, as they once thought. Adding to the confusion are the several variants of Petite Sirah grown throughout California. Most Petite Sirahs on the market today come from coastal vineyards or from the Delta and Lodi regions, where the grape typically yields inky-colored wines that are high in tannin and have simple, vinous flavors and few complex nuances. Its popularity is based mainly on the ability of its brawny structure to stand up to hearty foods. There are 13,200 acres in California; about one-third lie in the warmest regions of the Central Valley, where the grape retains its role in blended jug reds. About 80 wineries now produce Petite Sirah.

PINOT BLANC White vinifera grape that developed as a natural variant of Pinot Noir. It produces fruity, relatively high-acid wines that are often compared to simple versions of Chardonnay. Coupled with its modest flavors, the grape's typical low yield in the vineyard has kept it from gaining popularity. The few outstanding examples come from the dedicated efforts of small wineries and often carry Chardonnay-like price tags. A number of large wineries use Pinot Blanc in their better champagnes because of its natural acidity and clean flavor. There are 1,800 acres, half in Monterey County. 15 wineries offer Pinot Blanc as a varietal wine.

PINOT GRIS White, early-ripening variant of Pinot Noir. Offered by 3 wineries in Oregon and 2 in the Northeast.

PINOT MEUNIER (or Meunier). A red member of the Pinot family produced by 1 Oregon winery.

PINOT NOIR Red vinifera variety of high reputation in France—it is the principal red grape of Burgundy—that has proven a puzzle to California winemakers. In spite of large plantings (almost 10,000 acres) in a variety of soils and climates, California Pinot Noirs have too often been thin-flavored and simple. They have not offered the burgundian richness, complexity, and velvety texture on which the grape's reputation is based. Recent experiments with location, restricted crop level, fermentation technique, and clonal selections (over 200 strains of Pinot Noir exist) have begun to improve the wineries' performance—particularly for the producers with the patience and money to make a special effort. The favored vineyard locations are in cool areas, especially hillsides with limestone-enriched soils.

For the moment, however, the grape has lost its standing as California's number-two red variety (behind Cabernet), having been surpassed by Zinfandel for overall quality and popularity. The current surplus of Pinot Noir grapes has allowed the variety to be used increasingly and fairly successfully for Blanc de Noir, rosé, and champagne. 149 wineries offer Pinot Noir, including 14 in the Pacific Northwest and 8 further east (Colorado to New York).

PINOT ST. GEORGE Red vinifera grape (unrelated to Pinot Noir) that yields simple, vinous wines whether made in a thin, fruity style or pushed into becoming more full-bodied and tannic. 700 acres in California.

PORT Generic name for sweet fortified wine, usually red, made in the style of the port produced in the Douro region of

Portugal. Most U.S. ports are simple, cheap, quickly made sweet wines that are offered by large, full-line producers and bear little resemblance to their Portuguese namesakes. A handful of small wineries (and one or two of the big producers) treat the wine with more care and have offered ports that combine depth, richness, fruit, and aging potential.

RED TABLE WINE Generic name increasingly used by North American wineries for their blended, inexpensive red wine—instead of the borrowed names, burgundy or claret.

RHINE In the United States, a generic term for ordinary white table wine. Usually sweet.

RIESLING A legally acceptable name for wine produced from any grape variety carrying Riesling in its name (Johannisberg, Sylvaner, Grey, and Kleinberger). In actual use, it is most often produced from one of the lesser varieties, since Johannisberg on the label would seem to carry more prestige than the term Riesling itself. The wine is usually slightly to medium sweet.

RKATSITELI A Russian white vinifera with small acreages in California and New York. The grape yields a neutral, well-balanced wine with good acidity.

ROSÉ Pink wine made for early consumption and usually oversweetened. The best achieve a fresh, fruity taste and carry enough acid to balance the sweetness that most rosés have. Many rosés carry varietal names (Zinfandel Rosé, for example), but rosés made from blends of grapes are not necessarily less attractive. The wine's color is achieved either by blending red wine into white or by keeping the juice of red wine grapes (which starts out white and acquires color during fermentation) from extensive contact with the grape skins. Either way, the trick is to acquire a pleasing pinkish hue that suggests a lighter body and taste than red wine. Use with food depends on the degree of sweetness.

ROSETTE (also known as Seibel 1000) Red French hybrid lacking intense color, frequently used to make rosé. A half-dozen producers in the East and Midwest.

RUBY CABERNET A red vinifera grape developed by the University of California, Davis, in a search for a more productive, Cabernet-style wine. The grape, a cross between

Cabernet Sauvignon and Carignane, was expected to yield Cabernet character at Carignane's bountiful harvest levels. Unfortunately, it comes closer to the latter than the former and usually produces vinous, soft wines of jug quality—perhaps because 96% of the 18,400 acres are in the Central Valley. 30 wineries offer Ruby Cabernet.

SAUTERNE Generic name used by a few U.S. producers for white wine, usually sweet, always of jug wine quality. Fewer California wineries seem to be using the name these days, but it remains a popular product for Eastern wineries.

SAUVIGNON BLANC Very popular white vinifera grape, second only to Chardonnay for the production of dry white wines in California (many of which are identified as Fumé Blanc on the label). The grape typically has distinctly weedy, sometimes grassy aromas and flavors and can be intensely fruity. When produced as a dry wine, it is often aged in small oak barrels to round out its somewhat monochromatic character. In the dry style, Sauvignon Blanc often makes a suitable companion to fish and shellfish. A few wineries offer sweeter versions, but the number is decreasing due to the rapidly growing demand for the dry, crisp style. An occasional late harvest wine also appears. The 6,200 acres of Sauvignon Blanc are concentrated in the coastal counties of California, although highly respectable wines have also come from the Sierra foothills and from the Pasco area of Washington State. There are 77 producers of Sauvignon Blanc, mostly in California.

SAUVIGNON VERT All-but-forgotten white vinifera of modest aroma and flavor that is no longer grown commercially in France and is diminishing in California. 4 producers and 500 acres in California.

SCUPPERNONG Native American variety of the muscadine species grown mostly in Southeast and Gulf Coast states. It has a unique musky flavor and is usually sweet-finished. 5 wineries offer Scuppernong.

SEMILLON Vinifera grape popular from the 1930s through the 1960s as a dry, white, medium-bodied table wine with a figlike perfume. Acreage has expanded very slowly during the past decade, and the grape has been surpassed as a dry wine by Chardonnay and Sauvignon Blanc. A few very sweet dessert wines are made from Semillon. There are 15 producers in California, 4 in the Northwest, and 1 in New York. 2,754 acres in California.

SEYVAL BLANC This white French hybrid has become one of the mainstays of Eastern winemaking. It takes well to cold climates where it can be counted on to yield fruity, crisp wines. There are 48 wineries producing Seyval Blanc, mainly east of the Rockies; limited amounts are grown in the Northwest.

SEYVE-VILLARD Wine made from several varieties developed by French hybridist Seyve-Villard are labeled with his name by 4 wineries.

SHERRY Generic name in the United States for any fortified wine styled more or less after Spanish sherry. Though some follow the traditional *solera* system of aging, most U.S. sherries are "baked," or heated and briefly aged. The cream-style sweet sherries have been the best of the domestic products. The drier-style sherries are not competitive with the Spanish imports.

SOUZAO Portuguese grape used sparingly for port in California (200 acres). 2 wineries offer it as a varietal port.

SPARKLING BURGUNDY A generic name used for red sparkling wines in the United States. Some are attractive; none outstanding.

STEUBEN Native red hybrid made as varietal wine by 4 Midwestern and Eastern wineries. It has a light, grapey quality.

SYLVANER (also called Sylvaner Riesling and Franken Riesling) Not a Riesling at all, this white vinifera once enjoyed great popularity in California for its lightly spicy and floral qualities. However, increasing sophistication among wine drinkers and the change in style for Johannisberg Riesling seem to have reduced its popularity. Acreage has remained low: only 1,400 acres are planted. 10 wineries now offer it as a varietal.

SYRAH (also known as French Syrah and Shiraz) Low-producing grape of the Côtes du Rhône in France, yielding Hermitage wines among others, this red vinifera is attracting new attention among California winemakers who for years thought their Petite Sirah vines were this variety. 2 wineries make small lots of varietal wines. Less than 100 acres in California.

THOMPSON SEEDLESS Very versatile warm-climate white vinifera that produces wine with a bland character. It is widely

used in common white blends as a base for inexpensive sparkling wine and brandy. However, more than half the world's raisins are made from this variety, and it is also the foundation of California's fresh table grape business. 244,000 acres, over half in Fresno County.

TINTA MADEIRA Red vinifera grape used in some California ports for its rich flavor and deep color. 1,100 acres, mostly in the Central Valley.

TRAMINER A name used in California for various white varietal wines. Two decades ago, the name was mistakenly applied to the now abandoned Red Veltliner variety. Later the name Traminer was correctly used for the grape variety originating in Europe and grown sparsely in California. It is the parent of the now popular clone Gewurztraminer, which is far more intense and spicy than its progenitor. The term Traminer has disappeared except for references in wine books.

VIDAL BLANC This white French hybrid is rapidly gaining popularity because of its pleasant, fruity flavors and good balance. Successful versions, offered both in soft, slightly sweet and dry, crisp styles, are among America's most enjoyable wines coming from nonvinifera grapes. 29 wineries east of the Rockies produce Vidal Blanc.

VIGNOLES (also known as Ravat 51) 5 wineries vinify this white French hybrid, usually in a relatively dry, crisp style.

VILLARD BLANC Simple, fruity wine is made from this white French hybrid. 10 producers east of the Rockies. Interestingly, it is the most widely planted white hybrid in France.

WHITE RIESLING (known popularly as Johannisberg Riesling) The legally required name in the state of Oregon; used also by many vineyardists and wineries in other states, when an alternative to the borrowed Johannisberg name is desired.

ZINFANDEL Often called "the mystery grape" because its origins are unknown, this red vinifera variety is the most widely planted (30,000 acres) and also the most versatile wine grape grown in California. In medium-warmth coastal locations, especially sheltered hillsides, Zinfandel can yield full-bodied, intensely flavored wines with substantial tannin. The best wines of this type show Zinfandel's vigorous, berrylike, sometimes spicy varietal character. Late Harvest Zinfandels (usually high in alcohol, occasionally sweet) can come from coastal locations also.

Parts of Sonoma County—notably the Dry Creek Valley and the Geyserville area—as well as Amador County in the Sierra foothills have yielded most of the exceptional Zinfandels of the last decade. The grape is also widely grown in the Central Valley, including the Lodi area, which contains almost 40% of the state's total plantings. Lodi Zinfandels often display the variety's berrylike character, but tend toward flatter, earthier qualities at the expense of the lively, vigorous character found in other regions. Jug wine Zinfandels are also produced farther south in the Central Valley, and more often than not they exhibit the same lack of virtue found in most wines of the area.

A versatile grape, Zinfandel has proven successful in a variety of other styles, including light fruity red wine, rosé, Blanc de Noir, and Nouveau, and even as the base for champagne. There are 193 producers of Zinfandel, including several (Ridge, Carneros Creek, Fetzer, and Monterey Peninsula) who offer up to a half-dozen separate vineyard-designated Zinfandels.

California Vintages

Cabernet Sauvignon

1968 Copious vintage yielding wines that have big flavors, are tannic and long-lived. A number of successful bottlings offered a ripe, classic style. Many have reached their peak, but a few are still developing. Excellent vintage.

1969 An underrated vintage at first with most wines seeming light, short-lived, and lacking in full ripeness. With time the wines developed into nicely flavored, soft, and very likable Cabernets. Generally a good vintage, and a few wineries using hillside grapes offered very good quality. Most have peaked.

1970 A mild wet winter followed by severe spring frosts that reduced the crop by half. Fine warm late summer weather brought the grapes to full ripeness. Many wines are intense and ripe in character, but are revealing a lack of balance with aging. A few are ready now, whereas others remain magnificent and long-lived. An excellent vintage generally less classically styled than 1968.

1971 A cool spring followed by a long, unusually cool growing season. Good-sized crop. Most wines were average in quality, with the best coming from hillside and mountain vineyards. Generally on the thin, simple side and ready now.

1972 July heat spells reduced the crop. Late-season rains hurt the quality by creating mold. Most wines lacked varietal character and depth; they tended to be simple and short-lived. Quality generally ranged from dull to disastrous. A few exceptions were quite pleasant.

1973 Wet, cool winter followed by a warm spring and lovely long, moderate weather during the late season. The crop was large, and after some aging the quality now approaches excellent. Many wines possess fine character, balance, and harmony and have both tannin and a firm structure to hold for several more years. Above-average to excellent year.

1974 Cool spring and summer weather culminated in a warm harvest. The crop was large, and the grapes became very ripe. The best are dark, concentrated, tannic, and potentially long-lived. But some of the biggest, most tannic wines are fat and ponderous. Many medium-priced, less tannic versions are drinkable now, but will hold to 1982–83. A few of the special bottling types will mature close to 1990 and may last until the next century.

1975 Early frosts and rains were followed by a cool, unusually long season. Most wines are proving to be lightweights—pleasant, sometimes elegant—but few are superb versions. Straightforward in character, without great depth, the wines are likable and similar to the 1969s. Some are ready now, but the best have 4–8 years to go.

1976 First drought year, combined with heat spells and late rains. The grapes were tiny with high sugar levels and low acidity. The wines are dark, tannic, and high in alcohol, but generally lack intense fruit and firm structure. The best should peak in 1985–86; the majority before then. Atypical vintage.

1977 The second drought year was both drier and cooler. Wineries were better prepared, but the harvest experienced sporadic rains. The wines are better balanced than the 1976s, also less tannic and alcoholic. Generally average in varietal character, but lacking in depth and longevity. Average quality.

1978 Late September heat waves sent sugar levels soaring, sometimes too high. The crop was large. Early signs indicate wines ripe and tannic with high alcohol levels, making balancing acidity questionable.

1979 Heat waves followed by prolonged and persistent rain throughout September created chaos. At least 50% of the Cabernet went unpicked during the rains and developed rot and mold. Some vineyards, particularly in Sonoma, were never picked. Quality should be very uneven. Winemakers had to work hard to compensate for many deficiencies in the grapes.

Chardonnay

1972 Small crop due to hot July weather, but rather impressive quality. Almost all Chardonnay was picked before the mid-harvest rains. Many Napa versions were ripe, richly flavored, and oily in texture. They have also aged well. A fine vintage and probably the first with more than a handful of excellent renditions. Most are mature by now.

1973 Some frosts and a warm July. The grapes matured early, and it was a good-sized crop. Most wines possessed good varietal fruit and intensity, decent balance. The best are as developed as possible; some are faded by now. Above average.

1974 Odd—cold, wet, then a cool July. Adequate ripeness, decent acidity, generally average quality. Somewhat simple, light, fruity varietals. Most reached an early peak. Few exceptions.

1975 Good rainfall, a few frost scares, only light damage. Ideal May and June weather allowed a long, cool growing period perfect for Chardonnay. Ripe wines with tremendous flavors, complex, yet well balanced. Began as nicely structured, closed-in wines; now blossoming as harmonious, flavorful wines. Several long-agers from this exceptional vintage.

1976 Drought and dehydration; tiny berries and uneven ripeness. Picked during or after intense heat spell. Some Botrytis in Napa. Wines are ripe, fragrant, powerful, often low in fruit with insufficient acid to balance the high alcohol level. A real contrast to the classic wines of 1975.

1977 Second drought year with unexpected late August rains forcing some early harvesting of marginally ripe fruit. Those who delayed in this on-again, off-again vintage achieved more flavorful, better-balanced wines. A surprising number of successes with above-average intensity, depth, and balance in a pleasantly restrained style. The best will not develop until 1981–82. Many above-average wines; very few classics.

1978 Enormous rainfall (55 inches) and a cool spring without frost damage. September was warm, sending sugars very high, very quickly. Many wines are ripe and fragrant, full-bodied, but often excessively alcoholic. Some lack acid balance. The quality is above average, but the lack of balance makes longevity questionable.

1979 Grapes harvested before the heavy and continuing rains of September were relatively balanced in sugar and acidity. The rest of the harvest is less interesting.

Pinot Noir

1970 Hot harvest temperatures caused some raisining. Many wines were flabby; most matured very early. No major exceptions.

1971 Cool weather prevailed during the early season, enabling several wineries to produce above-average-quality versions. Even the best (Chalone, Hanzell, Sonoma Vineyards, Inglenook Cask, and Sterling) are ready now.

1972 An average, uneventful year overall with mostly dull wines. Hanzell, Mount Eden, Swan, and ZD excelled. Drink now with few exceptions.

1973 Another average-quality year offering many ordinary wines. Several rose above ordinary—Hoffman Mountain Ranch, Mondavi, Kenwood, and Chalone. Mount Eden was superb.

1974 A very consistent year yielding wines uniformly lackluster in character. Only Mount Eden, Swan, Fetzer, and Chalone offered wines of ✿✿ or better quality.

1975 The coolish, elongated growing season offered hope for major breakthroughs, but the quality was just above average overall. Santa Cruz Mountain Vineyard's wine was superb. All others should peak by 1981.

1976 Drought, dryness, and the first fruits of long-term experiments combined to make this an unusual vintage. Fine wines were made by Carneros Creek, Caymus, Burgess, and Hoffman Mountain Ranch. Others showed improvement, though suffering somewhat from a lack of balance.

1977 The crop was small, picked before the rains. The vintage produced more successes than 1976, and several wines have better depth and balance. This could prove to be a watershed vintage for Pinot Noir. Initial enthusiasm is being confirmed by the releases from Carneros Creek, Chalone, Firestone, Kenwood, Sanford & Benedict, ZD, and many others.

1978 Many vineyards were maturing when the heat spell arrived and the grapes ripened quickly, reaching high sugar levels. Wines should possess good color and strong alcohol, but balance could be a problem.

1979 Uncertain quality since most grapes were picked during the cool September weather at marginal ripeness. Those picked toward the end or after the rains developed mold and often had less than desirable acidity. Whether or not they will have fruit and balance after aging remains a big question.

Zinfandel

1970 Hot summer weather brought Zinfandel to full ripeness, but few wineries were taking the varietal seriously. Those who did made rich, well-flavored wines. Most have reached their peak.

1971 A cool vintage yielding wines of moderate ripeness. Joseph Swan and Kenwood's Lot #1 excelled, joining Ridge and Sutter Home as quality leaders. Others were generally of average quality. Wines now at peak or beginning to fade.

1972 Late-season rains hindered quality overall. Many wines were thin and early-maturing. Clos du Val and Fetzer Vineyards proved to be exceptions.

1973 An ideal warm harvest without any rains led to many successful barrel-aged, ripe fruit Zinfandels. Uniformly good conditions in Napa, Sonoma, Mendocino, and Amador counties. Many new wineries entered the field, and both Amador and Sonoma counties won recognition in 1973. Many ✪ versions and several were of ✪✪✪ quality. Excellent year. Most ready to drink now.

1974 Another fine, warm year resulting in numerous ripe, full-flavored Zinfandels. All regions fared well, but quality overall was just a shade below 1973. Some near full maturity.

1975 Generally cool with late-season showers. Napa versions were less intense; those from Sonoma and Amador generally above average in quality, but early-maturing. Ready now except for the most tannic.

1976 Drought and heat waves brought Zinfandel to extreme ripeness, making it the greatest success of the vintage. Many late harvest versions were offered. Others were heavy, intense, and tannic. An excellent vintage, the best of which need further cellaring.

1977 Another drought-year extravaganza for Zinfandel. Many outstanding ripe and balanced wines from Sonoma County. Again, an abundance of late harvest wines. Cellaring required for most.

1978 First reports show an overabundance of late harvest wines. Grapes ripened faster than most wineries could pick them.

1979 Very mixed quality. Some wines made from grapes picked before the heavy September rains will be of average quality. Those made afterwards lacked ripeness and were often low in acidity.

Amador County Zinfandel

1970 Only Sutter Home was involved to any extent. Above-average quality.

1971 Generally less ripe and average in quality. Matured early.

1972 An uneventful vintage of average-quality wines. Mayacamas late harvest Zinfandel was the only exception. Most are past prime.

1973 An above-average vintage. Monteviña joins Sutter Home and Harbor to focus greater attention on Amador. These wines are now fully developed.

1974 A warm year, but ideal. Many coastal wineries purchased Amador grapes and brought forth ripe, briary, sometimes brawny Zinfandels, often the vintage's finest. Carneros Creek, Mount Veeder, and Ridge contribute to the region's success. Many ✿ and several ✿✿ Zinfandels. Excellent vintage. Most are close to ready.

1975 Average quality, generally less intense than 1974. The best, however, were powerful, high-alcohol wines. San Martin and Monterey Peninsula entered the Amador sweepstakes. Most are drinking well now.

1976 Powerful, very ripe wines resulted from the drought conditions. Several late harvest Zinfandels were made. The style was heavy, tannic, and high in alcohol. Some versions are too dried out and lack fruit. The best will develop to 1983–84.

1977 Again the grapes became very ripe, but the early releases indicate the wines are better balanced than the 1976s.

1978 Good winter rainfall and a warm spring and summer. Rains in early September delayed the harvest and deprived the grapes of their usual dehydration. Most are balanced with ample flavors, lighter in body and tannin than in previous vintages.

1979 Fairly normal vintage, meaning wet in the winter and warm and dry in the summer months. Amador escaped the rains but not the September heat wave. Slightly dehydrated grapes led to fairly full-bodied, highly tannic wines, similar in style to 1973 and 1974.

Wine Geography

Place names listed here are in California, unless otherwise noted. Counties are indicated in parentheses following the place name.

ALAMEDA COUNTY Across the bay from San Francisco, this county has 2,000 acres of grapes grown primarily in the Livermore Valley and owned in large part by local winery interests, including Wente and Concannon. The leading varieties are Grey Riesling and Semillon (about 300 acres each). Other important varieties are Chardonnay, Chenin Blanc, Petite Sirah, Sauvignon Blanc, and Zinfandel (100–150 acres each). In the last several years, about a dozen small- to medium-sized wineries have sprung up in the Oakland-Berkeley area, the result of home winemakers' turning commercial. A few have full-time staff, but most are still at the hobby stage.

ALEXANDER VALLEY (Sonoma) Lying along the course of the Russian River from the point where it passes Cloverdale in the north until it sidles around Healdsburg before turning toward the sea, the Alexander Valley is a landlocked piece of topography every bit as temperate and hospitable as the Napa Valley. Near Geyserville, heat-loving varieties like Zinfandel bask in long sunny days and reach levels of ripeness similar to the adjacent Dry Creek Valley. In other pockets, especially those near the river and those at the southwestern corner of the valley near Healdsburg, growers do very well with Gewurztraminer and Johannisberg Riesling. There are more than a dozen wineries in this area, including such popular names as Simi, Souverain, and Geyser Peak. About half of Sonoma County's vineyard acreage is in the Alexander Valley.

AMADOR COUNTY Tucked into the Sierra foothills in an area southeast of Sacramento, logging- and vacation-oriented Amador County would be indistinguishable from all the other gold-country foothill locations save for the Zinfandel grown there. The major grape-growing areas are in the Shenandoah Valley and in Fiddletown (both near the town of Plymouth). It was the rediscovery of Shenandoah Valley Zinfandel in the late 1960s that put Amador County on the wine map and encouraged more than a dozen coastal wineries to go there for grapes. Amador County has about 1,000 acres in vineyard, of which 450 were in existence prior to the vinous rebirth of the area. Zinfandel is 80% of the acreage.

AMERICAN The least specific appellation of origin. It usually suggests that the wine was blended from grapes grown in 2 or more states.

ANDERSON VALLEY (Mendocino) Tucked into a narrow valley halfway between Ukiah and the Pacific Ocean is the very cool (Region I and Region II) Anderson Valley. Its 500 acres are mostly devoted to Gewurztraminer, Chardonnay, and Pinot Noir, with limited amounts of Zinfandel and Cabernet Sauvignon. Edmeades, Husch, and Navarro wineries are located in the Anderson Valley.

ARROYO SECO (Monterey) Lying west of Greenfield in a protected area nestling against the foothills of the coastal mountains, the Arroyo Seco area has, in its first decade as a wine-growing area, yielded the superb late harvest Rieslings from Wente and a brace of exciting Chardonnays under the MEV label. Wente, Masson, and Mirassou are the major growers in Arroyo Seco. Ventana Vineyards, a grower and new winery, also has extensive vineyards in the area.

CALIFORNIA The number-one state in population, cars per capita, wine and beer consumption, and natural beauty, California is also number one in vineyard acreage. Some 85% of all wine produced in the United States is grown there and, by some estimates, 95% of the premium wine is Californian by origin. Wine grapes are grown in 42 of California's 58 counties and are the third most important agriculture crop of the state. Today, California boasts more than 330,000 acres planted to wine grapes and produces 400 million gallons of wine annually. In the last decade, California's reputation for premium wine has gained nationwide and even worldwide acceptance. However, California specializes in the production of everyday table wine —as much as 80% of the annual output.

On wine labels the name California means that the grapes come from anywhere within the state and usually signifies a blend of grapes from areas that very often include the hot

Central Valley. (See table on pages 180–81 for grape acreage by county and variety.)

CALISTOGA (Napa) As the Napa Valley floor fans out north of St. Helena, the climate becomes increasingly warm. The area around the city of Calistoga is rated medium to high Region III in heat accumulation and is most noted for Zinfandel and fat-styled Cabernet Sauvignon. Wineries located in the Calistoga area include Sterling, Cuvaison, Stonegate, and Chateau Montelena.

CARMEL VALLEY (Monterey) Twisting inward from the Pacific Ocean near the town of Carmel is the Carmel Valley. The few vineyards occupy the uplands and receive enough sunlight and warmth to be somewhat more hospitable for red wine grapes than the Salinas Valley, several miles directly inland.

CARNEROS (Napa and Sonoma) Stretching across the southernmost parts of Napa and Sonoma counties, immediately adjoining San Francisco Bay, Carneros is a cold growing area (Region I and low Region II) by California standards and is suited mostly to early-ripening varieties: Chardonnay, Johannisberg Riesling, Gewurztraminer, and Pinot Noir. The climate is tempered by lingering fogs and early afternoon breezes off the bay. Much of the early wine activity of the Napa and Sonoma valleys was centered in Carneros. Today, such important wineries as Charles Krug, Beaulieu, Louis Martini, Chandon, Buena Vista, and Carneros Creek have substantial vineyard holdings in Carneros. In addition, Carneros has been identified on labels as the place of origin for a number of wines produced by Burgess Cellars, Veedercrest, Wine and The People, and ZD.

CENTRAL COAST The territory lying south of San Francisco and north of the city of Santa Barbara—San Mateo, Santa Cruz, Santa Clara, San Benito, Monterey, San Luis Obispo, and Santa Barbara counties—is known as the Central Coast. After a brief flirtation with the term North Coast, many wineries in this area are now identifying their wines with specific Central Coast appellations.

CENTRAL VALLEY California's Central Valley, the most productive agricultural area in the state, consists of 2 major sections. The Sacramento Valley runs north of Sacramento almost to the Oregon border; the San Joaquin Valley stretches south from the Sacramento-Stockton area to Bakersfield. There are isolated pockets of grapes in the north amounting perhaps to 8,000 acres. In the southern portion of the

Central Valley, spread across 8 counties, are approximately 195,000 acres of grapes—about 60% of California's total. Until recently, Central Valley wines were very often bad: low in acid, oversweetened to hide a multitude of faults, and possessing a cooked quality in aroma and flavors. The bad days are not totally past, but things have certainly changed. Varieties with higher natural acidity (French Colombard, Barbera, and Chenin Blanc) have been planted where once Carignane, Mission, and Grenache ruled. Grapes are picked with more care so that balance and ripeness are achieved. And the modern technology of temperature-controlled, stainless-steel fermentation keeps the fruit cleaner and retains whatever freshness is brought into the winery from the vineyard.

Central Valley products at their best are the cleanest, most flavorful everyday drinking wines in the world. Of course, at their worst they remain as unpalatable as ever.

CLARKSBURG (Yolo) Lying at the eastern edge of the Delta region, Clarksburg-area vineyards are heavily oriented toward Petite Sirah and Chenin Blanc. The area is fairly warm (Region III to low Region IV).

CLEMENTS DISTRICT (San Joaquin) Every now and then a winery will get hold of some Zinfandel from the Clements district, in the foothills east of Lodi, and bottle it up with its own appellation. We have never been fond of the results and apparently neither are they—judging by the one-time nature of most experiments.

CUCAMONGA (San Bernardino) This once burgeoning vine-growing region clings tenaciously to life in spite of air pollution and urban encroachment. The vineyards are old and fast disappearing, having dropped from 25,000 acres before World War II to under 8,000 acres now. Most wine from the area is of bulk quality, and even that which bears varietal nomenclature lacks interest. A sad fate for a proud winegrowing region.

DAVIS (Yolo) 90 miles northwest of San Francisco, on the doorstep of Sacramento, sits the pretty university town of Davis, home of the University of California, Davis. Its Viticulture and Oenology Department, the best in the country, has trained winemakers for more than half the premium wineries in the state and has contributed substantially to the high-technology orientation of most California wineries. The university is a world leader in studies of grapevine diseases, vineyard problems, and grape clones.

DELTA The watery lowlands lying in the triangle formed by the confluence of the San Joaquin and Sacramento rivers is known as the Delta. On some of the many islands and on the surrounding hills, there is a small but moderately successful winegrowing industry. The Delta is warm (Region III to low Region IV) but more moderate than its Central Valley neighbors because of the San Francisco Bay fog and wind that cool it. Its prominent grape-growing locations are Clarksburg in southern Yolo County and Mandeville Island in northern San Joaquin County.

DRY CREEK VALLEY (Sonoma) 6 miles long and (on the average) 1 mile wide, this valley runs northwest-southeast in Sonoma County near Santa Rosa and Geyserville. It has a medium temperature range and long-growing season and is home of Dry Creek, Preston, Lambert Bridge, and A. Rafanelli wineries. Most noted for the very fine Zinfandel (among California's best) grown on benchlands with southern and southwestern exposure. Dry Creek Zinfandels often exhibit archetypical, ripe Zinfandel flavors and are full-bodied and well-balanced with good aging potential. Its use as an appellation is spotty, but growing. Sauvignon Blanc and Chenin Blanc are often successful in cooler, lower grounds and in areas near the valley mouth bordering the Russian River Valley. The Lytton Springs area is immediately adjacent.

EDNA VALLEY (San Luis Obispo) In this coastal plain bordering the western edge of the Coast Range, about 600 acres have been recently planted. To date, Chardonnay seems to be the most successful. Pinot Noir is promising.

EDNA VALLEY VINEYARD (San Luis Obispo) A major supplier of grapes to leading Central Coast wineries, including Hoffman Mountain Ranch, David Bruce, and Chalone Vineyard (for its private label business and the Edna Valley Vineyard label). Chardonnay is the leading variety.

EISELE VINEYARD (Napa) This well-known Cabernet Sauvignon vineyard in the warm Calistoga area produces fat, generously flavored wines in years like 1971 and 1975, when wines from cooler climates tend to turn out on the thin side. In recent years, grapes from this vineyard have gone to the Joseph Phelps winery. They had gone to Ridge, Souverain (of Rutherford), and Conn Creek earlier.

FIDDLETOWN (Amador) Lying just across the ridge from the Shenandoah Valley, this area yields typical, ripe, concentrated Zinfandels in the Amador County style, but possibly a little less forceful in flavor and alcohol than those of the Shenandoah Valley.

FINGER LAKES REGION *New York* The largest wine region in New York, producing over 75% of its wines. Most of the 10,000 acres of vineyards are clustered around Keuka, Canandaigua, and Seneca lakes. Though moderated by the lakes themselves and Lake Ontario to the north, the weather is freezing in winter. The growing season is very short for wine grapes. Most of the state's vinifera are in this region. Labruscas, mainly Concord, predominate, but French hybrids now represent about 15% of the total acreage and are increasing. The region's wine production is primarily in the hands of Taylor, Gold Seal, Great Western, and Widmer's. Bully Hill, Glenora, Heron Hill, and Konstantin Frank are small, prestigious producers.

FRESNO COUNTY 38,000 acres of grapes grow in hot Fresno County; most are converted into jug and dessert wines. The list of plantings is typical of the Central Valley: French Colombard (7,000 acres), Barbera (6,000 acres), Ruby Cabernet (4,200 acres), Grenache (3,000 acres), Chenin Blanc (2,600 acres). At the other end of the scale is Chardonnay (400 acres).

GEYSERVILLE (Sonoma) Sitting on the northwestern edge of the Alexander Valley, Geyserville is the source of excellent Zinfandels, notably from Ridge Vineyards, and of fat-styled Cabernet Sauvignons. In low-lying areas, especially near the river, growers seem to succeed with Chardonnay and Gewurztraminer. The Geyserville area is the home of the Souverain, Geyser Peak, and Pedroncelli wineries.

GILROY (Santa Clara) The agricultural center of the southern Santa Clara Valley, Gilroy has long been home for a number of jug wine producers and small, family-owned wineries operating on a shoestring. The valley floor near Gilroy has substantial vineyard acreage, but the majority of the nearby wineries are located in the hills to the west in the Hecker Pass area.

GLEN ELLEN (Sonoma) North of the city of Sonoma, about halfway to Kenwood, the Sonoma Valley floor becomes a series of rolling hills and gullies. Recent experience in the area suggests that the tops of these "moguls" are warm enough to ripen Zinfandel and Cabernet Sauvignon, but the gullies are more appropriately planted to early-ripening varieties. Grand Cru Vineyards and J. J. Haraszthy are the major wineries in Glen Ellen.

GONZALES (Monterey) In the northern end of the Salinas Valley, this small community boasts 1 winery, the Monterey Vineyard, and a host of plantings in what is surely one of the windiest and coolest vineyard locations in California. At the time they were planted, virtually all of the grapes in the Gonzales area were destined for the town's single winery. When the winery did not grow as fast as expected, the grapes lost their intended home. Much of the output from Gonzales now ends up in jug wines, often from Central Valley producers who desire the high-acid grapes of Gonzales for blending with their own low-acid varietals.

GRAND TRAVERSE REGION *Michigan* Located in the northwest corner of the state, the region includes the Leelanau Peninsula and the Old Mission Peninsula, both running into Lake Michigan. The "lake effect" provides cooler summers and warmer winters than elsewhere in the state. The first vineyards were established here in the mid-1960s, and total acreage now exceeds 100. The predominant grapes are French hybrids; Chardonnay and Johannisberg Riesling are the only vinifera varieties of consequence. 5 wineries.

GREENFIELD (Monterey) A town in the northern Salinas Valley, Greenfield received heavy plantings of red and white varieties during the early 1970s. The first results in this cool growing area suggest that the whites will prosper, but reds may not. J. Lohr is the most visible producer and has already decided to convert much of its red grape acreage to whites. A new winery, Jekel Vineyards, has also enjoyed early success with white wines. Greenfield is capable of producing fruity, high-acid Pinot Blancs and floral, delicate Rieslings in good years. Arroyo Seco is immediately adjacent to Greenfield.

HEALDSBURG (Sonoma) About 20 miles north of Santa Rosa, the Healdsburg area is home to some 2 dozen wineries. 3 unique and important vineyard districts are nearby: the Alexander Valley to the east and north; the Dry Creek Valley to the northwest; and the Russian River Valley to the south and southwest.

HECKER PASS (Santa Clara) The Coast Range Mountains to the west of Gilroy open up ever so slightly to the coastal plain. This area, called Hecker Pass, is the location of a dozen wineries, most of which produce fair to indifferent jug wines and an occasional heavy red wine of interest.

HUDSON RIVER VALLEY *New York* This valley claims to be "America's oldest wine region." Attempts to grow vinifera in 1677 failed here; and until the 1950s, labrusca varieties were the rule. Today it has over 1,500 acres planted to French hybrids, mainly along the west bank of the Hudson River about 75 miles north of New York City. Concord still predominates, but is decreasing in acreage. Seyval Blanc and Baco Noir are the most successful varieties. Presently home to 10 wineries.

KENWOOD (Sonoma) Midway between the cities of Sonoma and Santa Rosa in the Sonoma Valley is the whistle-stop town of Kenwood. It is the home of Kenwood Vineyards and Chateau St. Jean, but is not the major source of their grapes. However, both wineries have made white wines from the cooler vineyards lying at the lowest, least sunny section of the valley floor.

KERN COUNTY 37,000 acres of grapes located here in the hottest, driest part of the Central Valley are oriented toward jug and dessert wines. Some vineyards are planted in the foothills above the valley floor, where the climate is thought to be more moderate. But one can scarcely detect the difference in Kern County wines that claim hillside provenance. The vineyards have the typical Central Valley mix: Ruby Cabernet (4,700 acres), French Colombard (4,700 acres), Chenin Blanc (4,300 acres), and Barbera (3,600 acres). Surprisingly, there are also 1,200 acres of Cabernet Sauvignon.

KING CITY (Monterey) Toward the southern end of the Salinas Valley, the temperatures become more hospitable for the medium-heat varieties that fail to ripen adequately farther north. The most enjoyable Petite Sirahs and Cabernet Sauvignons from Monterey County have been grown in the King City area.

KNIGHT'S VALLEY (Sonoma) Occupying its own bowl midway between the southern end of the Alexander Valley and the northern end of the Napa Valley is the small but increasingly vineyarded Knight's Valley. The area is cooled by tenacious morning fogs and afternoon breezes. Knight's Valley appears as the appellation of some Beringer wines.

LAKE COUNTY A northern coastal county lying inland from Mendocino County and north of Napa County, Lake County had about 100 acres of wine grapes 10 years ago; now, the total is close to 2,500. The expansion occurred in 1973 and 1974 with moderate growth after that. Over half the acreage is planted to Cabernet Sauvignon with another 30% split between Zinfandel, Napa Gamay, and Sauvignon Blanc. Everything else is planted in minuscule amounts. The few red wines from Lake County have, to date, been on the thin side, although there is reason to believe that some well-exposed vineyards will be able to ripen the medium-heat reds that dominate the current plantings. A few wineries have begun operations, but most of the harvest is trucked to wineries in neighboring counties.

LIVERMORE VALLEY (Alameda) Southeast of San Francisco, lying in its own enclosed pocket, is the Livermore Valley. Urban expansion has whittled away at vineyard holdings here, but both Wente and Concannon remain in the area and continue to produce a few genuine estate-bottled wines. Agricultural zoning has slowed the onslaught and encouraged new plantings. The valley is marked by medium-warm growing conditions (low Region III) and rocky soil. Almost 1,900 acres of vineyard survive.

LODI (San Joaquin) Located at the northern end of the grape-searing, hot San Joaquin Valley and cooled by the same coastal breezes as the Delta area, Lodi has produced heavyweight, sometimes overripe Zinfandels and Petite Sirahs. Flame Tokay grapes from Lodi, highly praised for table use, also find their way into bulk method champagnes, sherry, and brandy.

LYTTON SPRINGS (Sonoma) Small winegrowing area lying in the low hills that separate the Dry Creek Valley from the Geyserville area of the Alexander Valley. Zinfandel is the leading wine.

MADERA COUNTY 30,000 acres of wine grapes are planted in Madera County, and 2 wineries there, Ficklin and Angelo Papagni, are among the quality leaders of the Central Valley. Papagni is the only winery in the area that proudly displays its local appellation instead of the more general California appellation. The major plantings in the county consist of: Carignane (5,600 acres), French Colombard (5,400 acres), Grenache (4,000 acres), Barbera (3,600 acres), Chenin Blanc (2,500 acres), and Ruby Cabernet (2,300 acres).

MANDEVILLE ISLAND (San Joaquin) This peat bog of an island in the Delta region produces grapes that go to a variety of wineries. The combination of medium-warm temperature and rich soil yields good but rarely great wines; Chenin Blanc, Petite Sirah, and Cabernet Sauvignon are the main varieties.

MARTHA'S VINEYARD (Napa) This most famous Cabernet Sauvignon vineyard in California yields moderate amounts of exceptional wine from Heitz Cellars. The vineyard is located on the Rutherford benchlands along the western edge of the Napa Valley just north of Oakville and yields balanced, fairly hard wines marked by a distinctive blend of black currants and mint in aroma and flavors.

MAYACAMAS MOUNTAINS The mountain range, running north from San Francisco Bay, that forms the geographical boundary between the Napa and Sonoma valleys. Important vineyards and wineries are located on the mountainsides in both counties, including the Spring Mountain and Mount Veeder areas.

MENDOCINO COUNTY The northernmost of the coastal wine producers, Mendocino County has established a vinous identity of its own only in the past decade. Rough timber country, it has limited tillable acreage tucked away in a series of isolated valleys and canyons cut into the hills by the Russian River, including Anderson Valley, Redwood Valley, Potter Valley, and the Talmage and Ukiah areas. The growing season in Mendocino is generally shorter than elsewhere in California, but varies from very cool (Region I) near the coast to fairly warm (Region III) inland. Grape acreage has increased by 70% in the last decade to 10,100. The pre-1970 plantings of Carignane (2,100 acres) and French Colombard (1,100 acres) still show the way in Mendocino, but Zinfandel (1,300 acres) and Cabernet Sauvignon (900 acres) are making headway. The leading wineries are Parducci, Fetzer, Husch, and Edmeades.

MODESTO (Stanislaus) The incredible assortment of labels from Modesto, including Red Mountain, Carlo Rossi, André Champagne, Boone's Farm, and Madria-Madria Sangria, are all products of the Gallo Winery.

MONTE BELLO (Santa Clara) This is the famed home of Ridge Vineyards in the Santa Cruz Mountains west of San Jose. Both Cabernet and Zinfandel produce flavorful, full-bodied wines on Monte Bello Ridge.

MONTEREY COUNTY Grape growing in Monterey County (31,600 acres) is mainly in the Salinas Valley; a few hundred acres exist also in the Carmel Valley and the mountains near the Pinnacles National Monument. The county rates as cool (Region I to Region II) in its northern two-thirds to moderately warm (Region III) in its southern extremes. All but 2,000 acres of plantings are new since 1970, and

60% are in red varieties. However, the white varieties have seemed to fare best in the cool, windy climate. Johannisberg Riesling and Gewurztraminer have succeeded because of the intense fruitiness they develop. The fuller-bodied whites—Chardonnay, Sauvignon Blanc, and Pinot Blanc—have generally been less well received in spite of occasionally spectacular results. The reds are a different story. Thousands of acres of Cabernet Sauvignon, Zinfandel, and Petite Sirah were planted in locations too cool to ripen the grapes adequately in most years. The wines also displayed bothersome vegetal smells, although this problem is being eliminated to some extent as the vines mature. Even in the most hospitable areas, the best red wines from Monterey have yet to rise above ✿ rankings.

Monterey County plantings in order of acreage are Cabernet Sauvignon (4,200 acres), Chenin Blanc (3,200 acres), Chardonnay (3,100 acres), Johannisberg Riesling (2,800 acres), Zinfandel (2,800 acres), Petite Sirah (2,400 acres), and Pinot Noir (2,100 acres). Important Monterey County growing areas include Arroyo Seco, Carmel Valley, Gonzales, Greenfield, King City, Salinas Valley, and Soledad.

MORGAN HILL (Santa Clara) The first town south of San Jose in the southern portion of the Santa Clara Valley, Morgan Hill has a few wineries with poor to fair track records.

NAPA (Napa) A few wineries and a few vines lie within the city of Napa. Its major importance is as the urban center (if a town of 25,000 can be so described) for the Napa Valley, whose vineyards lie to the west and north.

NAPA COUNTY For years, wine labels reading Napa Valley have been allowed to refer to grapes from any location in Napa County. And although it is true that 95% of the 25,400 planted acres in the county actually lie in the valley proper, the new wine laws may now require grapes from outlying regions to be labeled as Napa County. With almost no exception among present plantings, these other areas have generally warmer climates and shorter growing seasons than the Napa Valley. Some, such as Pope Valley, already appear on wine labels while others, Gordon Valley and Wooden Valley, have not achieved separate recognition. As a way of calling attention to the nonvalley-floor origin of their grapes, a few wineries have chosen to use Napa County as an appellation in cases where their grapes come from the surrounding hills or from the Carneros region. The most widely planted varieties here are Cabernet Sauvignon (5,400 acres), Chardonnay (3,700 acres), Pinot Noir

(2,500 acres), Zinfandel (2,100 acres), and Johannisberg Riesling (1,400 acres).

NAPA VALLEY (Napa) The most famous winegrowing area in the United States, this land lives up to its Indian moniker of "the Valley of Plenty." It begins at the base of Mount St. Helena in the north, dissolving some 30 miles to the south into a flood plain as the Napa River enters San Francisco Bay. From Mount St. Helena to the city of Napa, the valley is defined by 2 north-south ridge lines of the Coast Range Mountains. The valley floor varies from 3 to 4 miles in width in the south to 1 mile or less in the north.

From its earliest days, the Napa Valley has been the home of some of California's most famous wine estates, including such well-known producers as Charles Krug, Beringer Brothers, Schramsberg, and Inglenook. Today, the valley boasts upward of 23,000 acres planted to wine grapes, making it California's most intensively farmed viticultural area. More than 60 wineries are in the Napa Valley, and most offer high-caliber, often expensive wines.

With few exceptions, the best California Chardonnays and Cabernet Sauvignons come from the Napa Valley, and much of the reputation of the valley is based on the success of these two varietals. But the valley is large and filled with varied growing conditions. The cold Carneros region by San Francisco Bay yields good Chardonnay and Riesling, shows great promise for Pinot Noir, but rarely produces well-ripened Cabernet Sauvignon. By the same token, the warm Calistoga region can produce nicely ripe Zinfandel, Gamay, and Petite Sirah, but overcooks Pinot Noir and the other heat-sensitive varieties. On wine labels the term Napa Valley has historically included all areas within Napa County. A recent change in federal wine-labeling rules will require a redefinition of the term and will limit its use to wines produced in a specific geographic area within the county. Approximately 95% of all vines in Napa County will be included within this appellation.

Over 20 major subareas have been identified within the Napa Valley; 12 are already important for viticulture and are described in the adjoining pages (see Carneros, Calistoga, Napa, Stag's Leap, Rutherford, St. Helena, Yountville, Spring Mountain, Mount Veeder, Silverado Trail, Oakville, and Pope Valley).

NEW YORK STATE The second most important wine-producing state in the United States now has close to 50 wineries, including several of the country's largest. Its vineyards are planted to labruscas, French hybrids, and vinifera, but are predominantly Concord. Only half of the total acreage

(50,000) is harvested for wine production. The other half goes into assorted fruit juices, jams, and jellies. The most important regions for winemaking are the Finger Lakes (about 80% of the state's total) and the Hudson River Valley. New York State as an appellation means that at least 75% of the wine's volume was derived from New York–grown grapes. New York is the second biggest wine-consuming state on a per capita basis.

NORTH COAST Once used to indicate the coastal counties north of San Francisco, this ill-defined suggestion of geographical heritage and wine quality has come to mean any portion of California north of Bakersfield and Santa Barbara and as far inland as the distinctly noncoastal Central Valley. It would be appropriate for the term to pass totally out of usage, and there is some indication that government rule makers will force that to happen. In the meantime, people who use the name North Coast on their wines are talking about Mendocino, Napa, Sonoma, and Lake counties, or they are pulling your leg—and ours.

NORTHERN CALIFORNIA One occasionally sees this appellation on wine labels. By most definitions it covers everything north of Los Angeles, or 97% of the grapes grown in the state. For all practical purposes, this term on a label is no more meaningful than the word California.

OAKVILLE (Napa) Situated in the southern end of the Napa Valley, halfway between Yountville and Rutherford, this way station is the home of several wineries (foremost among them the Robert Mondavi Winery) and adjoins some of the Napa Valley's best Cabernet growing turf. The superb Martha's Vineyard produced by Heitz Cellars, the vineyard yielding the Charles Krug Vintage Selection Cabernet, and a substantial portion of the Robert Mondavi Cabernet vineyards are in Oakville, along the western edge of the valley floor. Other wineries in the area are Villa Mt. Eden and an Inglenook production and bottling plant.

OREGON 30 small wineries and over 200 growers have become active since the early 1960s. Most vineyards are less than 5 acres, and many wineries depend on eastern Washington for grapes. The total acreage was approximately 1,300 acres; two-thirds of which lay on the western side of the Willamette Valley, west and south of Portland. The other major wine area is the Umpqua Valley in Douglas County. Almost all Oregon vineyards are dry farmed on shallow, light soils, on hilly sites. Predominant grape varieties are Chardonnay, Pinot Noir, and White Riesling.

PACIFIC NORTHWEST Burgeoning winegrowing area covering Oregon, Washington, and Idaho. Upward of 5,000 acres of grapes (approximately 75% in Washington; 23% in Oregon; 2% in Idaho) and 45 wineries. California has been a major influence, but winemakers and growers are increasingly successful at adopting their own special techniques to the problems and opportunities of cool climates, shorter growing seasons, and longer daylight hours in summer. Whites (especially Chardonnay, Sauvignon Blanc, and White Riesling) have been more successful than reds and dominate the plantings.

PASO ROBLES (San Luis Obispo) Lying in the lee of the Coast Range area is a series of vineyards near Paso Robles. The Hoffman Mountain Ranch, located in the hills to the west, is the only winery in the immediate Paso Robles area. Others are nearby in Templeton, and the Estrella River Winery lies on the rolling hills to the east. Grapes from the entire area are often labeled as being from Paso Robles.

POPE VALLEY (Napa) Nestled in the mountains east and north of the Napa Valley is the small, hot depression of land called Pope Valley. A few hundred acres of vines and 1 winery occupy this rustic area, removed from the sophistication of the Napa Valley floor. Zinfandel grows well, and there has been talk of planting Barbera. The area's lone winery, Pope Valley Winery, is suitably quaint.

POTTER VALLEY (Mendocino) The most northerly and highest in elevation of the county's grape-growing areas, Potter Valley contains approximately 700 acres of mostly new vineyard. Chateau St. Jean has produced late harvest Rieslings from the area, and Fetzer and Felton-Empire have made soft Rieslings.

RANCHO CALIFORNIA (Riverside) Another name for the new grape-growing area northeast of San Diego, which is more frequently called Temecula.

REDWOOD VALLEY (Mendocino) Among the most northerly and coolest of the many grape-growing valleys framing the Russian River, this moderately cool wine-growing area seems able to ripen most varieties adequately. The hills yield good Zinfandel and Petite Sirah, whereas the cooler valley floor is more suited to whites. The name Redwood Valley appears on many Fetzer wines, and the area has also contributed grapes to such non-Mendocino producers as Souverain and Wente.

RUSSIAN RIVER VALLEY (Sonoma) The Russian River is an important influence in several viticultural parts of Sonoma County—and each of these is a valley bearing its own name. As an appellation of origin, however, the name Russian River Valley has commonly been used to describe the low-lying, flat plain that extends south and west of Healdsburg and follows the river as it turns toward the Pacific Ocean. At Guerneville the coastal hills close off the area and mark its western boundary. Plantings are oriented to early-ripening varieties, especially Chardonnay and Johannisberg Riesling. Some Merlot and Pinot Noir also thrive in the coolest areas near the river. In the sheltered areas and hillsides, decent-quality red varieties can be grown. There are about a dozen wineries in the area, including the well-known Korbel and Sonoma Vineyards. Most, however, are new and small.

RUTHERFORD (Napa) Small community located in south-central Napa Valley between Oakville and St. Helena in a temperate Region II climate. Heat-retaining soils keep the hillsides warm; high clay content along the valley floor near Napa River and Conn Creek provides cooler growing conditions. The area is home for many important wineries—Beaulieu, Inglenook, Caymus, Rutherford Hill—and yields exceptional (up to ✿✿✿) Cabernet Sauvignon along benchlands at the western edge and also from scattered sites across the valley floor. Freemark Abbey and Spring Mountain have major vineyard holdings in slightly cool locations that yield good to excellent Chardonnay. The eastside hills have medium heat (up to Region III) suited to Zinfandel and Petite Sirah. Look for West Rutherford (Benchlands) to become an appellation of origin recognized for its superb Cabernet Sauvignon in the next decade.

SAGEMOOR FARMS (Washington) South Columbia Basin vineyard name appearing on some of the best wines produced in the Pacific Northwest. Sagemoor Farms has 465 acres and regularly sells to more than 20 wineries in the northern states and Canada, including Chateau Ste. Michelle, Preston, Ste. Chapelle, Sokol Blosser, and Eyrie. A third of the total acreage is in Cabernet Sauvignon and Merlot. Most of the remaining acreage is in white varieties, led by Johannisberg Riesling (96 acres) and Chardonnay (65 acres).

ST. HELENA (Napa) This picturesque town and its environs are home to no fewer than 35 wineries, including such historically important producers as Beringer, Charles Krug, Christian Brothers, and Louis Martini. Among newer properties, St. Helena can boast Freemark Abbey, Heitz Cellars, and Joseph Phelps. The vineyards surrounding St. Helena are not the valley's most noteworthy. On the valley floor east of the city, heavy soils and increased temperatures limit the area's suitability for the noble grape varieties.

But there are exceptions. The low-lying, wet clay soils that abut the Napa River have yielded above average to superb Chardonnays (up to ✿✿✿) and very likable Johannisberg Rieslings. The low hillside slopes west of the valley floor contain areas similar in exposure and soil to the best Cabernet Sauvignon vineyards of Rutherford and are expected to yield fine wines when the vineyards mature. The eastern side hills get the hot late-afternoon sun and are amenable hosts to Zinfandel and Petite Sirah.

SALINAS VALLEY (Monterey) Lying on a north-south axis behind the Coast Range hills, which protect it from direct ocean influence, the Salinas Valley is California's newest major winegrowing area. It contains almost all of Monterey County's 30,000-plus acres of grapes.

SAN BENITO COUNTY This is Almadén country. When its grape needs could no longer be met by Santa Clara vineyards, Almadén made a major commitment to San Benito County that now approaches 4,600 acres. There are a few other growers and producers in San Benito, but their output is small. This warm, dry area is planted substantially to early-ripening varieties that have fared only moderately well— like Chardonnay (1,000 acres), Pinot Noir (800 acres), Gamay Beaujolais (500 acres), Johannisberg Riesling (300 acres), Gewurztraminer (300 acres), and Pinot Blanc (200 acres). The later-ripening varieties planted there, Cabernet Sauvignon (500 acres) and Zinfandel (200 acres), have similarly failed to yield particularly interesting results.

SAN BERNARDINO COUNTY The remaining 7,300 acres of vineyard of the once vibrant Cucamonga district east of Los Angeles make up the plantings in San Bernardino County. The vines are old, the varieties are old-fashioned, and the grapes are made into wines of indifferent quality by local wineries. The leading varieties are Zinfandel (2,300 acres), Mission (1,500 acres), Grenache (1,500 acres), Palomino (800 acres), Burger (400 acres), and Alicante Bouschet (300 acres). There have been very few plantings in San Bernardino County in the last decade.

SAN JOAQUIN COUNTY The northernmost of the major Central Valley counties, San Joaquin (especially in the Lodi and Delta areas) is occasionally cooled by fog and winds flowing in from San Francisco Bay. This may account for the somewhat higher quality of its wines in comparison to its even hotter neighbors to the south. The plantings in the 39,000-acre San Joaquin County vineyards are a mix of old-fashioned varieties, of coastal grapes hoping to benefit from the occasional fog, and of the typical high-acid choices for new Central Valley plantings. 11,300 acres of Zinfandel concentrated in the Lodi area yield over 40% of the entire California crop. Other grapes include Carignane (7,500 acres), French Colombard (4,900 acres), Grenache (2,300 acres), Petite Sirah (2,300 acres), Barbera (1,500 acres), and Cabernet Sauvignon (700 acres).

SAN JOAQUIN VALLEY The southern portion of the Central Valley. Running south from the Sacramento-Stockton area to Bakersfield and containing San Joaquin, Stanislaus, Merced, Madera, Fresno, Tulare, Kings, and Kern counties, the San Joaquin Valley is the source of most California jug wine. A medium-warm area at the northern end of the valley (see Lodi and Delta) is cooled by breezes that flow in from the coast; Zinfandel, Petite Sirah, and Chenin Blanc grow well here. The rest of the valley is extremely hot in the summer (up to Region V) and rarely produces exceptional wine; it is common to refer to grapes and wines from this area as Central Valley.

SAN JOSE (Santa Clara) This major urban area (population 700,000) is home to 3 important wineries—Almadén, Mirassou, and J. Lohr. It also houses facilities for Paul Masson and Llords & Elwood.

SAN LUIS OBISPO COUNTY A recently developed major California grape-growing region, San Luis Obispo County contains approximately 4,600 acres located in 4 distinct areas. The newest are the Shandon region in the northern end of the county and the Edna Valley, stretching south from the city of San Luis Obispo toward Santa Barbara County. The wines of these areas have been of average to slightly above average quality to date, but the verdict is far from final. The older areas, Paso Robles and Templeton in the western foothills of the county, have a longer but no more distinguished history. The county's main grapes are Cabernet Sauvignon (1,000 acres), Zinfandel (900 acres), Chardonnay (600 acres), Sauvignon Blanc (500 acres), Chenin Blanc (400 acres), and Johannisberg Riesling (200 acres).

SANTA BARBARA COUNTY This coastal county north of Los Angeles is among the last decade's newcomers to grape growing. Its 117 acres in 1969 increased to 4,700 in 1973 and to nearly 7,500 today. The plantings are located in the Santa Ynez Valley, some 20 miles removed from the coast; in the Santa Maria area further north and inland; and to a limited extent in cooler, more coastally oriented climes. Approximately 75% of the acreage is in 4 varieties: Johannisberg Riesling (1,800 acres), Chardonnay (1,500 acres), Cabernet Sauvignon (1,400 acres), and Pinot Noir (800 acres).

SANTA CLARA COUNTY This fast-urbanizing area was once among the highest production winegrowing regions in California. Now its 1,700 acres of grapes represent about 0.5% of all vineyards. The once abundant vineyards to the north and east of San Jose are all but gone. The one remaining concentration of grapes, in the southern end of the Santa Clara Valley near Gilroy, serves the cluster of small, local wineries. The bigger wineries of Santa Clara County have stayed in place. Paul Masson, Almadén, and Mirassou all maintain large production facilities in the San Jose area, and they are joined by a growing list of small and medium-sized operations up and down the length of the valley. The leading grape in number of acres is Cabernet Sauvignon (about 200 acres). Others with more than 100 acres are Carignane, Chardonnay, French Colombard, Petite Sirah, and Zinfandel.

To supply their needs, many large and medium-sized wineries in Santa Clara County have invested heavily in vineyards in Monterey County and are major buyers of grapes from San Luis Obispo and Santa Barbara counties. The larger wineries also rely on grapes from the Central Valley.

SANTA CLARA VALLEY (Santa Clara) Nearly all the identifiable vineyard acreage of this county lies within the Santa Clara Valley. A few small but important mountain vineyards exist north and west of San Jose, but the bulk of the valley's northernmost winegrowing has faded under urban onslaught. A few thousand acres remain in production where the valley narrows south of San Jose in the Morgan Hill, Gilroy, and Hecker Pass areas.

SANTA CRUZ COUNTY A cool, coastal county south of San Francisco and north of Monterey. Fewer than 100 acres of grapes are made into wine here by a dozen small but dedicated wineries. The more successful varieties are Chardonnay, Johannisberg Riesling, and Pinot Noir. Grapes are brought in for crushing by most wineries to make up for the inadequate supply of local grapes.

SANTA CRUZ MOUNTAINS The coastal mountain range running south of San Francisco past San Jose has long been a hotbed of winemaking activity. Today, the two dozen wineries of the area, all fairly small, are scattered throughout southern San Mateo County and the low mountains west of San Jose on both the Santa Clara and the Santa Cruz sides of the ridge line. There is agreement among the wineries to call the entire area Santa Cruz Mountains, and the name has been appearing as an appellation of origin on a few wines from the area. Prominent wineries include Ridge, David Bruce, Felton-Empire, Mount Eden, and Roudon-Smith.

SANTA YNEZ VALLEY (Santa Barbara) In this new cold-climate vineyard area in the low mountains of Solvang, initial experience shows frequent success with whites and Pinot Noir, but less satisfactory results with other reds. The leading wineries of the area—Firestone, Zaca Mesa, Sanford and Benedict—are well financed and quality-oriented.

SHENANDOAH VALLEY (Amador) This major grape-growing district of Amador County was rediscovered in the late 1960s by the Sutter Home Winery. Its mature Zinfandel vines have become highly prized for the ripe, intense wines they yield. Shenandoah Valley grapes, mostly Zinfandel, are used now by more than a dozen wineries, including Carneros Creek, Mayacamas, Harbor, and Ridge. In the early 1970s the new Monteviña Winery opened and began experiments with many varieties, including Nebbiolo. An older winery, D'Agostini, has been in business for over 100 years, making wines of indifferent quality. The Deaver, Esola, and Ferrero vineyards are important sources of grapes.

SIERRA FOOTHILLS East of the Central Valley rise the majestic 10,000-foot-high Sierra Nevada Mountains. During the Gold Rush era, places like El Dorado, Placer, Calaveras and Amador counties in the Sierra foothills developed a burgeoning wine industry that reached 10,000 acres at its peak. In 1970 less than 1,000 acres remained, and most was in Amador. Recent years have seen a return to those foothill counties by vineyardists and winemakers alike, raising the foothill acreage to 1,500. El Dorado County, which had 5,000 acres of vines during the Gold Rush, seems likely to come back into prominence.

SILVERADO TRAIL (Napa) Technically not a wine district, the Silverado Trail is a lightly traveled roadway that traverses the eastern edge of the Napa Valley starting in the city of Napa and extending northward to the city of Calistoga. The vineyards east of the trail generally support grape varieties needing warmer growing conditions than those found in corresponding locations on the valley floor.

SOLEDAD (Monterey) Located in the middle of the Salinas Valley wind tunnel, the area around Soledad is definitely a cold winegrowing area. Many large wineries have holdings in the area, but none so large as Paul Masson, which has produced a series of vintage-dated wines from its vineyards near Soledad.

SONOMA (Sonoma) The home of the Sebastiani, Hacienda, and Buena Vista wineries. This quaint town was the wine capital of the North Coast from the 1830s to the 1860s, when it sported the most successful and progressive vineyards of the area. Vineyards to the south and west of Sonoma are cooled by proximity to San Francisco Bay, making them suitable for white grapes. The hills north of Sonoma are more sheltered and have direct southern exposure. For almost 150 years they have produced good to very good Cabernets and Zinfandels.

SONOMA COUNTY Except for the mid-1800s, when North Coast winemaking was centered in the city of Sonoma, the nicely situated vineyards of Sonoma County have somehow always taken a back seat to the Napa Valley. In the late 1960s the vineyards of Sonoma County were still more heavily oriented toward jug wines than fine varietals. Almost 30% of the county's 14,000 vineyard acres were in Zinfandel, which had yet to be recognized as an important varietal wine. Another 30% was in Carignane, French Colombard, and Petite Sirah (another as yet unrecognized variety). Less than 25% of the vineyards were devoted to premium table wine varieties. At the time, only 6 of the then two dozen producers in Sonoma County offered varietal wines.

But what a difference a decade makes. Today, Sonoma County's acreage has increased to 27,200, and almost all of the new plantings are in the better varieties. In addition, the new popularity of Zinfandel and Petite Sirah has created a legacy of mature vineyards in outstanding locations. Superb wines from distinctly identified appellations —Carneros, Sonoma Valley, Russian River Valley, Alexander Valley, and Dry Creek Valley—are coming to market from 40 new and refurbished wineries. Among the great wines of Sonoma County are ripe, distinctive Zinfandels; lush late harvest Rieslings; and forward, spicy Gewurztraminers.

SONOMA VALLEY (Sonoma) Almost one-quarter of Sonoma County's planted vineyards lie in the picturesque Sonoma Valley. The area contains a mix of climatic, topographical, and soil variations that may one day be divided into a dozen or so separate appellations of origin. Sonoma Valley's 6,000 acres of grapes stretch from San Francisco Bay northward through the narrow valley until they reach the suburban outskirts of the city of Santa Rosa. The coolest growing district, Carneros, abuts San Francisco Bay and is best suited to early-ripening varieties. Following the valley northward, one passes through the city of Sonoma, Glen Ellen, and Kenwood. The hills that line the valley regularly produce good Cabernet Sauvignon and Zinfandel, whereas the valley floor is generally cooler and is more heavily devoted to whites.

There are a dozen producing wineries in the Sonoma Valley, of which the oldest is Buena Vista and the biggest Sebastiani. Although the Sonoma Valley was the first winegrowing area to develop north of San Francisco, during the early to mid-1800s, it was soon surpassed by neighboring Napa Valley, losing its prominence by the early 1900s. Almost two-thirds of the current plantings in the Sonoma Valley, as well as two-thirds of its wineries, are relatively new.

SOUTH COLUMBIA BASIN *Washington* Rather large horseshoe-shaped land mass in eastern Washington defined by the course of the Columbia River as it heads toward the Oregon border and then reaches west for the Pacific Ocean. The region is arid, mountain desert relying on heavy irrigation of the sandy soils for agriculture. The several wineries and growers cultivating sites ranging up to hundreds of acres include Chateau Ste. Michelle, Preston Wine Cellars, and Sagemoor Farms (a grower only). Temperatures are moderately warm but not excessive, allowing most whites and many reds to ripen well with high levels of acidity.

SOUTHERN CALIFORNIA To a Californian, anything south of Santa Barbara is part of Southern California. As a grape-growing area, sometimes called South Coast, it consists of the Temecula area in the southwestern corner of Riverside County, the vineyards in the Cucamonga district, and the coastal vineyards of San Diego County.

SPRING MOUNTAIN (Napa) A distinctly identifiable watershed area known as Spring Mountain lies west of St. Helena in the Napa Valley and forms part of the Mayacamas Mountain Range, the boundary between the Napa and Sonoma valleys. This picturesque stretch of hillside has a long and fabled history of grape growing that dates back to the nineteenth century. It maintained itself fitfully after Prohibition, but many of Spring Mountain's great estates are only now being reopened and put back into winegrowing. (Chateau Chevalier and Spring Mountain Vineyard occupy two of the loveliest refurbished properties.) Soils and exposures on Spring Mountain vary considerably, allowing the successful cultivation of most varieties. York Creek Vineyard is near the top of Spring Mountain. Other wineries here include Yverdon, Keenan, and Smith-Madrone.

STAG'S LEAP (Napa County) About a mile east of Yountville is the picturesque Stag's Leap area. Known primarily for Cabernet Sauvignon, this superb viticultural pocket has distinctly red soil and is bounded on the east by a rocky knoll with red rock outcroppings. It is thought that the red soil and rock absorb heat and keep the vines at moderate growing temperatures long after the sun's warming rays are lost. Although only 400–600 acres of vines exist in the Stag's Leap area, the quality of wines produced by Clos du Val, Stag's Leap Wine Cellars, and Stags' Leap Vineyards makes it one of California's most important winegrowing microclimates.

STANISLAUS COUNTY 19,600 acres of grapes in the hot Central Valley geared primarily to bulk and dessert wine production: French Colombard (3,300 acres), Chenin Blanc (2,500 acres), Ruby Cabernet (2,300 acres), and Grenache (2,100 acres). Located in this county is Modesto, the home of Gallo.

STELTZNER VINEYARD (Napa) This Stag's Leap area vineyard has yielded dry, full-bodied Chenin Blancs and round, inviting Cabernets typical of its viticultural area. Wineries using grapes from this vineyard have included Burgess, Markham, Cakebread, and Veedercrest.

TALMAGE (Mendocino) Near Ukiah, on a broad fan of land that extends to the east and south and occupies the foothills as well, are some 4,000 planted acres of grapes in the Talmage area. The majority of plantings (most of which are less than a dozen years old) are in the medium-warm reds—Zinfandel, Cabernet, and Petite Sirah. Sprinklings of whites, mainly Chardonnay, French Colombard, and Chenin Blanc, also appear.

TEMECULA (Riverside) This burgeoning winegrowing area projects inland from the ocean north of San Diego. It is home to the Callaway Winery and several newer and smaller enterprises. Grape-growing conditions seem to be nearly perfect for cool to medium-warmth varieties of reds and whites, but the current track record is spotty indeed. Rancho California is another name used to denote the area.

TEMPLETON (San Luis Obispo) Just south of Paso Robles, located in the Santa Lucia Mountains, sit the 3 wineries of the Templeton area—York Mountain, Pesenti, and Las Tablas. These old-line establishments survive mainly on local clientele and the tourist trade that passes through. The area is noted for Zinfandel.

UKIAH (Mendocino) The urban center of the Mendocino County winegrowing areas and home of the Parducci, Weibel, and Cresta Blanca wineries. About 1,000 acres of grapes are grown directly north of Ukiah in the light bench soils and hillsides above the Russian River.

UMPQUA VALLEY *Oregon* Contemporary winemaking began in this valley, the watershed of the Umpqua River, when Hillcrest Vineyard established vineyards in 1961. 6 wineries and about 17 growers (200 acres) now exist. The area is a cool Region I, well suited to its major variety, White Riesling.

VALLEY OF THE MOON (Sonoma) The name given to the Sonoma Valley by author Jack London (whose winery existed there until the early 1900s) derived from the Indian expression "Valley of the Seven Moons." The moon would appear and disappear behind 7 hilltops as it rose.

VENTANA VINEYARDS (Monterey) This 300-acre vineyard in Soledad was planted to 8 varieties in 1973. The leading grapes are Chardonnay (46 acres), Pinot Noir (44 acres), Chenin Blanc (40 acres), and Johannisberg Riesling (33 acres). Grapes are sold to many small wineries, including Chardonnay to MEV, Roudon-Smith, Pendleton (formerly Arroyo), and Martin Ray Vineyards. 34 new acres of Chardonnay were added in 1980.

WASHINGTON Most of Washington's grape vines are Concords (19,000 of 24,000 acres). The Yakima Valley (Yakima and Benton counties) and the South Columbia Basin area further east—where the Columbia, Snake, and Yakima rivers converge (Benton, Franklin, and Walla Walla counties)—are the centers for grape growing. These are dry areas with barren hills, warm summer temperatures, and cold winters. The acreage in vinifera wine grapes more than doubled, to 4,000 acres, between 1975 and 1980. Major varieties are Riesling and Cabernet, and other large plantings include Grenache, Chardonnay, Chenin Blanc, Gewurztraminer, Sauvignon Blanc, and Semillon. The largest blocks of vineyards belong to Chateau Ste. Michelle with approximately 2,000 acres, Sagemoor Farms with 500 acres, and Preston Wine Cellars with 200 acres. 15 wineries.

WILLAMETTE VALLEY *Oregon* Principal grape-growing and wine-producing area in Oregon. As a river valley/watershed, the Willamette Valley (cool Region I) starts below Eugene in the south and extends northward to Portland, where the Willamette River merges with the Columbia River. The flat plain of the valley is rich agricultural land, but the vineyards are all in the hills on the west side of the Willamette River. The central section from Salem to the Chehalem Mountains (mainly Yamhill County) contains a dozen wineries. There are 400–500 acres in vines, and prime locations for more than 20,000 acres of vines exist. To the north, in the hilly portions of Washington County and in the foothills of the Coast Range Mountains, are 400 or more acres of vineyard and a half-dozen wineries. The vines in the Willamette Valley are planted on their own roots and enjoy adequate groundwater and rainfall. Chardonnay, White Riesling, and Pinot Noir are the main varieties of grapes grown.

WINERY LAKE VINEYARDS (Napa) Situated on a hilly site in the middle of the Carneros district is the sculpture-studded, baronial estate of art collector René Di Rosa. From these 100-plus acres, grapes go out to 14 wineries, many of whom put the vineyard name prominently on the label. One that does not, Robert Mondavi, derives much of its Pinot Noir from this property. Excellent wines bearing the Winery Lake designation include Chardonnay and Johannisberg Riesling from both Burgess and Veedercrest, Merlot from Wine and The People, and Pinot Noir by ZD Wines.

YAKIMA VALLEY *Washington* A major agricultural region located in the south-central part of the state. The south-facing slope holds about 500 acres of vinifera vines with a capacity of up to 20,000 acres. The area is relatively dry and subject to temperature drops as low as 20° F. below zero. Chateau Ste. Michelle has a major winemaking facility here, and there are several new wineries.

YOLO COUNTY Lying west of Sacramento in an area that is technically part of the Central Valley, Yolo County vineyards (700 acres) experience cooler growing conditions because of fog intrusions from San Francisco Bay up the Sacramento River lowlands. The majority of vineyards are planted in the southern part of the county in the Delta region and are primarily Chenin Blanc (300 acres) and Petite Sirah (100 acres). The Chenin Blanc is reported to go primarily to big wineries that use it to supplement their own grapes.

YORK CREEK VINEYARD (Napa) High on Spring Mountain sits the 125-acre York Creek Vineyard, belonging to washing-machine heir Fritz Maytag. Best known for its Petite Sirah (from 10 acres) that yield brawny, tannic wines at Freemark Abbey and Ridge, it has also produced Cabernet Sauvignon (35 acres) and Zinfandel (30 acres) bottled by Ridge. A limited amount of Napa Gamay (6 acres) goes to Chappellet.

ROBERT YOUNG VINEYARDS *(Sonoma)* Located in the Alexander Valley, this property ranks alongside Winery Lake Vineyards as California's most widely heralded. Its name has appeared prominently on the labels of the unsurpassed late harvest Rieslings of Chateau St. Jean and on the exceptional Chardonnays of St. Jean, Dry Creek Vineyards, and MEV. The property has also yielded Cabernets for Smothers and Felton-Empire.

YOUNTVILLE (Napa) Lying just 6 miles north of the city of Napa, the little town of Yountville is the first major wine community that one encounters when entering the Napa Valley. Surrounding Yountville are a variety of important growing areas and wineries. Lying to the south in relatively cold growing conditions are Chardonnay vineyards that supply Chateau Montelena, Trefethen, and Beringer. To the west lies the dramatic new home of Domaine Chandon, and the eastern side of the valley contains the small Stag's Leap microclimate that produces the superb Cabernets of Stag's Leap Wine Cellars and Clos du Val.

❧❧❧ An exceptional wine, worth a special search.

❧❧ A distinctive wine, likely to be memorable.

❧ A fine example of a given type or style.

♀ A wine of average quality. The accompanying tasting note provides further description.

ᚦ Below average. A wine to avoid.

♯ A wine regarded as a "best buy," based on price and quality.

Wineries and Wines
in California

Location by county and date established is indicated in italics within each winery entry.

ACACIA WINERY *Napa 1979* Primarily using Carneros-grown grapes, the winery is concentrating on barrel-fermented Chardonnay and ripe, full-bodied Pinot Noir. First wines, about 13,000 cases, were made in leased facilities. A Carneros winery is planned. Ambitions are high.

AHERN WINERY *Los Angeles 1978* Small hobbyist operation (1,000 cases) emphasizing barrel-aged Sauvignon Blanc and Chardonnay. Amador County Zinfandel will be offered.

AHLGREN VINEYARDS *Santa Cruz 1976* A 1,200-case winery offering several varietals made from purchased grapes. Quantity of each varies from 40 to 400 cases. Its red wines, particularly Petite Sirah, are quite successful.

ALATERA VINEYARDS *Napa 1977* First wines appeared in 1979. Winery will specialize in Pinot Noir, Cabernet Sauvignon, and Gewurztraminer from grapes grown in partner's vineyards (70 acres) near Yountville. Efforts to date have been unexciting save for an exceptional, intense, honeylike late harvest Johannisberg Riesling. Current wine production is 3,000 cases.

ALEXANDER VALLEY VINEYARDS *Sonoma 1975* Family-run 120-acre vineyard is among the best in the Alexander Valley region. The winery is slowly building to 20,000 cases, mostly of white varietals. Cabernet blended with Merlot and recently released Pinot Noir are the only reds. Enjoys a good reputation for the whites with Chardonnay being the most consistent. All wines are made from its own vineyards. Reasonably priced.

Cabernet Sauvignon: *Herbaceous, soft, some oak* ♥
Chardonnay: *Ripe, moderate oak, balanced* ♥/✿

Johannisberg Riesling: *Flowery, delicate, slightly sweet* ♀/❀

ALMADÉN VINEYARDS *Santa Clara 1852* The fourth largest U.S. winery now sells 11 million cases and is still expanding. The company operates 5 facilities to offer some 60 wines under its labels. It owns 6,700 acres of vineyards, including large holdings in Monterey and San Benito counties. Both appellations appear on its vintage-dated varietals, most of which struggle to attain average-quality status. A high percentage of Almadén's production is in jug wines (generics and varietals), and the generic blends are not keeping pace with the competition. Yet Almadén is one of the largest champagne producers under its own and the Le Domaine labels, and a few of the Almadén sparkling-wine offerings are above average. The line is rounded out by numerous dessert wines headed by popular sherries. (See Charles Le Franc for review of Almadén's newest label.)

Blanc de Blancs Champagne: *Fruity, yeasty, slightly sweet* ♀/❀
Burgundy: *Light, dull* ♀/δ
Cabernet Sauvignon: *Fruity, vegetal, soft, simple* ♀
Chablis: *Flat, overly chemical* δ
Eye of the Partridge Champagne: *Fresh, fruity, soft, slightly sweet* ♀/❀
Flor Fino Sherry: *Yeasty, thin, sharp* ♀
Gewurztraminer: *Spicy, sometimes flat, slightly sweet* ♀/❀
Zinfandel: *Light, fruity, vinous* ♀

ALTA VINEYARD CELLAR *Napa 1979* In a historic pre-Prohibition winery currently being refurbished, the owner aged and bottled 1,000 cases of oak-aged Chardonnay. Present 6 acres of Chardonnay will be increased to 10, and optimum output is pegged at 2,500 cases, all Chardonnay.

AMADOR WINERY *Amador 1967* The second oldest winery in Amador, offering 8 generic wines from purchased grapes. Low quality. 3,500 cases per year.

AMBASSADOR (PERELLI-MINETTI WINERY) A large line of vintage-dated, cork-finished varietals and generics, most of which are jug wine quality. Also included are vermouth, Marsala, and a good inexpensive bulk process *brut* champagne, finished slightly sweet. All wines are low-priced. Production is now at 75,000 cases total.

ANDRÉ (E. & J. GALLO) Made by bulk process, this is likely the largest selling line of U.S. champagne. Ranges from slightly sweet to very sweet, including even those labeled dry. Inexpensive, but often bland in flavor and low in acidity.

ARGONAUT WINERY *Amador 1976* This 2,000-case winery makes Amador Zinfandel and Barbera. Over the first few vintages, it did not make them well.

ARROYO SONOMA A private label backed by vineyards in Carneros (Chardonnay), Dry Creek Valley (Cabernet Sauvignon), and Ukiah (Sauvignon Blanc). Early wines were made at Phelps; more recently at Buena Vista. Continuing rumors of a winery to go along with the label have never borne fruit. They continue, however.

Cabernet Sauvignon: *Ripe, brawny, full-bodied* ✪

ARROYO WINERY The early name for the winery now known as Pendleton. Wine was offered under Arroyo through the 1977 vintage.

ASSUMPTION ABBEY (BROOKSIDE CELLARS) Assumption Abbey is the top line offered in Brookside's tasting rooms. Some varietals now carry vintage dates and Temecula or Sonoma appellations. Emerald Riesling and Petite Sirah are best sellers of a fairly full line. Quality has never been high.

BALLARD CANYON WINERY *Santa Barbara 1978* 2,000-case production from the winery's 39 acres is expected to reach 10,000 cases when vines mature. Cabernet Sauvignon (23 acres) and Johannisberg Riesling (16 acres) will be offered.

BALVERNE CELLARS *Sonoma 1979* Located 2 miles south of Healdsburg along the eastern hillsides are 175 acres of vineyards and a winery finished in 1980. 5 white and 2 red varietals are in the program of this presently 15,000-case— ultimately 40,000-case—winery. First wines made elsewhere were simple and inexpensive.

BANDIERA WINES *Sonoma 1975* The winery was founded in 1937 and remained active for decades before winemaking ceased. Reopened by the founder's descendants, the winery began a modernization program. All grapes are purchased, and its 3 red varietals carry the Alexander Valley appellation. Their quality has been erratic to date. About 80% of total 5,000-case output consists of inexpensive generics.

BARENGO VINEYARDS *Stanislaus 1934* Old-time large-scale (over 500,000-case) Central Valley producer in the Lodi area. Run by Dino Barengo until early 1970s. Line has concentrated on jug wines and locally grown varietals, but it has expanded now to include grapes from other areas, including Central Coast. Production techniques have changed to reflect modern technology, but the wines have not always kept pace. A related product, Barengo's strong, pungent wine vinegar, is very highly regarded.

BARGETTO WINERY *Santa Cruz 1933* A broad line of varietals and fortified wines (35,000 cases in all) is offered. The winery owns no vineyards, so wines are from purchased grapes and often from purchased wines brought to the winery and bottled. As a result, quality has varied widely. Bargetto is also well known for fruit and berry wines.

Chardonnay (Santa Barbara): *Fruity, crisp, slightly floral, light oak* ♥/✿

BEAULIEU VINEYARDS *Napa 1900* Once the proudest Napa Valley name, this fabled winery has more than tripled its output (to 350,000 cases) since its acquisition by Heublein in 1969. Its most important wines—Cabernet Sauvignon, Pinot Noir, and Burgundy—have not maintained their earlier depth and richness. Except for the whites noted below, much of the rest is only of average quality. The winery offers a broad line including dessert wines, champagne, and an expanding proportion (50,000 cases) of generic wines in magnums.

Burgundy: *Fruity blend made in drinkable style* ♥
Cabernet Sauvignon/Private Reserve: *Generous, ripe style, fairly tannic, oaky* ✿/✿✿✿ *with good to great depth until 1970;* ♥/✿ *thereafter*
Chardonnay: *Crisp, fruity, moderate oakiness* ♥/✿
Johannisberg Riesling: *Medium sweet, fruity* ♥/✿
Pinot Noir: *Simple, fruity, some oak and tannin* ♥

JOHN BECKETT CELLARS *Napa 1975* Beckett owns 110 acres in Lake County and an aging cellar in Napa that is being expanded into a winery. The first wines, Cabernet and Fumé Blanc, were made at Rutherford Hill. Production is at 4,000 cases, as most grapes are being sold pending completion of Beckett's own winery.

Fumé Blanc: *Fruity, elegant, medium-bodied, crisp* ♥/✿

BEL ARBRES (FETZER VINEYARDS) A fast-growing second label now over the 25,000-case-per-year mark. It consists of an assortment of red and white table wines, some "produced by" and others "cellared by" Fetzer. Its appellations also vary from Mendocino to California. Most reds are fruity and simple; the whites, highly variable. The best seller is the Blanc de Blancs. All offerings are low-priced.

BELL CANYON CELLARS (BURGESS CELLARS) Its second label, used for small lots of wine purchased from other producers and bottled at the winery. The quality has varied widely and often failed to keep pace with price.

BERINGER VINEYARDS *Napa 1876* This historic winery was completely restored and returned to current tourist appeal by Nestlé, its owner since 1970. The old winery with aging cellars is a showcase; all wines are now made in large modern premises across the highway. The vineyard holdings have increased to 1,400 acres in varied Napa locations and 400 acres in Sonoma's Knight's Valley. Major emphasis is now on varietals; the whites represent good value. Reds include the standard varietal mix. Production is close to 300,000 cases under the Beringer label. The company's Los Hermanos line of jug wines is twice as big. Steady quality improvement has been registered since 1975.

Cabernet Sauvignon: *Modest varietal, light tannins* 🍷
Chardonnay: *Appley, medium varietal, light oak* 🍷
✦ **Chenin Blanc:** *Aromatic, fruity flavors, medium sweet* 🍷/✿
Fumé Blanc: *Varietal, crisp, fruity, light oak* 🍷
Johannisberg Riesling: *Fragrant, lively, medium sweet* ✿

BERNARDO WINERY *San Diego 1898* Produces generic table wines and dessert wines. Mainly direct retail sales at the winery. 75 acres of vineyards.

BERTERO WINERY *Santa Clara 1919* Aging Hecker Pass winery (5,000 cases) offering jugs and inexpensively priced varietals of low—often the lowest—quality.

BOEGER WINERY *El Dorado 1973* As part of a small-scale wine revival in the Sierra foothills, the Boegers planted 20 acres, leased 7 more, and now make around 5,000 cases per year. Cabernets and Zinfandels are noteworthy. They also make a blended red and a Chablis and in 1979 added Chardonnay and Sauvignon Blanc to their varietal program.

✦ **Cabernet Sauvignon:** *Spicy, rich, complex* ✿
Zinfandel: *Berryish, woody, rough* 🍷

BOUNTY VINEYARDS A privately owned label for generics and varietals made at the Growers Winery. No discernible difference between Bounty wines and the Growers products.

BRECKENRIDGE CELLARS (GIUMARRA VINEYARDS) Line of inexpensive, uninteresting varietals offered east of the Rockies since 1976. Sales at the 50,000-case level.

BRONCO WINERY *Stanislaus 1973* When their fathers sold Franzia Brothers to Coca-Cola of New York in the early 1970s, the cousins Franzia started their own winery just a half-dozen miles down the road. For years they have bought wine in bulk and sent it to market in jugs and carafes at extraordinarily low prices under the Bronco, JFJ Winery (for John, Fred, and Joseph Franzia), and CC Vineyards labels. In 1979 they crushed their first grapes, a massive 100,000 tons (6 million cases). Bronco Winery also makes a bulk process, sweet-tasting, low-acid champagne that is no worse than other inexpensive champagnes.

BROOKSIDE CELLARS *San Bernardino 1832* This large winery has been a division of the Beatrice Foods conglomerate since 1973. The Brookside label appears on a broad range of specialty wines, generics, dessert wines, champagne, and brandy, all cheap. Brookside owns 780 acres of vineyards and leases another 1,100. Its top-priced labels are E. Vache and Assumption Abbey, sold primarily through the winery's chain of 30 tasting rooms. These are located mostly in California with a few in Nevada, Arizona, and Illinois.

DAVID BRUCE WINERY *Santa Cruz 1964* Smallish (5,000-case) producer dedicated to heavyweight, wood-aged wines. Dr. Bruce was one of the first to espouse the minimum handling concept of letting the wine make itself. His late 1960s late harvest Zinfandels were among the first and the best. Bruce has always proclaimed himself a Burgundian and devotes his attention first to Chardonnay and Pinot Noir. Some Chardonnays have been superb; some simply big and dull. Other wines have been variable: occasionally awful, never spectacular. 25 acres grow next to the winery in the Santa Cruz Mountains.

Chardonnay: *Oaky, full-bodied, ripe* ♥/✿✿
Pinot Noir: *Oaky, sometimes rich, often thin* ♥/✿
Zinfandel: *Usually intense, often exotic and heavy* ♥

BUEHLER VINEYARDS *Napa 1978* Quality-minded growers with 60 acres in eastern Napa hills who are now beginning to ease into winemaking. First vintage of Cabernet, Sauvignon Blanc, and Zinfandel totaled 1,000 cases. Production doubled in 1979.

BUENA VISTA WINERY *Sonoma 1857* This historic property, established by the flamboyant Count Agoston Haraszthy, sat vacant for four decades until being returned to winemaking in the early 1940s. Drawing on its own vineyards nestled against the hills backing up to the city of Sonoma, Buena Vista produced hearty reds and usually uninspiring whites for 30 years. In 1968 the winery was sold to new owners with plans for change. 700 acres of vineyard were planted in the cooler Carneros district and a new, up-to-date winemaking facility was built alongside. Production is now in the 100,000-case range. Whites are showing improvement. At the end of 1979 the winery was sold to German interests.

Cabernet Sauvignon: *Muted varietal, medium light* ♥
Chardonnay: *Modest varietal, light oak, lemony* ♥
Zinfandel: *Berryish, moderately tannic, a bit lacking in vigor* ♥/✿

BURGESS CELLARS *Napa 1972* Fairly modern winery occupying a site used for wine growing since 1880 and located in the hills east of the Napa Valley floor. The first Souverain winery structure, built here in the 1940s, was purchased by former airline pilot Tom Burgess in 1972 when Souverain moved. Production is now 20,000 cases, versus 14,000 in 1972. Most grapes are purchased; Chardonnay and Johannisberg Riesling from Winery Lake Vineyards and Chenin Blanc from Steltzner. Wines are high-quality and priced accordingly.

Cabernet Sauvignon: *Hard, moderately tannic, not always intense* ♥/✿
Cabernet Vintage Selection: *Rich, hard, ripe, weedy, fairly tannic, ages well* ✿/✿✿✿
Chardonnay *(Winery Lake Vineyards): Fruity, good varietal, big, crisp, oaky* ✿
Chenin Blanc: *Dry, fruity, lots of oak* ✿/✿✿
Zinfandel: *Fairly refined, fruity with good varietal and oak tastes* ✿/✿✿

DAVIS BYNUM WINERY *Sonoma 1975* Bynum ran a storefront winery near Berkeley from 1965 until moving to the present Russian River location. Most varietal offerings are made from grapes grown locally. The 20,000-case production leans toward the reds. Though there is a hit-or-miss quality record, the hits are generally with red wines.

Chardonnay: *Very oaky, fairly big, variable* ☾/✿
Fumé Blanc: *Assertively varietal, strong flavors, not complex* ♥/✿

Petite Sirah: *Ripe, plumlike, oaky, imperfect* ♥/❀
Pinot Noir: *Complex, ripe fruit, high acid* ♥/❀

CADENASSO WINERY *Solano 1906* Much of the output (50,000 cases) is sold in bulk to others; some is available at the winery—the best of which is Zinfandel. Winemaking follows the "overlong aging in too old tanks" school.

CADLOLO WINERY *San Joaquin 1913* 5 acres and substantial amounts of purchased grapes yield the standard generic table wines and dessert wines. They are enjoyed mainly by local patrons.

CAKEBREAD CELLARS *Napa 1973* Vineyard owner's 22 acres of wine, along with Cabernet from Steltzner vineyards and Zinfandel from hills, contribute to the winery's 10,000-case output. Wines to date, made in big barrel-aged style, have possessed admirable intensity, although some wines have exhibited exotic, often unpleasant characteristics.

Cabernet Sauvignon: *Good fruit and varietal, tannic* ♥/❀
Chardonnay: *Oaky, spicy, earthy, good acid balance, fairly big in the mouth* ♥/❀
Sauvignon Blanc: *Big, dry, oaky, not always clean* ♥/❀

CALERA WINE *San Benito 1976* Aspires to make great Pinot Noir from its 24-acre vineyard. Meanwhile, it produces Zinfandels from different vineyard sources and in different styles that range from pleasant and heavy to unpleasant and overripe. 4,000 cases.

CALISTOGA VINEYARDS (CUVAISON) Currently a second label used for Cabernet, Chardonnay, and Zinfandel made from lots that were not used for Cuvaison's bottlings. Over recent vintages the Chardonnay, though coarse, has been the best value.

CALLAWAY VINEYARD AND WINERY *Riverside 1974* As Southern California's first well-financed new winery, it began with some panache. Over the first few vintages the table wines met with mixed acceptance. The white varietals, though understated in character, were better than the reds. Beginning with the 1977 vintage, the reds have been improving slowly in quality. Callaway occasionally offers a late harvest Chenin Blanc subtitled Sweet Nancy. Production has reached 60,000 cases with grapes supplied from the winery's 150 acres and neighboring vineyards.

Chenin Blanc: *Fruity, simple, soft, slightly sweet* ♥

Fumé Blanc: *Grassy, round, soft, some wood* ♥/✿
Zinfandel: *Ripe, pruney, heavy, warm* ☖/♥

CAMBIASO VINEYARDS *Sonoma 1934* An old jug winery modernized by a new corporate owner. Most of its 50,000-case sales are in generics, but a small varietal line has been added. Uses 1852 House as another generic brand. Owns 52 acres. Buys some grapes and still sells to other wineries. Most varietals are weak. The slightly tanky Burgundy is barely acceptable for the price.

CAREY CELLARS *Santa Barbara 1978* 47 acres of Cabernet Sauvignon, Merlot, Chardonnay, and Sauvignon Blanc will provide grapes for the planned production level of 4,000 cases. First wine, released in 1979, was a tart, fruity Cabernet Sauvignon Blanc.

RICHARD CAREY WINERY *Alameda 1977* Biology-professor-turned-winemaker Richard Carey produces 25,000 cases of wine. The wide range of average-quality varietals sells at a moderate $3–6 price, but an occasional special bottling costs more.

CARMEL BAY WINERY *Monterey 1977* Small, hobbyist winery (400 cases) producing Zinfandel and other red wines, primarily from Central Coast grapes.

CARNEROS CREEK WINERY *Napa 1972* Small (10,000-case) winery making high-quality varietals. Chardonnay and Pinot Noir are Carneros-area grown. Cabernet from 1977 vintage onward comes from Fay vineyard in the Stag's Leap area. Zinfandel is from Amador County. A small experimental plot of Pinot Noir grows next to the winery. Prices are generally reasonable, even the $12 Pinot Noir.

Chardonnay: *Dry, crisp, oaky, sometimes needing greater intensity* ♥/✿
Pinot Noir: *Rich, intense varietal and oak, good depth* ✿/✿✿✿
✦ **Zinfandel:** *Occasionally late harvest, always typically ripe-tasting, usually very tannic* ♥/✿✿✿

CASSAYRE-FORNI CELLARS *Napa 1977* Small winery (1,000 cases) operated by full-time engineering consultants; very successful first wines. Cabernet is a blend of 2 vineyards—one near the winery in Rutherford and the other across the valley near the Silverado Trail. Chenin Blanc is from a cool-climate vineyard near the city of Napa. Zinfandels are from Dry Creek and Amador.

Cabernet Sauvignon: *Mediumweight, oak-aged, moderately tannic* ♥/✿

Chenin Blanc: *Dry, good acid, lots of citrusy fruit, no oak* ♥/✿

CAYMUS VINEYARDS *Napa 1972* The transition from growers to winemakers was distinguished by the production of superb-quality Cabernet and by a pioneering Blanc de Noir labeled Oeil de Perdrix. Drawing from a 55-acre vineyard in Rutherford and some purchased grapes, Caymus makes close to 12,000 cases and sells another 8,000 under the Liberty School label. Recently added a Reserve Cabernet and Reserve Pinot Noir and expanded the line of varietals to include Chardonnay and Petite Sirah. High-quality varietals at reasonable prices; reds generally more exciting than whites.

⚘ **Cabernet Sauvignon:** *Minty, complex, tannic* ✿/✿✿✿

Pinot Noir: *Ripe, fruity, tannic, woody* ✿

Sauvignon Blanc: *Oaky, medium–full-bodied, varietal, usually fruity, dry* ♥/✿

Zinfandel: *Berrylike, rich, moderately tannic* ✿/✿✿✿

CC VINEYARDS (BRONCO WINERY) One of the labels used by the Bronco Winery for its array of wines; it seems reserved for inexpensively priced, dull-tasting jug wine. Also used for sweet-tasting bulk process champagne.

CEDAR RIDGE Distributor's private label sold mainly to restaurants for use as house wine.

CHALONE VINEYARD *Monterey 1960* A small, much-revered winery located high in the hills east of the Salinas Valley. Famous for ripe, oak-aged wines of the highest quality. Early success with Pinot Noir, Chardonnay, Chenin Blanc, and Pinot Blanc inspired other wineries to emulate the Chalone style—and often to exceed it in quality. Still, demand for Chalone wines remains high because their best continues to be superb. Limited production (fewer than 2,000 cases) will expand substantially as winery's 110 acres (including 50% Chardonnay, 25% Pinot Noir) come into full bearing.

Chardonnay: *Ripe, oily, very oaky; sporadic quality in recent vintages, 1978 was superb* ♥/✿✿✿

Pinot Blanc: *Usually ripe, powerful, balanced, oaky; occasionally flawed* ♥/✿✿✿

Pinot Noir: *Often thin, sometimes intense and complex, always oaky* ♥/✿✿✿

CHANDON *Napa 1973* French-owned (Moët-Hennessy of Moët
& Chandon champagnes and Hennessy cognac) champagne label produced at the architecturally sparkling new
winery called Domaine Chandon. Two-thirds of the
100,000-case sparkling-wine output is labeled Brut, a blend
of Chardonnay (60%), Pinot Noir (30%), and Pinot Blanc
(10%). The other offering, Blanc de Noir, is 100% Pinot
Noir. Both are aged up to 2 years on the yeast *(en tirage)*.
The winery owns 400 acres of vineyards mostly in the
Carneros area. Production reaches 250,000 cases in 1981.

Blanc de Noir: *Same dry-tasting balance as Brut, a bit
more body, slight onion-skin color* ✪
Brut: *High acid balanced by slight sweetness, tight,
hard fruit* ✪/✪✪

CHAPARRAL A private label owned by a group of Southern California retailers. The wines, Pinot Noir and Chardonnay,
are produced by Chalone from grapes grown in the Edna
Valley.

CHAPPELLET VINEYARDS *Napa 1969* From 100 acres located on
the eastern side of the Napa Valley, Chappellet is making
Chardonnay, Chenin Blanc, Riesling, and Cabernet. The
quality of Cabernet varies widely. Recent vintages of
Johannisberg Riesling are slightly sweet, but the Chenin
Blanc remains dry. Production has reached the maximum
25,000 cases, which include the blended white and red
Pritchard Hill bottlings.

Cabernet Sauvignon: *Ripe, hard, slow ager* ♥/✪✪
Chardonnay: *Average varietal, firm, oaky* ♥/✪
Chenin Blanc: *Fruity, full crisp, some oak* ✪
Johannisberg Riesling: *Floral, delicate, balanced* ♥/✪

CHARLES LE FRANC (ALMADÉN VINEYARDS) This line, introduced in 1978, represents Almadén's foray into the world
of limited-production, higher-priced wines. It consists of
well-known varietals along with some odd and exotic types
(Pinot St. George, sweet Zinfandel, and aged port). Also
there are 2 blended wines—Maison Blanc and Rouge—
both high-priced. Most are improvements over Almadén's
regular offerings.

Chardonnay: *Light fruit and oak, dry* ♥
Johannisberg Riesling, late harvest: *Low fruit,
somewhat flat, very sweet* ♥

CHATEAU CHEVALIER *Napa 1972* This old (1891) estate on
Spring Mountain was revived in 1969 when 60 acres of

hillside vineyards were established, primarily to Cabernet Sauvignon and Chardonnay. The first wines appeared in 1972, and production reached 8,000 cases by 1980. Other varietals offered on a small scale include Pinot Noir, Johannisberg Riesling, and Merlot. A Reserve Cabernet was made in 1975. Wines made from purchased grapes are sold under the Mountainside Vineyards label. Prices so far are in advance of quality.

Cabernet Sauvignon: *Dark, ripe, tannic* ♥/✿

Chardonnay: *Modest intensity and flavor* ♥

CHATEAU MONTELENA *Napa 1972* Noted from its outset as one of California's premier Chardonnay producers, Montelena gained worldwide fame in 1976, when its wine was chosen best among 12 leading California and French offerings by a highly regarded French tasting panel. Now producing approximately 20,000 cases per year, the winery is heading toward 50% Cabernet Sauvignon, about 35% Chardonnay, and 15% Zinfandel. In spite of critical success with Johannisberg Riesling, it plans to drop that variety.

Cabernet Sauvignon: *Elegant, moderately tannic, balanced wines, good fruity qualities, a little lacking in intensity* ✿

Chardonnay (Napa): *Among the best. Rich oak and deep fruit, superb balance* ✿/✿✿✿

Chardonnay (California): *Usually contains Central Coast grapes, often tastes simpler than Napa wine, sometimes grassy* ♥/✿✿

CHATEAU ST. JEAN *Sonoma 1973* This white wine specialist (97% of its 50,000-case production) has established solid credentials for highest-quality wines often produced from single vineyards. About 25% of production is in Chardonnay with smaller amounts in Johannisberg Riesling, Sauvignon Blanc, Gewurztraminer, and Pinot Blanc. The current array of red wines is being reduced to a single bottling of Cabernet Sauvignon from a neighboring vineyard. Chateau St. Jean has had extraordinary success with late harvest Johannisberg Riesling and Gewurztraminer. Among the Chardonnays, those labeled Robert Young Vineyard and Wildwood Vineyard have been our favorites.

Chardonnay: *Fruity, oaky, fairly full-bodied style; quality varies among bottlings, but is usually high* ♥/✿✿✿

Johannisberg Riesling: *Late harvest bottlings are usually clean, honeyed wines. The most expensive reach 23–28% sugar in the finished wines and are remarkable achievements on an international scale. Regular*

bottlings are usually medium sweet, very clean, and fruity ♥/✿✿ *for regular bottlings;* ✿/✿✿ *for most late harvest;* ✿✿/✿✿✿ *for the supreme efforts*
Sauvignon Blanc (Fumé Blanc): *Small-lot Paulsen and Crimmons bottlings are intense, fresh, fruity, and varietal with light oakiness* ✿/✿✿; *the other bottlings (designated by county only) are less attractive versions (except for Napa 1978* ✿✿) ♥/✿

CHATEAU SONOMA Label owned by S. S. Pierce for a red and white table wine made from Sonoma grapes at Souverain Cellars. About 2,500 cases annually. Light-style wines.

L. CHERPIN WINERY *San Bernardino 1934* Old firm continuing to sell its generics at the winery and local restaurants.

CHISPA CELLARS *Calaveras 1976* First new winery to materialize in Calaveras since Prohibition. Without vineyards, it buys Ruby Cabernet and Zinfandel from Amador and El Dorado counties. Makes 2,500 cases.

CHRISTIAN BROTHERS *Napa 1882* This venerable producer offers a full line of wines and brandies. It has 1,600 acres and 3 facilities in Napa, where it makes table wines and champagnes. Dessert wines and brandies are produced in the Central Valley. The wines total 2 million cases, consisting of the proprietary La Salle bottlings and the top-line Napa Valley varietals. It is beginning to use vintage dates, but most wines are nonvintage blends. The white varietals are consistent and nicely priced; the reds tend to be light and overaged.

Cabernet Sauvignon: *Light varietal, modest and mature* ♥
⚘ **Chardonnay:** *Appley, medium-bodied, clean, crisp* ♥/✿
⚘ **Chenin Blanc:** *Fresh and fruity, medium sweet* ✿
Fumé Blanc: *Herbal, light wood, flavorful* ♥/✿
Gamay Noir: *Tired, mature, woody* ♥
Zinfandel: *Vague fruit, thin, simple* ♥

CILURZO & PICONI WINERY *Riverside 1978* Small (2,000-case maximum) Temecula winery producing Cabernet, Petite Sirah, and dry Chenin Blanc from Mt. Palomar Vineyard grapes. First releases in 1980.

CLOS DU BOIS VINEYARDS *Sonoma 1976* Several partners own 1,200 acres of vineyards in the Dry Creek and Alexander Valley regions. Wines labeled Clos du Bois are made at Souverain and subsequently aged at the partners' facility in the Dry Creek area. Gewurztraminer and Johannisberg Riesling vie for top honors and have ranked in the 🏆🏆 category from 1977 on. Chardonnay, Cabernet, and Pinot Noir in both regular and special bottling versions occasionally rise above average quality. Annual production is about 40,000 cases.

Chardonnay: *Appley, light oak, monochromatic* 🏆
Gewurztraminer: *Intense varietal fragrance and flavors, slightly sweet* 🏆/🏆🏆
Johannisberg Riesling: *Floral, delicate, slightly sweet* 🏆/🏆; *the Private Reserve, complex, medium sweet* 🏆🏆

CLOS DU VAL *Napa 1973* The winemaker is French, and the winery's emphasis is on a Bordeaux-style Cabernet-Merlot blend. About 80% of the 20,000-case output is Cabernet. The remainder is divided equally between Zinfandel and Chardonnay. There are 120 acres planted. Any excess production is bottled under the Granval brand. So far, Zinfandel has overshadowed the Cabernet. We wish there were more Zinfandel.

Cabernet Sauvignon: *Weedy, hard, tannic, ages well* 🏆/🏆🏆
Chardonnay: *Has improved steadily; 1978 was best effort to date; crisp, rich with oak* 🏆/🏆
Zinfandel: *Complex, minty, firm, tannic* 🏆🏆/🏆🏆🏆

COAST RANGE Negociant's label for wines purchased ready-made and bottled at various wineries. The annual offerings are subject to what is available. Close to 10,000 cases were bottled in 1980.

COLOMA CELLARS *San Joaquin 1974* This old Gold Country label is now applied to a range of generic, dessert, champagne, and specialty wines. All are made from purchased wines. Offered 7,500 cases in 1979.

COLONY *1887* Founded at Asti in northern Sonoma County under the name Italian Swiss Colony, the winery eventually found its way into increasingly larger wine conglomerates until it was purchased a decade ago by Heublein. As recently as 10 years ago, ISC wines bore various North Coast appellations. Now most of the wine is produced and bottled at plants in the Central Valley. All the wines, including the reds, have noticeable sweetness.

Cabernet Sauvignon: *Relatively clean, slightly sweet, low varietal, jug wine* 🏆
Ruby Cabernet: *Medium sweet with little interest* ◿/🏆
Chenin Blanc: *Decidedly sweet, bubble-gummy, no varietal* ◿/🏆

Zinfandel: *Overripe, sometimes cooked taste; occasionally offers varietal taste* ♥

COLUMBIA CELLARS *Tuolumne 1974* The only winery crushing in this county. Its 2,000-case output consists of an Amador Zinfandel, several generics, and bulk process champagnes. Quality reputation yet to emerge.

CONCANNON VINEYARDS *Alameda 1887* Medium-sized producer (75,000 cases) in the Livermore Valley offering a broad line of vintage-dated varietals grown primarily on 250 acres of immediately adjacent estate-owned vineyards. Winery's staid image is changing due to vastly changed winemaking technology and continued emphasis on innovation. Concannon offered the first varietally labeled Petite Sirah in the mid-1960s, is the only California winery to offer varietal Rkatsiteli, and helped initiate trend-setting Zinfandel Rosé from Amador County and Muscat Blanc. Production is 70% white wine, but Petite Sirah is its leading seller.

⚘ **Muscat Blanc:** *Perfumed, floral and spice, medium sweet to sweet* ✪/✪✪
Petite Sirah: *Clean, fruity, slightly ripe, moderately tannic; less brawny than most competitors* ♥/✪
Sauvignon Blanc: *Dry, fruity, no oak style* ♥/✪
⚘ **Zinfandel Rosé:** *Slightly sweet, intensely fruity, best of breed* ✪

CONGRESS SPRINGS VINEYARDS *Santa Clara 1976* Promising winery located in the Santa Cruz Mountains. Current production of 4,000 cases is expected to double. Early results have been mixed, with greatest success in Sauvignon Blanc and Zinfandel.

Sauvignon Blanc: *Dry style, labeled Fumé, is weedy, spicy, strong* ✪; *slightly sweet, called Sauvignon Blanc, is fruity, pungent* ♥/✪
Zinfandel: *ripe, spicy, vanilla oakiness* ✪/✪✪

CONN CREEK VINEYARD *Napa 1974* First 2 Cabernets were good enough to justify building a new winery on the Silverado Trail and leasing over 100 acres. The wine roster consists of 4 varietals and a burgundy. Early record was fine for reds. First Chardonnay was promising. In a few years, production will reach 20,000 cases.

Cabernet Sauvignon: *Complex aroma, ripe, tannic* ✪/✪✪
Chardonnay: *Oaky, ripe, medium-full-bodied* ♥/✪
Zinfandel: *Brawny, full-bodied, variable* ♥

CONROTTO WINERY *Santa Clara 1933* Old-time generic wine producer selling to local restaurants and stores. An occasional varietal is offered.

CONTI ROYALE Viewed by its owner, East-Side, as the premium label, it encompasses a range of varietals, generics, and brandies. The red varietals sometimes offer good value. Ports and sherries are among the best of the inexpensive California offerings. Conti Royale 10-year-old brandy is extremely good.

CORTI BROTHERS A private label owned by a Sacramento delicatessen/wine store. Since 1968 it has offered Amador Zinfandel (made at Sutter Home and aged in Corti's cooperage). Other wines are offered occasionally.

Zinfandel: *Spicy, ripe, woody, tannic* ✿

CRESTA BLANCA WINERY *Mendocino 1971* A famous brand established in 1880 in Livermore. Underwent several changes in ownership until acquired by the Guild cooperative, which reestablished it in Ukiah. The winery has been expanded and has a storage capacity of 2.3 million gallons. Most of the table wines carry vintage dates, and a few bear a Mendocino County appellation. Recently, several varietals have been made from Central Coast grapes. The quality to date is inconsistent. The white wines are generally thin and low on character; the reds, including the top-selling Zinfandel, are variable. The brand's most consistent good-quality wines are the sherries, which are made at other facilities.

Chenin Blanc: *Weak varietal, rough, medium sweet* ◌/♥
Cream Sherry: *Aromatic, full-bodied, very sweet* ♥
Zinfandel: *A nonvintage bottling varying from flat and dull to slightly berrylike and balanced* ◌/♥

CRIBARI WINES This historic name is now just a label owned by the Guild cooperative. A large line of inexpensive, sweet-finished, flat-tasting table and dessert wines. Quality ranges from dull to dismal.

Mellow Burgundy: *Heavy, flabby, sweet* ◌
Zinfandel: *Flat, raisiny, sweet* ◌

CUCAMONGA VINEYARD *San Bernardino 1870* This million-case producer is California's Bonded Winery No. 1 and proud of it. Its major labels are Cuvee d'Or and Bonded Winery No. 1. The bulk process champagne is fairly interesting for the price. Much of the production is sold to other wineries.

CUVAISON *Napa 1970* Medium-sized (20,000-case) producer of quality-oriented, full-bodied varietals. Offers only Chardonnay, Cabernet Sauvignon, and Zinfandel, made from purchased grapes. Hillside vineyards are preferred, except for Winery Lake Chardonnay.

> **Cabernet Sauvignon:** *Medium–full-bodied, tannic, oak-aged style* ♥/❀
> **Chardonnay:** *Oaky, good varietal, sometimes low on intensity* ♥/❀
> **Zinfandel:** *Ripe, brawny style* ♥/❀❀

CYGNET CELLARS *San Benito 1977* 3,000-case winery offering 4 varietals from purchased grapes. Quality of the first offerings ranged from flawed to uninteresting.

D'AGOSTINI WINERY *Amador 1856* The oldest in Amador, this winery has been family-owned since 1911. The 125-acre vineyard is mixed—Zinfandel and Mission mostly. The wines are old-style generics, Zinfandel being the one varietal. The generics are inexpensive; the Zinfandel is an overaged, tanky blend of vintages. It is not modern Amador fare. Production averages 80,000 cases per year.

DEHLINGER WINERY *Sonoma 1976* One of our favorites for quality and price. It has 14 acres and buys grapes from hillside vineyards in Sonoma. Production is 6,000 cases limited to 4 varietals. Crushed its first Pinot Noir in 1977. Its performance over the first several vintages places it among the best of the new Sonoma wineries.

> ⚘ **Cabernet Sauvignon:** *Dark, ripe, flavorful, stylish* ❀/❀❀
> ⚘ **Chardonnay:** *Varietal, medium full, light oak* ♥/❀❀
> ⚘ **Zinfandel:** *Briary, rich, woody, ages well* ❀/❀❀

DELICATO VINEYARDS *San Joaquin 1935* A large (12-million-gallon capacity) winery selling wines to other brands, but beginning to expand its own line of generics and varietals rapidly. Bottled around 700,000 cases in 1979. All wines are low-priced, but not bargains.

DEVLIN WINE CELLARS *Santa Cruz 1979* A 2,000-case winery, with a capacity for 5,000 cases, offering 4 varietals from purchased grapes. First releases included a barrel-fermented Pinot Blanc, a dry Zinfandel Rosé, a slightly sweet Malvasia, and Zinfandel.

DIABLO VISTA WINERY *Solano 1977* Tiny, part-time producer (400 cases) offering small lots of a half-dozen varietals. Zinfandel from Sonoma tops the list.

DIAMOND CREEK VINEYARDS *Napa 1972* A Cabernet-only winery offering 3 distinct bottlings each vintage. Its 20-acre vineyards are situated in 3 adjoining sites, each of which exhibits significant differences in soil composition and exposure. The separate bottlings carry the vineyard names: Gravelly Meadows, Red Rock Terrace, and Volcanic Hill. However, all three share a dark color, ripe flavors, and extremely tannic character. About 2,500 cases in total are produced per year.

Cabernet Sauvignon: *Ripe, rough, sometimes complex, tannic* 🍷/✿✿

DOMAINE LAURIER *Sonoma 1978* Small winery using its 20-acre vineyard in Forestville for several varietal wines. Production over the first two vintages was 3,000 cases each year. The vineyard site is favorable for both Chardonnay and Pinot Noir.

DRY CREEK VINEYARDS *Sonoma 1972* This 20,000-case winery has advanced the cause for both the Dry Creek region and for Fumé Blanc wines. It was also among the first new, small wineries to settle in Sonoma. Although noted more for the whites, the quality of all varietals is above average. Over half of its grapes come from 50 acres surrounding the winery.

Cabernet Sauvignon: *Modest varietal, fruity, soft* 🍷
Chardonnay: *Medium intense, lemony, oaky, crisp* 🍷/✿
Chenin Blanc: *Fruity, crisp, but slightly sweet* 🍷/✿
Fumé Blanc: *Assertive varietal, medium-bodied, balanced* 🍷/✿✿
Zinfandel: *Spicy, berryish, tannic* 🍷/✿✿

DURNEY VINEYARDS *Monterey 1976* From 80 acres located in the Carmel Valley, Durney produces close to 10,000 cases today, half of its maximum capacity. Major emphasis is on Cabernet, but small amounts of Chenin Blanc and Gamay Beaujolais are produced. Showing annual quality improvement.

Cabernet Sauvignon: *Ripe varietal, full, round, moderately tannic* 🍷/✿

EDMEADES VINEYARDS *Mendocino 1972* After a rough beginning Edmeades is now making good red varietals in better vintages and light-style whites. From 35 acres in the Anderson Valley and purchased grapes it produces about 10,000 cases. Also offers blended proprietary wines and apple wines.

Cabernet Sauvignon: *Herbaceous, earthy, thin to balanced* ♥/✿
Gewurztraminer: *Light varietal, delicate, slightly sweet* ♥/✿
Zinfandel: *Berrylike, variable depth and tannin* ♥/✿✿

EDNA VALLEY VINEYARD *San Luis Obispo 1980* A 50,000-gallon winery operated as a joint venture by Chalone Vineyard and a local grower. Prior to construction of the winery, the 1979 vintage (1,000 gallons) was made at Chalone and sold only through the Chalone mailing list. The 1980 vintage (also limited in size) was crushed in leased facilities in San Luis Obispo County. The completed winery is expected to be occupied in early 1981. Production will be two-thirds Chardonnay, one-third Pinot Noir.

ELEVEN CELLARS (PERELLI-MINETTI WINERY) Napa Valley varietals made from purchased grapes were once offered under the Fino Eleven Cellars brand. Recently, the name was changed to Eleven Cellars. The parent company plans to phase out the line. Any wines remaining are likely to be over the hill.

EMILE'S CAVALCADE (EMILIO GUGLIELMO WINERY) Label for good-sized (30,000-case) line of jug wines. Mostly inexpensive generics in a heavy style.

Burgundy: *Vinous, full-bodied, aged flavors* ♥

ENZ VINEYARDS *San Benito 1973* Offers an assortment of varietals, most of which were not well made in the first few vintages. Production is 3,500 cases. Owns 35 acres.

ESTRELLA RIVER WINERY *San Luis Obispo 1977* A large vineyard with 500 acres planted to wine varieties, currently using only 25% of its crop for a line of table wines. Annual production quickly climbed to 45,000 cases by 1979 with Chardonnay and Cabernet Sauvignon representing the two best sellers and the most successful wines. The other varietals are made in a fruity, simple style. The winery plans to offer a French Syrah soon.

Cabernet Sauvignon: *Spicy, herbaceous, moderate tannins* ♥/✿
Chardonnay: *Grassy, light fruit flavors, oaky* ♥
Sauvignon Blanc: *Vague varietal, flat, light oak* ♥

FELTON-EMPIRE VINEYARDS *Santa Cruz 1976* About 80% of 10,000-case output consists of Johannisberg Riesling from different regions made in a variety of styles. Winemaker prefers Rieslings either in a low-alcohol style and/or from Botrytis-affected grapes. Efforts with Cabernet and Zinfandel attract less attention. The winery owns 45 acres.

White (Johannisberg) Riesling: *Fruity, fresh, soft, medium sweet to sweet finish* ♥/✿✿

FENESTRA WINERY *Alameda 1976* Smallish producer (3,500 cases) located in Livermore. Most offerings are produced from Central Coast grapes. A few very good wines but most have been average or worse. Called Ventana Winery until 1978.

Chenin Blanc: *Dry, green apple aroma, clean* ♥
Zinfandel: *Ripe, slightly earthy, rich* ♥/✿

FETZER VINEYARDS *Mendocino 1968* This family-owned winery built a reputation for sturdy red varietals that represent 80% of its 50,000-case production. Since 1977 it has made headway in erasing a dreadful record for white varietals and is expanding the list of white wines. It has 200 acres and buys grapes from Mendocino growers and others in Lake and Sonoma counties. Among its best wines are the vineyard-identified Zinfandels and a Reserve Petite Syrah. Red and white table wines are popular items. Bel Arbres is Fetzer's second label.

Cabernet Sauvignon: *Ripe, fruity, oaky, tannic* ♥/✿
Chardonnay: *Low varietal, fairly oaky, little excitement* ♥
Gewurztraminer: *Spicy, medium light, slightly sweet* ♥/✿
Petite Syrah: *Peppery, medium full, rough, tannic* ♥/✿✿✿
Zinfandel: *Spicy, ripe berries, woody* ♥/✿✿

FICKLIN VINEYARDS *Madera 1946* The first port specialist and still highly regarded. Follows a 4 1/2-year aging policy and releases about 5,000 cases annually. The nonvintage port improves with age.

Port: *Dark, rough, complex, warm* ♥

JAMES ARTHUR FIELD *Alameda 1975* San Francisco advertising executive James Arthur Field solved his mid-life crisis by dropping into the wine business. At his Emeryville bottling facilities, Field blends dry, mainly coastal-county wines into tasty jug blends, Chablis and Burgundy.

FIELD STONE WINERY *Sonoma 1966* A 9,000-case winery drawing from its 140 acres of vineyards in the Alexander

Valley region. All grapes were sold until the winery was completed in 1977. Its white varietals and Blanc de Noirs (subtitled Spring wines) are field crushed and pressed. The red wines, headed by Petite Sirah from an old parcel, are conventionally handled. Most wines are sold through a mailing list.

Chenin Blanc: *Fresh, citrusy, spritzy, medium sweet* ♀/✿
Johannisberg Riesling: *Intensely fruity, light, medium sweet* ✿
Petite Sirah: *Forwardly fruity, good varietal, medium tannins* ✿

FIELDBROOK VALLEY *Humboldt 1976* Tiny (200-case) winery owning 1 acre and buying some grapes from Napa to make 3 varietal wines. Sells direct to consumers through a mailing list.

FILIPPI VINTAGE COMPANY *Riverside 1934* Under Chateau Filippi and J. Filippi primary labels, it sells a range of table wines, dessert wines, and bulk process champagnes. Virtually all of its annual 150,000-case sales are at the company's 6 tasting rooms in Southern California. Part of the production for the 36 different wines comes from 322 acres under lease.

FIRESTONE VINEYARD *Santa Barbara 1974* This dynamic venture is owned by members of the Firestone tire family, and a one-third interest belongs to Suntory of Japan. It has 300 acres planted in the Santa Ynez Valley and is moving close to its 65,000-case maximum level. Over the first few vintages, Firestone had better success with white varietals than reds, although its Pinot Noir is improving rapidly.

Chardonnay: *Ripe, sometimes grassy, medium full, oaky* ♀/✿
Gewurztraminer: *Spicy, firm, balanced* ♀/✿
Johannisberg Riesling: *Complex aroma, balanced, slightly sweet* ✿
Pinot Noir: *Good fruit, herbal, oaky, fat in good years* ♀/✿✿

FLORA SPRINGS WINES *Napa 1979* New, small winery crushing estate-owned Cabernet Sauvignon and purchased Chardonnay. Wines debut in 1981.

FOPPIANO VINEYARDS *Sonoma 1896* This family-run 200,000-case winery located south of Healdsburg is gradually sloughing off its jug wine image. It offers 9 varietals and 4 generics, heavily oriented toward red wines in both types. Wines from its 200-acre vineyard carry a Russian River Valley appellation. New stainless steel tanks and small casks have resulted in cleaner and better varietals of late. Average-quality wines with reasonable prices.

Cabernet Sauvignon: *Vinous, medium-bodied, vague* 🍷
⚘ **Petite Sirah:** *Good fruit, medium weight and tannins* 🍷/⚘
Sonoma Fumé: *Modest varietal, simple, crisp* 🍷
Zinfandel: *Vaguely varietal, dull* 🍷

FORMAN WINERY *Napa 1979* Ex-winemaker at Sterling went off on his own, planted 50 acres on hilly Spring Mountain sites, and built a winery. In 1979 totaled 1,400 cases of Merlot and a Sauvignon Blanc–Semillon blend, from purchased grapes. Future vintages will offer a Merlot-Cabernet blend and a 70% Sauvignon Blanc/30% Semillon blend. Maximum production goal is 8,000 cases.

FORTINO WINERY *Santa Clara 1948* Produces a wide variety of table wines in the low-priced end. The reds are heavy and coarse and often represent good values. Most of its 10,000-case production is sold at the winery.

⚘ **Zinfandel:** *Berryish, rough, woody* ⚘

FOUNTAIN GROVE (MARTINI & PRATI) Famous late 19th- and 20th-century winery closed in 1951. The label occasionally shows up on not-so-famous wines bottled by bulk-wine-producer Martini & Prati.

FRANCISCAN VINEYARDS *Napa 1973* Acquired in 1979 by a West German firm, the fifth owner since it opened. Produces a wide variety of table wines ranging in quality from good to indifferent. The vineyards total 450 acres, and present production of 100,000 cases could easily treble in a few years. Prices remain average.

⚘ **Burgundy:** *Mature, flavorful, balanced* 🍷
Cabernet Sauvignon: *Light varietal, fruity, simple* 🍷
Chardonnay: *Appley, medium-bodied, crisp* 🍷/⚘
Johannisberg Riesling: *Modest varietal, fruity, slightly sweet* 🍷

FRANZIA BROTHERS *San Joaquin 1906* Giant winery (10-million-case storage capacity; 4,000 acres of vineyards) producing jug wines and limited amounts of locally grown, mass-produced varietals. A host of secondary labels usually adorning very uninspiring wines can be identified as Franzia products by the Ripon, California, bottling location. Winery was purchased in 1973 by Coca-Cola of New York.

Chenin Blanc: *Medium sweet, clean, light flavors* 🍷
French Colombard: *Slightly sweet, dull* 🍷
Robust Burgundy: *Lightweight but clean, flirtation with Gallo Hearty Burgundy* 🍷
Zinfandel: *Clean, but hot and dull* 🍷

FRED'S FRIENDS (DOMAINE CHANDON) Second label of this champagne producer used for still wines made from the second pressings of its sparkling wine grapes. Chardonnay and Blanc de Noir (Pinot Noir) are offered. 8,000 cases.

FREEMARK ABBEY *Napa 1967* After 55 years of inactivity the dormant Freemark Abbey site was modernized into a new winery (25,000 cases) by a consortium of 7 partners, including Charles Carpy (whose grandfather was partner in the now defunct Uncle Sam Cellars, 1887–1916), noted vineyardist Laurie Wood, and oenologist Brad Webb. Winery and partners hold substantial vineyard acreage that supplies greatest part of winery crush. Very successful Petite Sirah is from the York Creek Vineyard.

Cabernet Bosche: *From a select vineyard in Rutherford; good depth, some complexity; 1970 was superb* ✿✿✿; *later vintages rate* 🍷/✿
Cabernet Sauvignon: *Pleasant, medium intensity, but lacking depth* 🍷
Chardonnay: *Intense varietal and oak-aged style, classic dimensions in great years* ✿✿/✿✿✿
Edelwein: *Late harvest Johannisberg Riesling with richness, depth, and complexity* ✿✿/✿✿✿
Johannisberg Riesling: *Fruity, slightly spicy, slight to medium sweet* 🍷
Petite Sirah: *Brawny, tannic, distinct black-pepper spiciness* 🍷/✿✿

FRETTER WINE CELLARS *Alameda 1977* Tiny (500-case) producer of good-quality wines owned by wine seller Travis Fretter.

FRICK WINERY *Santa Cruz 1977* Barrel-fermented Chardonnay and Pinot Noir are the focus of this small (2,000-case) winery with high ambitions. Its first release, however, was a not very interesting Chenin Blanc.

GALLEANO WINERY *Fresno 1933* Makes generic and dessert wines of all types and a Zinfandel. All sales are from the tasting room.

E. & J. GALLO WINERY *Stanislaus 1933* This could well be the world's largest winery. Headquartered in Modesto, it has 4 facilities with a total storage capacity of over 250 million gallons. Though it owns 4,000 acres, it must purchase 95% of its grapes crushed. Predominantly a generic wine producer with screw caps, in 1975 it started a line of varietals with cork closures. Over recent years, it has been using grapes from cooler regions, particularly the North and Central Coasts. A massive underground aging cellar is now finished to provide longer aging and also to augment the varietal offerings. Champagnes are bottled under both Gallo and André labels. Table and dessert wines are sold under numerous labels. All Gallo labels combined represent one-third of California wine sales. The white wines often represent good value.

Chablis Blanc: *Fruity, simple, light, medium sweet* ♟
Chenin Blanc: *Clean varietal, fresh, slightly sweet* ♟
French Colombard: *Modest, fruity, medium sweet* ♟
Hearty Burgundy: *Vinous, medium full, medium sweet* ᕐ/♟
⚡ **Sauvignon Blanc:** *Light grassy aroma and flavor, simple* ♟
Zinfandel: *Vinous, light, balanced* ♟

GAVILAN VINEYARDS (CHALONE) A label used for French Colombard made from purchased grapes and Pinot Noir-Blanc from its own vineyard. The style is dry and oaky. Output today is close to 10,000 cases, and the quality is average.

GEMELLO WINERY *Santa Clara 1934* Known through the 1960s for hearty, long-aged, and long-lived reds from nearby vineyards. Now it buys all grapes and releases its wines earlier, while remaining primarily a red wine producer. The quality is average at best. Most of its 10,000-case production is in Cabernet Sauvignon and Zinfandel from different appellations.

Zinfandel: *Fruity, woody, rough, astringent* ♟

GEYSER PEAK WINERY *Sonoma 1972* A long-time producer of bulk wines acquired by Schlitz of Milwaukee in 1972 and given a label. It has since been modernized and expanded, producing close to 200,000 cases today under this label. The first several vintages were made from purchased grapes, and the wines with California appellations were of marginal quality. Many varietals now come from Sonoma County, where the winery owns 600 acres. With few exceptions, the quality level has yet to rise above average. The whites are simple, sometimes thin. Most reds are fruity, sometimes tanky. Summit Wines is a second label.

Fumé Blanc: *Light fruit, soft, clean* 🍷
Gewurztraminer: *Slightly spicy, muscatty* 🍷/❀
Pinot Noir: *Varietal fruit, earthy, sometimes good depth* 🍷/❀

GIBSON WINE COMPANY *Fresno 1934* A large winery specializing in fruit and berry wines. It offers a range of generic, dessert, and sparkling wines that have not attracted much interest.

GIUMARRA VINEYARDS *Kern 1975* A large (12-million-gallon capacity) winery owned by a family active in the bulk wine business since 1946. First attempt with a line of varietals and generics failed; a second attempt in 1979 was based on blending Central Coast wines with wines from the family-owned Central Valley vineyards. Prices are low; quality is still inconsistent. Annual sales of about 1.5 million cases.

GOLD MINE WINERY *San Joaquin 1974* This label is part of Coloma Cellars and is used for generic wines and several flavored table wines, including one called Columbian Gold.

GRAND CRÚ VINEYARDS *Sonoma 1970* Two former engineers share the duties in running this 12,000-case—ultimately 20,000-case—winery. They favor fragrant, light white varietals. The Gewurztraminer ranks among the best in California. They also make tiny amounts of Cabernet, Zinfandel, and intensely sweet "induced Botrytis" Gewurztraminer.

Chenin Blanc: *Fruity, soft, slightly sweet* 🍷/❀
Gewurztraminer: *Spicy, rich flavors, round, medium sweet* ❀/❀❀❀

GRAND PACIFIC VINEYARDS *Marin 1974* Small (8,000-case) winery buying all grapes from Sonoma County. Offers Cabernet, Merlot, and Chardonnay, all of which have varied in quality. Saumon is its Blanc de Noir.

GRANVAL (CLOS DU VAL) This label first appeared on second-quality wine. It has reappeared for 2 vintages of 100% Cabernet Sauvignon, a style deviating from Clos du Val's usual Cabernet-Merlot blends. Both—1975 and 1977—were good Cabernets. Also appeared recently on a flurry of Chardonnays, 1975 to 1977.

GRGICH HILLS CELLARS *Napa 1977* Winemaker Grgich built a reputation with Chateau Montelena and then started his own winery with coffeeman Austin Hills. Hills owns 140 acres in Napa that over time will go toward this winery's 15,000-case production. The varietal lineup includes regular and late harvest Johannisberg Rieslings, Chardonnay, and Zinfandel.

Chardonnay: *Medium ripe, oaky, fat* ✿
Johannisberg Riesling: *Medium varietal, fruity, medium sweet* ♥/✿✿
Zinfandel: *Ripe, warm, complex, tannic* ✿

GROWERS BRAND *Tulare 1936* A highly visible broad line of wines and brandies are produced at a large (19-million-gallon capacity) facility called California Growers Winery. Other labels used by this winery include Setrakian Vineyards, L. Le Blanc Vineyards, and Bounty Vineyards. Most Growers table wines are of low, jug wine quality. Its varietals are light and thin at best; most often they are dull and occasionally flawed.

GUASTI (PERELLI-MINETTI) WINERY Historical label revived recently by the parent winery. It covers a line of table wines, champagne, vermouth, and brandies. The table wines are vintage dated with California appellations. Most are blends of Central Valley and Central Coast grapes. The first offering totaled 300,000 cases, and most wines were simple, fruity, and inexpensive. The most noteworthy wines are a medium sweet French Colombard, a light, vinous Zinfandel, and a fruity, deeply colored rosé.

EMILIO GUGLIELMO WINERY *Santa Clara 1925* Long-time producer of relatively high quality jug wines under the Emile's Calvacade label. Also offers 10,000 cases of low-priced, vintage-dated varietals, of which 80% is Petite Sirah, Zinfandel, and Cabernet Sauvignon, all made in a rough, hearty style under E. Guglielmo. 150 vineyard acres are devoted primarily to the varietal program.

Petite Sirah: *Medium-bodied, vinous, dull* ♥

GUNDLACH-BUNDSCHU WINERY *Sonoma 1973* 125 years of grape-growing and 50 years of pre-Prohibition wine-making preceded the reopening of this family-owned winery. Half of the crop from the 350 acres is used in the winery. The rest is sold to Sebastiani. Production, now 24,000 cases, is split evenly between red and white wines. So far the reds seem to be of better quality.

Cabernet Sauvignon: *Full-bodied in good years, ripe flavors, some oak* ♣/❀
Chardonnay: *Fruity, round, oaky* ♣/❀
Zinfandel: *Ripe flavors in big years, often brawny* ♣/❀

HACIENDA WINE CELLARS *Sonoma 1972* Located in the Sonoma Valley, the winery now makes 10,000 cases of varietals per year. It uses grapes from the adjacent 50-acre vineyard that once belonged to Buena Vista. Recent Zinfandels come from a partner's 60-acre vineyard in Cloverdale. The winery is at its best with Gewurztraminer. Its other varietals are generally of average quality. However, it has occasionally offered a fine late harvest Johannisberg Riesling and an above-average Cabernet Sauvignon.

Cabernet Sauvignon: *Minty, medium-bodied, tannic* ♣/❀
Chardonnay: *Medium intensity, balanced, oaky* ♣/❀
Gewurztraminer: *Spicy-floral, balanced, slightly sweet* ❀/❀❀
Pinot Noir-Blanc: *Fruity, simple, slightly sweet* ♣

HALE CELLARS *Santa Barbara 1974* Growers with 350 acres planted to numerous varieties make a few thousand cases of varietals in an old dairy barn. Zinfandel represents a major percentage of production, but the first few vintages have been unattractive. Chardonnay and Riesling made at a Monterey County winery were not much better. Through 1979 Hale was called Los Alamos Vineyards.

HANZELL VINEYARDS *Sonoma 1956* The original showcase winery designed by the late Ambassador James D. Zellerbach, who modeled it after a French chateau. It was among the first to produce Chardonnay in a ripe, balanced, oak-aged style. The Pinot Noirs are less consistent, but the finest are often big, fat, complex, and high in alcohol. After several ownership changes, it continues to offer exceptional wines. Production from its 34-acre vineyard is about 3,000 cases annually. Plans to add Cabernet Sauvignon in a few years. Its wines carry Sonoma Valley appellations.

Chardonnay: *Ripe, supple, oaky, slow ager* ❀/❀❀
Pinot Noir: *Dark, complex herbal, ripe, tannic* ❀/❀❀

J. J. HARASZTHY & SON *Sonoma 1978* Run by direct descendants of Agoston Haraszthy, founder of Buena Vista, this winery offers only Zinfandel and Gewurztraminer. All grapes are purchased locally and crushed elsewhere, pending construction of a winery. 8,000 cases produced in 1979; predominantly Zinfandel.

HARBOR WINERY *Sacramento 1972* In his amateur days in the late 1960s, Harbor's winemaker discovered Amador Zinfandel. Today he makes Amador Cabernet, Zinfandel, Mission del Sol, and Napa Chardonnay. Total production is 1,000 cases, sold only in California.

Chardonnay: *Fruity, flavorful, complex*✿/✿✿
Zinfandel: *Ripe fruit, medium-bodied, tannic*♛/✿

HAVELOCK GORDON A negociant's label for varietal wines selected by Paul Draper, winemaker at Ridge Vineyards. Most of the first offerings (20,000 cases) were produced at Sonoma Vineyards. The quality is average, no better than most other private labels despite Draper's involvement.

HAWK CREST (STAG'S LEAP WINE CELLARS) Label often used for sweet-finished, fragrant Johannisberg Riesling and occasionally for light, early-maturing Cabernet.

HECKER PASS WINERY *Santa Clara 1972* Red varietals and dessert wines are made by this 3,000-case winery. The prices are low, the quality variable. Sales are mainly at the winery.

HEITZ CELLARS *Napa 1961* Moderately sized winery (approximately 30,000 cases) of high repute. Makes superb and expensive Cabernet from Martha's Vineyard. Other Cabernets have been ordinary except for newly offered Fay vineyard, which should become Heitz staple. Also well known for Chardonnay and for estate-grown Grignolino rosé. Many lesser wines are purchased in bulk, aged, and blended. Others (sparkling and dessert wines) are bottled especially for Heitz. Colorful, outspoken, often irascible owner.

Cabernet Martha's Vineyard: *Always distinctively minty with deep, rich, black currant; ages well; 1968 and 1974 are classic; 1969, 1970, 1972, 1973, 1975 not far behind* ✿/✿✿✿
Chardonnay: *Fragrant, sometimes spicy, oily texture, good depth* ♛/✿
Grignolino Rosé: *Tart, fruity, nice for its type* ♛
Johannisberg Riesling: *Dry, fruity, acceptable but not outstanding for type* ♛

JAY HEMINGWAY VINEYARDS *Napa 1977* A former sculptor, Hemingway is specializing in Zinfandel. He has 4 acres planted. 700 cases were made in 1978.

WILLIAM HILL WINERY A label owned by investors and vineyard developers who have established 400 acres of vineyards in sites along Mount Veeder in Napa. Most of the current acreage is planted to Cabernet and Chardonnay. The first wine, made elsewhere, is a 1976 Cabernet (400-case total released in 1980). 1979 production of the 2 varietals was 5,000 cases, combined. At last notice, the search for a winery site was under way.

HILLS CELLARS A label owned by Austin Hills for Chardonnay from his Napa Valley vineyards. The label was retired when Hills united with Grgich to form Grgich Hills Cellars.

HOFFMAN MOUNTAIN RANCH *San Luis Obispo 1972* A 30,000-case winery offering a line of varietals and determined to make outstanding Pinot Noir. Its 60-acre vineyard is planted mostly to Pinot Noir and Chardonnay and contains soils rich in chalk and limestone. The winemaking style emphasizes ripe grapes and traditional fermentations—barrel fermentation for Chardonnay and inclusion of stems during red wine fermentation. To date, its Chardonnays are variable; Pinot Noirs are usually good. The other varietals are of average quality. Prices tend to be high for all wines.

Chardonnay: *Ripe, toasty, medium full, complex, oaky* ♥/✿
Pinot Noir: *Ripe, herbal, good depth, sometimes raisiny, heavy, oaky* ♥/✿✿
Zinfandel: *Fruity, round, oaked, lacks depth* ♥

HOP KILN WINERY *Sonoma 1975* This 3,000-case winery, a state historical landmark, is a stunning hop kiln on the outside, a threadbare winery within. The adjacent 65-acre vineyard is in the Russian River region. A small percentage is used to produce rather heavy-styled red varietals and an interesting dry, oak-aged French Colombard.

Petite Sirah: *Heavy, astringent, low fruit* ♥
Zinfandel: *Ripe and briary, woody, tannic* ♥/✿

HORIZON WINERY *Sonoma 1977* Tiny (under 2,000-case) winery making only Zinfandel from vineyards in Healdsburg and Dry Creek areas in fruity, ripe, moderately tannic style.

HUGO'S CELLARS *Riverside 1979* A home winemaking operation grew into hobbyist scale commercial operation. Production is pegged at 500–800 cases.

HUSCH VINEYARDS *Mendocino 1968* The oldest of the Anderson Valley wineries, this 4,000-case producer makes all of its wine from its own 23-acre vineyard.

Chardonnay: *Floral, appley, tart, with vanillin overtones* ❦/❦
Gewurztraminer: *High acid, spicy* ❦
Pinot Noir: *Cherrylike aromas, balanced* ❦/❦

INGLENOOK VINEYARDS *Napa and Central Valley 1879* Inglenook labels now appear on wines from every part of the state and in every price range. In total, Inglenook sales are in the 1-million-case range. The top of the line, (loosely) labeled Estate Bottled, consists of vintage-dated, Napa Valley wines whose sales are about 250,000 cases annually. Inglenook also offers 2 lines of jug wines that are neither produced nor bottled in the Napa Valley. The so-called Vintage lines consists of average-quality, lower-priced wines. The Navalle wines (not related to Napa Valley) are the high-volume, jug wine end of the line. In 1969, Inglenook was purchased by corporate giant Heublein, owner of Beaulieu Vineyards and Italian Swiss Colony.

ESTATE BOTTLED
Cabernet Cask Bottling: *Ripe, medium-full-bodied, some tannin* ❦/❦
Cabernet Sauvignon: *Medium body, some varietal, moderate tannin* ❦
Chardonnay: *Good varietal, never intense, light oak* ❦/❦
Chenin Blanc: *Medium sweet, fruity, moderate varietal* ❦

NAVALLE
French Colombard: *Medium sweet, somewhat floral* ❦
Ruby Cabernet: *Vinous, clean jug wine* ❦

INVERNESS WINE CELLARS 25,000 cases of red, white, and rosé marketed by a San Francisco distributor. Early efforts with varietals have ceased.

IRON HORSE VINEYARDS *Sonoma 1978* The 130-acre vineyard located in the Sebastopol region is planted primarily to Chardonnay and Pinot Noir. The winery was finished during 1979, in time to make 7,500 cases; the previous vintage was made elsewhere. Other wines offered include a Blanc de Noir and a Cabernet Sauvignon, grown in the Alexander Valley. First Chardonnays were quite successful. Production is now approaching 10,000 cases annually.

Chardonnay: *Appley, fruity, medium intense, crisp, some oak* ❦/❦

ITALIAN SWISS COLONY The century-old name belonging to a winery in Asti (northern Sonoma County) that is now owned by Heublein. The winery still exists, but the wines are now called simply Colony and are not necessarily bottled at Asti.

JEKEL VINEYARDS *Monterey 1978* Its first Riesling and Chardonnay were excellent. The roster is rounded out by Cabernet, Gamay Beaujolais, and Pinot Blanc. Using only grapes from 140 acres planted in 1972, Jekel is making about 25,000 cases. Its Greenfield location is better suited to white varietals.

Chardonnay: *Ripe, grassy, medium full, balanced, oaky* ✿
Johannisberg Riesling: *Floral, delicate, balanced, medium sweet* ✿

JFJ WINERY (BRONCO WINERY) Wines, sold mainly in jugs and carafes, vary in quality and type according to availability in the bulk market. Generic wines are sweet, sometimes passable. Varietals, usually the cheapest and least attractive of their type, have been known to offer reasonable value if you hit the right batch.

JOHNSON'S WINES *Sonoma 1975* An affable family of growers removed pears and prunes and planted 50 acres of wine varieties. They make 5,000 cases annually from their Alexander Valley grapes. So far they've been totally erratic with most varietals. All whites finished with residual sweetness have been poor to marginal in quality, while the reds have been low on varietal character. A dry-styled Rosé of Pinot Noir is the only consistent wine.

JORDAN VINEYARD *Sonoma 1976* Instead of buying a French château, a Denver geologist built a handsome estate in the Alexander Valley and established a 275-acre vineyard along the valley floor. Wanting to make 1 wine only, he planted Cabernet Sauvignon and Merlot in hopes of replicating a Bordeaux wine, but since then he has added considerable Chardonnay acreage. The first Cabernet, made in 1976 and released in 1980, showed promise of greater excitement as vineyards mature. Chardonnay was crushed in 1979. Beginning in 1978, the Cabernets follow a 5-year aging (barrel and bottle) regime prior to release. Peak production for the 2 varietals is set at 60,000 cases.

Cabernet Sauvignon: *Herbaceous, refined, supple, balanced* ✿

KALIN CELLARS *Marin 1976* High-energy experimenter with small lots of wine. Reds are oak-aged, handled for refinement. Track record is good, though ambition occasionally exceeds success.

KEENAN WINERY *Napa 1977* Atop Spring Mountain, this producer plans to offer Chardonnay, Cabernet Sauvignon, and Pinot Noir from its young 17-acre vineyard. The vines are not yet mature, however, so the same varieties are purchased. Limited first offerings, especially Chardonnay, have been successful and expensive.

Chardonnay: *Oaky, oily, lemony, good varietal* ❂/❂❂❂

KATHRYN KENNEDY WINES *Santa Clara 1979* Very small winery producing Cabernet Sauvignon from 8-acre vineyard in the hills of Saratoga, near Mount Eden Vineyards.

KENWOOD VINEYARDS *Sonoma 1906* This former jug wine facility was refurbished starting in 1970, when the new owners began emphasizing varietals. Zinfandel heads the list of reliable reds, but the whites are improving. Most of the 40,000-case total consists of red wines made from grapes purchased in the Alexander and Sonoma valleys. The winery is now stressing locally grown, Sonoma Valley varietals, especially Chardonnay and Pinot Noir. Average prices.

Cabernet Sauvignon: *Herbaceous, fruity, soft, woody* ♥/❂
Chardonnay: *Medium fruit, oaky, balanced* ♥
Chenin Blanc: *Fruity, light, well-balanced, slightly sweet* ♥/❂
Zinfandel: *Ripe, full, warm, tannic* ♥/❂❂

KIRIGIN CELLARS *Santa Clara 1976* The old Bonesio Uvas Brand winery was purchased by the Kirigins in 1976 and now produces a broad range of varietals and generics. Total production nears 10,000 cases. Wines are priced low but are not bargains.

French Colombard: *Clean, light fruit* ♥

KONOCTI CELLARS *Lake 1975* After 4 years of selling grapes and making small amounts of wine from their 524 acres, the 34 growers in a cooperative started a winery in 1979. 20,000 cases were made with a Cabernet Blanc and a Cabernet as the mainstays. They also have small acreage of white varieties and Zinfandel. Production could grow to 150,000 cases, but growth depends on the acceptance of Lake County Cabernet.

KORBEL *Sonoma 1862* Largest (over 300,000-case) U.S. producer of *méthode champenoise* champagne, Korbel also sells 500,000 cases of brandy. Vineyards (600 acres) are located in cool climates suited to champagne grapes. A new Blanc de Noir champagne has been well received.

Brut: *A bit more fruit, slightly sweeter than the Natural* ♥/❁
Demi-Sec: *Sweet taste, but low on elegance* ♥
Natural: *Very slightly sweet, austere* ♥/❁

HANNS KORNELL CHAMPAGNE CELLARS *Napa 1952* Specializing in champagnes. It makes 7 types, all by the *méthode champenoise,* and sales average 80,000 cases per year. The driest style is the house specialty, Sehr Trocken, but most others are on the sweet side. Except for the muscat wine, the cuvées often hint of Johannisberg Riesling. The style in general is light in body with a softness and excellent effervescence. The quality ranges from average to ❁. The top seller is the Extra Dry.

Brut Champagne: *Vinous, soft, slightly sweet* ♥
Extra Dry Champagne: *Fruity and yeasty, crisp, medium sweet* ♥
Muscat of Alexandria: *Strong muscatty aroma, medium sweet* ♥

CHARLES KRUG WINERY *Napa 1861* Founded by immigrant Charles Krug, who ran it until the 1890s; winery then experienced 50 years of instability until purchased by Cesare Mondavi in the 1940s. Sales are in the million-case range, including jug wines under the C. K. Mondavi label and varietal and generic wines under Charles Krug. Winery is now run by Peter Mondavi. Red varietals are of middling quality; whites generally better; Chenin Blanc was first to have sweetness. Reasonably priced.

Cabernet Sauvignon: *Medium body, flavors lack depth* ♥
Cabernet Vintage Select: *Somewhat ripe, distinct varietal, medium tannins when young, best vintages age 10–15 years* ♥/❁
Chardonnay: *Fruity, but often with disturbing grassy or vegetal notes* ♥
Chenin Blanc: *Medium sweet, fruity, fresh, reliable* ❁
Johannisberg Riesling: *Floral, fragrant, medium intensity* ♥/❁

THOMAS KRUSE WINERY *Santa Clara 1971* Enthusiasm exceeds the quality of wines, which all too often exhibit the consequences of winemaking peccadilloes. 2,500-cases.

RONALD LAMB WINERY *Santa Clara 1976* Small lots of Gamay Beaujolais, Pinot Noir, Cabernet Sauvignon, and Zinfandel are produced by this fledgling winery aiming for 2,500-case production level. Early experimentation has been with Gamay Beaujolais and Zinfandel in different types of oak barrels. Quality has varied from pleasant to dull.

M. LA MONT WINERY *Kern 1966* This former, large, growers' cooperative experienced lean years and was sold to a Canadian corporation in 1978. It ranks as the sixth largest U.S. producer, and sells 2.5 million cases under its own labels. Grapes come from neighboring vineyards in this hot area. The varietals are the usual Central Valley fare, joined in the market by a range of dessert and generic wines. The most difficulty was experienced with white wines, which were poorly made. But all current table wines are of low quality. Its other labels used for cheap generics are Mountain Gold and Mountain Peak.

LAMBERT BRIDGE *Sonoma 1975* Located in the Dry Creek region, this efficient, well-financed winery makes only Cabernet and Chardonnay. With 78 acres, it is building toward a 10,000-case limit. So far the Chardonnays have been much better, the Cabernets have ranged widely in quality.

Chardonnay: *Medium intensity, variable, oaky* ♥/✿

LANDMARK VINEYARDS *Sonoma 1974* This winery is just beginning to settle down after a few variable vintages. It has 80 acres and an expanded winery (as of 1978). The 25,000-case production is evenly divided between red and white varietals. Chardonnay and Pinot Noir show the best potential. Prices remain relatively reasonable.

Cabernet Sauvignon: *Weedy, lightly oaky, moderate tannins* ♥
Chardonnay: *Grassy varietal, medium-bodied, light oak* ♥
Chenin Blanc: *Fruity, thin, dry* ♥
Pinot Noir: *Fruity, somewhat complex, rich oak* ♥/✿

LA QUESTA VINEYARD (WOODSIDE VINEYARDS) Cabernet Sauvignon, grown in the historic La Questa Vineyard in the Santa Cruz Mountain foothills near Palo Alto, is vinified by Woodside Vineyards. The wines are less interesting than the vineyard's history.

LAS TABLAS WINERY *San Luis Obispo 1890* This old facility in the Templeton Hills, known until recently as Rotta Winery, is under new ownership that changed the name but not the reputation for hearty jug-styled wines of more weight than elegance. Most sales are at the winery.

LAWRENCE WINERY *San Luis Obispo 1979* The first large-sized winery in the county. Turned out around 200,000 cases in 1979. The partners own close to 700 acres, and the maximum production of the winery is 350,000 cases. The first wines, the usual assortment of varietals and generics, were generally weak in character and high-priced. The Lawrence Table Wine trio represented no bargains either.

LE DOMAINE (ALMADÉN VINEYARDS) Almadén's second-quality champagnes. Both Brut and Extra Dry are made by the transfer method. Once fine values, they have become flat, oversweetened wines geared to the mass market.

LE FLEURON (JOSEPH PHELPS VINEYARD) Second label used primarily for wines from young vineyards or for an occasional surplus wine. To date, the quality has been quite adequate for the $5–7 price tags of its mixed bag of issuances.

LEJON A label belonging to Heublein (owners of Inglenook and Colony) and used for its low-quality champagnes and brandies. It is now attached to a new line of soft generic table wines. The Burgundy, Chablis, and Rosé are sweet, low in alcohol, and low in character. The first batch (more than 100,000 cases) carried vintage dates.

LEEWARD WINERY *Ventura 1979* Small winery (2,000 cases) producing Chardonnay from San Luis Obispo County and Zinfandel from Amador County. First wines will reach market in late 1980 or 1981.

LELAND STANFORD CHAMPAGNE (WEIBEL) Inexpensive, bulk process sparkling wine named for Leland Stanford, governor, senator, and university founder. He also established the original winery at Warm Springs in Alameda County that is now Weibel.

LIBERTY SCHOOL VINEYARDS (CAYMUS VINEYARDS) A second label used primarily for nonvintage Cabernets purchased and aged. Identified by lot numbers, they offered good value through Lot #6. The label now includes Zinfandel, Red Table Wine, and White Table Wine on a regular basis. Other wines are offered depending on the availability of surplus grapes and wine. Combined sales now reach 8,000 cases per year.

✇ **Cabernet Sauvignon:** *Fruity, varietal flavors, light oak* ♟

LIVE OAK WINERY *Santa Clara 1912* Produces 25,000 cases of generic table wines and wine vinegar. Except on rare occasions, the vinegar is the better product.

LIVERMORE VALLEY VINEYARDS *Alameda 1978* Long-time grower turned winemaker, taking advantage of well-developed 34-acre vineyard. Vines are a potpourri of varieties including French Colombard, Golden Chasselas, Grey Riesling, and 10 acres of mixed whites consisting of equal parts Chenin Blanc, Pinot Blanc, and Chardonnay. All wines are fermented to dryness in stainless-steel, temperature-controlled tanks and then aged in small oak barrels. Production reaches 3,000 cases in 1980.

LLORDS & ELWOOD WINERY This operation owns neither vineyards nor winery. Aging and blending are performed in leased space at Weibel. Sales have reportedly reached 25,000 to 30,000 cases, but the varietals may be slipping since new technology and technique have seemingly bypassed this winemaker. Sherries and ports are its most successful products.

J. LOHR WINERY *Santa Clara 1974* Partners developed 280 acres of vineyards in Greenfield and built a winery now operating at its annual 100,000-case capacity. Best known for white varietals with Monterey appellations. However, it has recently bought Zinfandel and Petite Sirah from warmer regions, produced Cabernet Sauvignon as a rosé, and added a *nouveau*-style Gamay.

Chardonnay: *Grassy varietal, crisp, balanced, light oak* ♂/♥
Johannisberg Riesling: *Floral, delicate, citrusy, slightly sweet* ♥/♣

LONG VINEYARDS *Napa 1977* Small winery (2,000-case maximum) owned by Simi's winemaker and her husband, who operate this winery in their spare time. The 14-acre vineyard (Chardonnay and Johannisberg Riesling) supplied Mount Veeder's excellent Chardonnays in previous vintages. First releases were exceptional.

Chardonnay: *Rich varietal aroma, balanced, oaky* ♣♣/♣♣♣

LOS ALAMOS VINEYARDS See Hale Cellars.

LOS HERMANOS (BERINGER VINEYARDS) Fast-growing, unpretentious, and inexpensive line of generics and varietals. Production is over 600,000 cases. The line is made from purchased grapes and bulk wine from the North Coast and Central Valley, all under the California appellation. Generally, they are light, clean, and palatable wines; the white generics are medium sweet. The two most attractive offerings are the proprietary wines—Barenblut and Traubengold—once sold under Beringer.

Chardonnay: *Appley, thin, light fruit, dry* ❦
Chenin Blanc: *Low fruit, heavy, medium sweet* ❦
Traubengold: *Muscatty fruit, lively, medium sweet* ❦
Zinfandel: *Varietal fruit, light, simple* ❦

LOST HILLS VINEYARDS A label belonging to a group of agricultural investors who own 3,200 acres of vineyards in Kern County. The California appellation wines, totaling about 100,000 cases, are produced under contract by this label without a winery, but with a full-time winemaker. Additionally, about 10,000 cases of North Coast varietals are offered under the Lost Hills label. The varietals are of average quality and often priced attractively. The California varietals and generics made from Kern County grapes are generally low in price, but weak in quality.

LOWER LAKE WINERY *Lake 1977* First Lake County winery since Prohibition. All grapes are purchased from local growers. Opened with a White Cabernet (900 cases) in 1978 and is specializing in Cabernet under specific vineyard designations. 1979 production was close to winery's 8,000-case maximum.

LUCAS HOME WINERY *San Joaquin 1978* This label belongs to Lodi growers (15 acres of Zinfandel and 15 of Tokay) supplying grapes to home winemakers across the country. It made 700 cases of Zinfandel in 1979.

LYTTON SPRINGS WINERY *Sonoma 1975* A well-known Zinfandel vineyard in the area, once selling to Ridge, has become a real winery. The 50-acre vineyard averages 80 years of age and contains a smattering of Petite Sirah. The winery's first vintage was 1976. By 1978 it had reached the optimum 5,000-case output. Hard to find a better example of ripe Sonoma County–style Zinfandel.

Zinfandel: *Ripe, spicy, complex flavors, oaky* ✿/✿✿

M. MARION A private label owned by negotiant M. Dennis Marion, who buys wine from several sources and has it bottled to his specifications. To date, price and quality have been modest with an occasional bargain popping up.

MARIO PERELLI-MINETTI WINES Private label (owned independent of the Perelli-Minetti Vineyards) for Cabernet

Sauvignon and Chardonnay purchased ready-made. First releases were light and simple in character. About 1,000 cases in total.

MARKHAM WINERY *Napa 1978* A well-financed, large (over 1-million-gallon capacity) winery owning 300 acres and using only a small portion of its premises and vineyards for Markham wines. Production is now at 15,000 cases. Line includes a broad range of medium to expensive varietals. First releases were interesting, but were not the equal of similarly priced wines.

LOUIS M. MARTINI WINERY *Napa 1923* Well-known winery noted for its inexpensive line of varietals and generics. Close to 75% of the annual 400,000-case output consists of red wines. The family owns 800 acres, half in Sonoma County and 350 acres in the Carneros district. All wines carry a California appellation. The family philosophy is to age red wines primarily in large cooperage and to finish the white varietals on the dry side. Most wines are light, fruity, simple, and intended for early consumption. The exceptions among the reds are the Barbera and occasionally special bottling type Cabernet. The best white wines are Gewurztraminer and Johannisberg Riesling, both often rising above average quality. Recent Chardonnay vintages reflect quality improvements.

⚄ **Barbera:** *Ripe berry character, powerful, ages well* ♥/✿
Cabernet Sauvignon: *Simple varietal, light-bodied* ♥
⚄ **Gewürztraminer:** *Spicy aroma and flavor, firm, dry* ♥/✿
Johannisberg Riesling: *Floral, spicy, balanced, dry* ♥/✿
Zinfandel: *Vinous, medium-bodied, fruity* ♥

MARTINI & PRATI WINES *Sonoma 1951* An old, large (2 1/2-million-gallon capacity) winery that sells 90% of its wines in bulk to various large wineries. It bottles 20,000 cases under its label, both varietals and generics. All are low-priced; most are tanky and unappealing.

PAUL MASSON VINEYARDS *Santa Clara 1852* One of the oldest and one of the biggest. Sales now exceed 6 million cases, covering almost every possible wine type. Most wines are nonvintaged, fairly low priced, and aimed at the broadest levels of acceptance. Limited quantities of vintage-dated varietals, champagnes, and fortified wines have managed to reach somewhat higher quality levels.

Masson owns 4,500 acres of vineyard in Monterey County.

Brut Champagne: *Dry, crisp, clean, lightly fruity* 🍷/❀
Cabernet Sauvignon: *Soft, dull, vegetal* ☉/🍷
Chardonnay: *Vintage versions are fruity, citric, oaky, but thin* 🍷; *nonvintage wine is heavy and less interesting* 🍷
Chenin Blanc: *Medium sweet, fruity, simple* 🍷
✡ **Emerald Dry:** *Medium sweet, good acid, clean* 🍷
✡ **Rare Souzao Port:** *Rich, fruity, powerful* 🍷/❀❀
Zinfandel: *Light, soft, low varietal* 🍷

MASTANTUONO WINERY *San Luis Obispo 1977* A Zinfandel-only winery, making 1,000 cases from its 11-acre vineyard. First vintages were made in three styles: regular, rosé, and *nouveau.*

MATANZAS CREEK WINERY *Sonoma 1978* This winery attracts attention because of its winemaker's successful record with Mount Eden Vineyards. Its 50 acres are planted in the Bennett Valley adjacent to Sonoma Valley. The major varieties are Cabernet, Chardonnay, Pinot Noir, and Merlot. The first releases, all successful, were made from purchased grapes. Production will level off at 5,000 cases.

MAYACAMAS VINEYARDS *Napa 1941* Consistent, high-quality Cabernet and Chardonnay have been offered by this Mount Veeder producer. It has 45 acres on hillsides and purchases some grapes to supplement its production. Both Cabernet and Chardonnay require long cellaring. Although most of its 5,000-case output consists of these varietals, it also makes small lots of late harvest Zinfandel and an induced-Botrytis Semillon.

Cabernet Sauvignon: *Ripe, powerful, tannic* ❀/❀❀
Chardonnay: *Rich, complex, oily, and oaky* ❀❀/❀❀❀

MCDOWELL CELLARS *Mendocino 1979* Success of other wineries with McDowell Valley grapes encouraged this large vineyard operation to open its own 25,000-case-capacity winery. 8 varietals are being produced.

MEV (MOUNT EDEN VINEYARDS) A second label used for wines produced from purchased grapes (the main label being reserved for estate-grown wines). The quality has been high and the prices somewhat less shocking than those charged for the main label.

Chardonnay: *Oaky, fat, rich, lacking refinement* 🍷/❀❀

MILANO WINERY *Mendocino 1977* Attractive new winery in a refurbished hop kiln. The near-term goal is 12,000 cases composed of small-lot production from low-tonnage, hillside vineyards. Zinfandel and Petite Sirah come from a Talmage-area vineyard. First Chenin Blanc was attractive; first Sauvignon Blanc much less so.

MILL CREEK VINEYARDS *Sonoma 1976* After planting a 70-acre vineyard in 1965, the owners completed a winery in 1975. Current offerings are Cabernet, Chardonnay, Pinot Noir, and Blanc de Noir. Most have achieved average-quality status to date. Production is close to 10,000 cases.

Cabernet Sauvignon: *Herbaceous, soft, fruity* ♥/❀
Chardonnay: *Ripe appley, medium flavors and oak* ♥/❀

MIRASSOU VINEYARDS *Santa Clara 1966* Family winery involved for decades in the bulk wine business and now producing and bottling close to 300,000 cases annually. Owns over 1,000 acres, mostly in Monterey, with some holdings (300 acres) in Santa Clara County. The Monterey-grown grapes are field crushed after mechanical harvesting. 60% of production is in white wines, which in the early 1970s were fruity and dry to slightly sweet finished but which have for the most part been rather sweet since. Conversely, the red varietals, once overly vegetal in character, have improved recently. Uses Harvest Selection for its Reserve bottlings. A blended white, Monterey Riesling, is the best seller. Close to 10,000 cases of *méthode champenoise* champagnes are made by Mirassou Vineyards each year.

Cabernet Sauvignon: *Slightly herbaceous, thin, tart* ♥
Chardonnay: *Grassy varietal, average flavors, crisp* ♥
Chenin Blanc: *Recently unreliable; 1977 was below average and 1978 average with modest fruit and slightly sweet finish* ♥
Johannisberg Riesling: *Light varietal, citrusy, medium sweet* ♥
Monterey Riesling: *Light floral, light-bodied, medium sweet* ♥
Zinfandel: *Fruity, medium-bodied, grassy, hard* ♥

C. K. MONDAVI WINES (CHARLES KRUG WINERY) A popular label covering a variety of jug generics and a Zinfandel. The C. K. Mondavi wines likely represent a high percentage of Krug's annual 2-million-case sales. Although C. K. Mondavi whites have slipped recently, the reds offer simple inexpensive drinking.

ROBERT MONDAVI WINERY *Napa 1966* Robert Mondavi left the Charles Krug Winery to make wines in his own style. The winery is without equal in design and equipment and now makes 300,000 cases of generally high-quality wines. It owns 1,000 acres and buys high-quality grapes at high prices. Mondavi pioneered slightly sweet Chenin Blanc with Krug and dry, balanced Fumé Blanc more recently at Mondavi. Highly innovative, the Mondavi family buys small oak barrels from numerous regions and continues experimenting with different theories of barrel aging and vinification. The popular Table Wines, about 500,000 cases, are made at a winery in Lodi. Oakville Vineyards is a second label.

Cabernet Reserve: *Complex, lush, long-ager* ✿/✿✿✿
Cabernet Sauvignon: *Elegant, supple, appealing* ♥/✿✿
Chardonnay: *Medium ripe, balanced, lightly oaky* ♥/✿✿
Fumé Blanc: *Herbal, smooth, stylish, light oak* ✿/✿✿
Gamay and Gamay Rosé: *Fruity, balanced, best of types*
Johannisberg Riesling: *Fragrant, delicate, medium sweet* ✿/✿✿✿
Red Table Wine: *Juglike, fruity, balanced* ♥

MONDAVI-ROTHSCHILD *Napa 1979* The likely name for a Cabernet-type wine produced in concert by the owners of Robert Mondavi Winery and of Château Mouton-Rothschild. The Cabernet Sauvignon and Cabernet Franc blend will be given a proprietary name. First crush was in 1979 at the Mondavi winery with the first wine scheduled to be released in 1983. Maximum production is 5,000 cases.

LA MONTAÑA (MARTIN RAY VINEYARDS) A second label devoted mainly to purchased wines. Quality has been erratic; some Cabernet Sauvignons reach ✿ heights. Volume is tiny (under 1,000 cases).

MONTCLAIR WINERY *Alameda 1975* Small (1,000-case) winery operated on a part-time basis. Buys grapes from leading Napa and Sonoma County vineyards, but has displayed inconsistent results to date. Zinfandel has been best to date.

French Colombard: *Dry, oak-aged, fairly big style* ♥/✿
Zinfandel (Dry Creek): *Oaky, ripe, berryish, sometimes late harvest* ♥/✿

MONTEREY CELLARS (MONTEREY PENINSULA WINERY) Second label used mostly for generics made from press wine and for less expensive varietals that the winery feels are of lower quality.

MONTEREY PENINSULA WINERY *Monterey 1974* A try-grapes-from-anywhere attitude prevailed in this 10,000-case winery over its first few vintages. Preference now falls on red varietals, mainly Zinfandel and Cabernet, made from very ripe grapes, fermented long, and intended for long aging. Owning no vineyards, it buys from Amador growers and others in the Central Coast. Inconsistent, but has made some of the best Monterey-grown Cabernet Sauvignon. Chardonnays vary from excellent to awful.

Cabernet Sauvignon: *Pungent and peppery; sometimes complex; sometimes tart* ♥/✿
Zinfandel: *Usually ripe and briary, tannic, inconsistent* ⌂/✿; *late harvest versions from concentrated to overly raisiny* ♥/✿

MONTEREY VINEYARD *Monterey 1973* A 2-million-gallon capacity winery that began with high aspirations for Monterey County varietals only to find the going rough. Now owned by Coca-Cola of Atlanta, it has no vineyards, but makes close to 40,000 cases. Production will likely grow rapidly over the next few years. Although in flux, it made better whites than reds, consistent with the experience of others in northern Monterey recently. Now buying grapes from San Luis Obispo for blended red and white wines.

Classic Red: *Vinous, slightly vegetal, medium-full bodied* ♥
⚲ **Johannisberg Riesling:** *Floral, citric, fruity, slightly sweet* ♥

MONTEVIÑA VINEYARDS *Amador 1973* A well-regarded winery best known for its Zinfandels and its experimental batches of other varietals. The Zinfandels, including those made in *nouveau* and white styles, are among the best. Occasionally some of the wines go unchecked in intensity and alcohol. About 6,000 cases in total are made. A high percentage of grapes (80%) from the 160 acres is sold. The most interesting experiments have been with Barbera and Ruby Cabernet.

Cabernet Sauvignon: *Ripe, powerful, tannic* ♥/✿
Sauvignon Blanc: *Intense, big, harsh, unrestrained alcohol* ♥/✿
Zinfandel: *Complex, spicy, ripe berries, unrestrained tannins* ✿/✿✿
Zinfandel Nuevo: *Jamlike, delicious, best of type* ✿

J. W. MORRIS PORT WORKS *Alameda 1975* A small but growing winery (12,000 cases) rapidly losing its port-only reputation. Red wines now account for 50%, port for 30%,
and whites for 20% (first whites were from 1979 harvest). Grapes are purchased, mostly in Sonoma County.
Most wines are made in full, rich style.

> **Pinot Noir:** *Fairly heavy for variety, oaky, wants
> elegance and complexity* ♀/✿
> **Vintage Port:** *Ripe grape nose, good fruit, complex
> notes, and good depth* ✿/✿✿
> **Zinfandel (Sonoma):** *Heavy, tannic, ripe berry style,
> needs age* ✿

MOUNTAINSIDE VINEYARDS (CHATEAU CHEVALIER) Second
label wines usually made from purchased grapes. The first
few vintages were produced from the winery's young vineyards. Chardonnays have recently been weak, whereas the
Cabernet Sauvignons are average-quality.

MOUNT EDEN VINEYARDS *Santa Clara 1972* A prestigious,
high-quality producer located on an isolated hilltop in
the Santa Cruz Mountains. 2,000 cases of estate-bottled
wines are produced from the 22 acres of vineyard (10
Cabernet Sauvignon; 8 Pinot Noir; 4 Chardonnay) surrounding the winery. The second label, MEV, is used
for wines made from grapes grown elsewhere. Recent
vintages have been atypical, dirty, disappointing. Prices
are never modest for Mount Eden wines.

> **Cabernet Sauvignon:** *Complex, oaky, herbal, ripe,
> tannic, occasionally lacking refinement* ✿/✿✿✿
> **Chardonnay:** *Fat, mouth-filling, oaky, spicy,
> intense* ♀/✿✿
> **Pinot Noir:** *Oaky, rich, good varietal, often superb
> depth and balance* ♀/✿✿

MOUNT PALOMAR WINERY *Riverside 1975* Located in the
Temecula region, where it has 160 acres planted, this winery sells most of its current 12,000 cases either in its tasting
room/gift store or through Southern California outlets.
Its top sellers are a Chenin Blanc and a sweet-finished
Cabernet Sauvignon. The winery is developing a sherry
solera.

MOUNT VEEDER WINERY *Napa 1972* Small winery (4,500
cases) located high on Mount Veeder in the Mayacamas
Mountains west of Napa. Brawny reds are made from
own vineyard and until 1978 from a variety of other
sources. Chenin Blanc is home grown.

Cabernet Sauvignon (Estate): *Brawny, tannic, deeply colored, weedy and currants flavors* ♥/✿✿

Chenin Blanc: *Dry, intensely fruity, sometimes lemony and crisp* ✿/✿✿✿

J. MUELLER CELLARS A private label for limited amounts (400 cases) of white wines produced in leased space at Parducci by consulting engineer Mueller. The two whites (Chardonnay and Chenin Blanc) are light, fragrant, and fruity.

NAPA WINE CELLARS *Napa 1975* Located north of Yountville, this winery is surrounded by 3 acres of Chardonnay. It makes several varietals, mostly from purchased grapes. Its grape sources change each vintage, but the winery's style emphasizes very ripe grapes and high alcohol. Zinfandel, late harvest and regular style, is its most successful varietal. The Chardonnays are well oaked; the other wines of average quality. Production has grown to 10,000 cases.

Chardonnay: *Fruity, round, oaky* ♥/✿

Zinfandel: *Ripe berries, full-bodied, variable style* ♥/✿

NAVARRO VINEYARDS *Mendocino 1975* This 4,000-case winery focuses on Gewurztraminer grown on 30 of its 33 planted acres. It also has 3 acres of Pinot Noir and purchases grapes for Cabernet, Riesling, and Chardonnay. First wines were average-quality for type.

NEPENTHE CELLARS *Santa Cruz 1967* Small-scale operation earning little critical success in a decade of operation.

NICHELINI VINEYARDS *Napa 1890* Located in the Chiles Valley, away from the main wine road, this old winery relies on faithful customers or tourists on their way to Lake Berryessa. It makes 6,000 cases of varietals, including a Sauvignon Vert. The wines are low-priced, but the quality (oxidized whites and poorly handled reds) prevents them from being bargains.

NIEBAUM-COPPOLA ESTATES *Napa 1978* Movie director Francis Ford Coppola acquired the historic Niebaum mansion (long associated with Inglenook's founder) and the adjacent 90-acre vineyard. Present plans are to produce a Cabernet Sauvignon (blended with Cabernet Franc, Merlot, and Malbec) and a Chardonnay. Both are scheduled for 1983 debuts.

A. NONINI WINERY *Fresno 1935* This family-owned winery makes a variety of generics along with a Barbera and a

Zinfandel from its own 200-acre vineyard. Most sales are through the quaint tasting room.

NOVITIATE WINES *Santa Clara 1888* This aging winery in Los Gatos is undergoing modernization. Long known for good-quality dessert wines and mediocre table wines, it is trying to maintain the former and improve the latter, especially the whites. Most of the winery's vineyards have been either leased or sold to others. It now buys all grapes for its 50,000-case annual output, still led by the dessert wines. Current table wines reflect transitional uncertainty.

Black Muscat: *Strong muscat character, full-bodied, sweet* ♥
Pinot Blanc: *Fruity, thin, sometimes crisp* ♥

N.V. (NAPA VINTNERS) *Napa 1975* There has been wine under this label for several years, but it was not until 1978 that the owners formed their own winery. Production is 3,000 cases.

Sauvignon Blanc: *Dry, fruity, good varietal, noticeable oak* ✿

OAK BARREL WINERY *Alameda 1960* Produces 600 cases of lackluster varietals sold at low prices only at its Berkeley, California, winery. Also 4,000 cases of purchased bulk wines.

OAKVILLE VINEYARDS (ROBERT MONDAVI WINERY) After a winery by this name went out of business, Robert Mondavi acquired the trademark and aging inventory. He intends to convert the varietals under Oakville into fruity, uncomplex wines. However, to date, most Oakville wines have been tired and slightly oxidized.

OBESTER WINERY *San Mateo 1977* Offers a broad range of varietals, all made from purchased grapes. First vintages evidenced good quality overall, the Zinfandel being above average. Production is near 4,000 cases. Most sales are direct.

PAGE MILL WINERY *Santa Clara 1976* Small (2,000-case) winery producing big, oak-aged but often flawed wines from purchased grapes, including Napa Valley Chardonnay, Chenin Blanc, and Zinfandel.

ANGELO PAPAGNI VINEYARDS *Madera 1973* Long-time grape grower Angelo Papagni had a better idea: Take the best of his several thousand acres of wine grapes, build a winery, and make limited amounts of wine. Benefiting from the latest technology, most wines have turned out clean, fresh, and a beat above the usual Central Valley fare. In spite of the winery's capacity (1.2 million cases), sales of Angelo Papagni labeled wines are limited to 80,000 cases. Reds and a few whites are barrel aged. Some 20 wines are offered, including the only Alicante Bouschet and late harvest Emerald Riesling in California.

Alicante Bouschet: *Vinous, tannic, clean* ♥

Chenin Blanc: *Fruity, slightly sweet, best when young* ♥

♦ **Moscato d'Angelo:** *Very sweet, fragrant, easy to sip* ✿

PARDUCCI WINE CELLARS *Mendocino 1931* During the past decade Parducci converted from a bulk operation to a producer of quality wines at low prices. This early champion of Mendocino-grown grapes now has 350 acres in vineyards and produces in excess of 170,000 cases annually, red wines representing a slightly higher percentage. The winery's style is to avoid excessive oak aging. Despite rapid expansion and an increased line of varietals and jug generics, the overall quality level has continued to be reliable. Lots Parducci deems special are labeled Cellar Masters Selection.

Cabernet Sauvignon: *Medium varietal, fruity, balanced* ♥/✿

♦ **Chardonnay:** *Appley, crisp, tart* ♥/✿

♦ **Chenin Blanc:** *Fruity, lively, delicate, slightly sweet* ✿/✿✿

♦ **Petite Sirah:** *Peppery, medium-bodied, tannic* ♥/✿

Zinfandel: *Fruity, round, light tannins* ♥

PARSONS CREEK WINERY *Mendocino 1979* Small operation (4,000 cases) that sold off much of its early production. Limited amounts of Johannisberg Riesling and Chenin Blanc are held back for the winery's label.

MICHAEL T. PARSONS WINERY *Santa Cruz 1976* Small, 500-case winery operated as a sideline by dentist Parsons, who aspires to make great Pinot Noir.

PASTORI WINES *Sonoma 1975* A pre-Prohibition name in the bulk wine business was revived and a small winery built. Its first wines, released in 1975, consisted of tired, tanky, purchased wines. It is now making wines from its 60-acre vineyard. The reds are overaged, and the whites are even less interesting. Production is close to 10,000 cases, and the generics are made from purchased grapes.

ROBERT PECOTA WINERY *Napa 1978* 40 acres of vineyard surrounding the Calistoga winery provide 8,000 cases of wine per year. First releases were youthful, fruity wines. Still to come is a dry, oaky Sauvignon Blanc.

French Colombard: *Dry, fruity and somewhat oaky* ❀
Gamay Beaujolais: *Intense fruity nouveau style* ♥/❀

PEDRIZZETTI WINERY *Santa Clara 1938* An old roadside winery modernized in 1976 after being reacquired by the family. New equipment and renewed effort are bringing quality closer to acceptability. Hearty reds are the more interesting wines, and recent whites remain inconsistent. From 40 acres adjacent to the winery and another 40 under contract, the winery makes 60,000 cases annually.

Chardonnay: *Oxidized, undrinkable* ☪
Petite Sirah: *Hearty, robust, fairly tannic* ♥
Zinfandel: *Fruity, light-bodied, tart* ♥

PEDRONCELLI VINEYARDS *Sonoma 1904* A long-time bulk wine producer, it began bottling wines under its own labels in the early 1960s. It has 135 acres under vine and, having expanded to the current 10,000-case level, it purchases grapes in Sonoma County. Through 1973, Pedroncelli red wines offered both quality and value, but quality suffered in 1974 and 1975. By 1976 the reds returned to form, but the whites revealed quality problems. Chardonnay and Gewurztraminer from 1978 indicate that most problems have been solved. All wines, including popular jugs, carry Sonoma County appellation.

Cabernet Sauvignon: *Vague varietal, simple fruit* ♥
⚘ **Chardonnay:** *Appley, light varietal flavors, crisp* ♥/❀
Gewurztraminer: *Slightly spicy, firm, slightly sweet* ♥
Zinfandel: *Fruity, simple* ♥
Zinfandel Rosé: *Fruity, spritzy, slightly sweet* ♥

PENDLETON WINERY *Santa Clara 1976* Moved into a new, 6,000-case winery in 1979 and changed name from Arroyo. First 3 vintages were made elsewhere. Major emphasis is on Monterey-grown Chardonnay and Pinot Noir, with small amounts of Chenin Blanc and Cabernet. Early efforts with Chardonnay and Pinot Noir resulted in above-average quality. Reasonable prices.

PERELLI-MINETTI WINERY This old name in California wine is now a new label for a line of varietals. Although the winery is in Delano, the varietals are from grapes purchased in the North and Central Coast regions. Total production is 12,000 cases. The most interesting wine is a Monterey Fumé Blanc.

PESENTI WINERY *San Luis Obispo 1934* A 100,000-case producer of dessert, generic, and inexpensive varietal wines for consumers in the San Luis Obispo area, especially those at the local college.

Zinfandel Rosé: *Fruity, overly sweet* ♟

PETRI WINES Label for fairly sweet, inexpensive, cooked-fruit-tasting jug wines bottled by Heublein (Inglenook, Colony). Below average in quality.

JOSEPH PHELPS VINEYARD *Napa 1973* Handsome 40,000-case winery producing wines of very high quality. Its early reputation for success with Riesling and Gewurztraminer now extends to Cabernet Sauvignon, Zinfandel, Chardonnay, and almost every other varietal it has offered. Late harvest Riesling and Gewurztraminer always rate ✿✿ to ✿✿✿. The winery's own vineyards (170 acres) will supply 80% of capacity soon.

Cabernet Sauvignon: *Fruity varietal, fairly full* ♟/✿✿
Chardonnay: *Oaky, medium-full-bodied, fat style* ♟/✿✿
Fumé Blanc: *Light, fruity, elegant, blended with Semillon* ♟/✿
Insignia: *Winery's best blend from available Cabernet, Merlot, and Cabernet Franc; content varies each year although wine maintains depth and charm* ✿/✿✿✿
Johannisberg Riesling: *Floral, good varietal, fruity, medium sweet* ✿/✿✿
Zinfandel: *Ripe, berryish, fairly tannic* ♟/✿✿

PLEASANTON VINTNERS (STONY RIDGE WINERY) A line introduced in 1978 consisting of inexpensive table wines made generally from bulk wines or tired wines inherited by new owners.

POPE VALLEY WINERY *Napa 1972* This family-run (8,000-case) winery makes a variety of wines that most often vary from awful to average. The winery has been modernized, and improvements should be coming. All grapes are purchased, and the annual offerings depend on what is available. Direction in varietal wines remains whimsical.

PHILIP POSSON (SIERRA WINE COMPANY) The only label used by the gigantic (30-million-gallon capacity) Central Valley bulk wine producer. Dry Flor Sherry, made by the "submerged flor" technique, is the only retail offering. It is one of California's best. Under 5,000 cases annually.

Dry Flor Sherry: *Yeasty, flavorful, medium-bodied, dry* 🏵

PRESTON VINEYARDS *Sonoma 1975* From 80 acres in the Dry Creek region, Preston has settled on making Fumé Blanc and Zinfandel as major parts of its 5,000-case production. Each year it experiments with other varietals—Gamay, Cabernet, and Sirah to date. Its most popular bottlings are the blended red and white table wines.

Fumé Blanc: *Intense varietal, good fruit, dry* 🏵
Zinfandel: *Fruity, rough and tannic* 🍷/🏵

QUADY WINERY *Madera 1977* Quady is part of the new interest in port wine production. Andrew Quady prefers to use only Zinfandel grown in either Amador or Paso Robles and to age the wine 2 years in American oak. Though working full-time for a major wine company, he makes 3,500 cases of Vintage Port in his small winery. First 2 vintages were appealing; whether long cellaring will improve them remains to be seen.

Vintage Port (Amador): *Rich, intense, moderately tannic* 🏵/🏵🏵

QUAIL RIDGE WINERY *Napa 1978* Small producer (1,200 cases in 1979) will grow to 2,500 cases when 20 acres of Chardonnay and Cabernet on Mount Veeder mature. Winery owners have set high goals for quality and price.

QUERCUS VINEYARDS A privately owned label for Lake County Cabernet Sauvignon. About 2,000 cases per year, made at Souverain Cellars. Variable quality in a light style.

A. RAFANELLI WINERY *Sonoma 1974* With 25 acres in Dry Creek, this 3,000-case winery offers only Gamay Beaujolais and Zinfandel. The first releases were vintage blends. The more recent vintage Zinfandels are good both for the type and region.

Zinfandel: *Dark, ripe berries, tannic, powerful* 🏵

RANCHITA OAKS *San Luis Obispo 1979* 6,000-case production of Zinfandel, Cabernet Sauvignon, and Petite Sirah from 1979 crush will debut in 1981 or 1982. Winery is seeking tannic, long-aging style. Vineyard and production facility are located in hills near Shandon.

RANCHO SISQUOC *Santa Barbara 1977* Small (1,300-case) winery located in the midst of a 38,000-acre diversified agricultural development. Close to 200 acres of vineyards are established, half of which are planted to Cabernet Sauvignon. Most grapes are sold. To date, the wines made have been uneven in quality. Sales have been primarily to winery visitors.

RANCHO YERBA BUENA Private label owned by sales arm of Papagni Vineyards. The first wines, Cabernet Sauvignon and Blanc Natur, have been clean and worth their moderate price tags.

RAPAZZINI WINERY *Santa Clara 1962* No longer making wine. This roadside sales operation relies on its own aged reds and augments them with wines purchased from others and bottled.

RAVENSWOOD WINERY Winemaker and equipment operating out of leased space in Sonoma County. Limited amounts of Zinfandel and Cabernet Sauvignon are produced from El Dorado and Amador counties and the Dry Creek Valley grapes. First Zinfandels were ripe, briary, intense. Total production is 1,000 cases.

MARTIN RAY VINEYARDS *Santa Clara 1946* Established by the late Martin Ray after he sold his interest in Paul Masson. His son, a professor at Stanford, now oversees the winery's 1,500-case output. Chardonnay is the volume leader; Cabernet Sauvignon and Pinot Noir are also offered. Prices are among the highest in California; quality has lagged.

Chardonnay: *Very oaky, fat, ripe, sometimes lovely, frequently dirty and oxidized* ☼/✿✿

RAYMOND VINEYARDS *Napa 1974* The Raymond family is directly related to the Beringer clan and was long involved with that winery. The Raymonds established an 80-acre vineyard in 1971 and completed their own winery in 1978, designed to make 20,000 cases. The early record ranges from a rich late harvest Riesling through average-quality Gamay, highly variable Cabernet and Chenin Blanc. Given the vineyard site, Johannisberg Riesling and Chardonnay are the best bets for now.

Cabernet Sauvignon: *Herbaceous, oaky, and tannic* ♥/✿
Chardonnay: *Medium varietal, very oaky, round* ♥/✿✿

REGE WINES *Sonoma 1939* Jug wines lead the way for this aging Sonoma-based winery (34,000-case output). Its Chateau

Rege label is a favorite among San Franciscans who pick it up at the winery's outlet in the city's North Beach section.

RICHERT PORT AND SHERRY CELLARS *Santa Clara 1954* A dessert wine specialist (sherries and ports) offering unexciting wines in recent years. A new generation has taken over and is determined to improve quality. About 20,000 cases are produced annually, including fruit and berry wines. Richert Cellars is a new label for varietal wines.

RIDGE VINEYARDS *Santa Clara 1962* Among the first wineries to demonstrate that Zinfandel can be made into a first-class wine. It did so by scurrying about to locate the finest hillside vineyards. Ridge red wines were once the biggest and brawniest; the style today is a bit more restrained. Current production is 25,000 cases, about half in Zinfandel and 40% in Cabernet Sauvignon. It buys Cabernet and Petite Sirah from York Creek in Napa. Monte Bello refers to several vineyards located along the ridge near the winery. Prices are ordinarily high, but the Central Coast Zinfandel, a flavorful, less tannic wine, often is a good value.

Cabernet Sauvignon, Monte Bello: *Earthy, oaky, tannic, recently variable* ♥/✿✿
Petite Sirah: *Briary, tannic, intense, hot* ♥/✿✿✿
Zinfandel (Geyserville): *Ripe, intense, powerful* ✿/✿✿✿
Zinfandel (York Creek): *Spicy and berrylike, brawny* ♥/✿✿✿

RITCHIE CREEK VINEYARDS *Napa 1974* This label represents a small trickle. 6 acres of Cabernet Sauvignon, along with a little plot of Chardonnay, are planted on Spring Mountain. Annual production is well under 1,000 cases. Cabernets from recent vintages have been medium-full-bodied with ample tannin, but far from harmonious.

RIVER BEND CELLARS (DAVIS BYNUM WINERY) A second label for lower-priced wines aged for shorter periods than the first label. Most offerings are simple and carry Sonoma County appellations. Quantity sold is a maximum of 5,000 cases annually.

RIVER OAKS VINEYARD This label belongs to a partnership of growers and investors with 600 acres under vine in the Alexander Valley area. The wines are made at 4 different facilities, and in 1979 over 75,000 cases were produced. It is a line of inexpensive varietals that are, at best, fruity, straightforward versions. The whites are more appealing. All are low-priced.

RIVER ROADS VINEYARDS *Sonoma 1978* Another instance of growers' beginning to test the market by selling under their own label (70 acres in Forestville and another 30 being planted). 5,000 cases of their own wine was made in 1979 at Sonoma Vineyards, divided among Chardonnay, Fumé Blanc, and Johannisberg Riesling. The Chardonnay is of good quality.

RIVER RUN VINEYARDS *Santa Cruz 1978* Orchard owner Will Hangen has started a small winery on his riverfront property. Output is limited (2,000 cases), and grape sources vary from year to year.

CARLO ROSSI VINEYARDS (E. & J. GALLO) This highly visible Gallo label now covers 4 generics in the inexpensive, jug wine end. It has recently been consolidated with the former Red Mountain Vineyards label. Carlo is really a cousin of the Gallos.

ROUDON-SMITH VINEYARDS *Santa Cruz 1972* New winery for this 6,000-case producer was finished in 1979. It has settled on making Cabernet, Zinfandel, and Chardonnay from purchased grapes and limited amounts of other varietals. Quite successful with the reds, especially Zinfandel, but results with various white varietals are mixed. Recent Chardonnay comes from Monterey; Cabernets from San Luis Obispo; Zinfandels from Sonoma.

Cabernet Sauvignon: *Complex, fruity, round, early-maturing* ♉/❀
Zinfandel (Chauvet): *Ripe berrylike fruit, good depth, fairly tannic* ❀
Chardonnay: *Fresh, appley, crisp, medium oak* ♉/❀

ROUND HILL VINEYARDS *Napa 1975* Began as a blender and bottler of purchased wines, now also produces 18,000 cases at its own winery. The 6 varietals produced carry Napa Valley appellations. Most of the 60,000 cases bought in bulk bear less specific place names, such as North Coast. All wines are inexpensive; a few are good values.

Cabernet Sauvignon: *Weedy varietal, soft, round* ♉
Chardonnay (Napa Valley): *Fruity, fresh, lightly oaky* ♉/❀

ROYAL HOST A primary label for wines and brandies made by Lodi's East-Side Winery. Its ports and sherries, particularly those finished sweet, win numerous awards. The label also appears on many inexpensive, low-quality generics and an excellent 6-year-old brandy.

CHANNING RUDD CELLARS *Alameda 1977* Label designer Rudd operates his 400-case winery part-time, emphasizing big reds (Zinfandel, Cabernet), port, and occasionally offering barrel-aged whites.

RUTHERFORD HILL WINERY *Napa 1976* This is a new label, although the winery was operated by Pillsbury as Souverain of Rutherford earlier. Several partners behind Freemark Abbey, who own large acreage in Napa, decided to acquire these premises instead of building a new winery. The first series of varietals released was of average quality (the reds were inherited in the transaction). By the 1978 vintage the white varietals were of above-average quality, and the reds more interesting also. Production will level off at 100,000 cases soon.

Cabernet Sauvignon: *Medium-bodied, some fruit, noticeable oak* ♥/✿
Chardonnay: *Fruity, round, oaky* ♥/✿
Johannisberg Riesling: *Flowery, balanced, slightly sweet* ♥/✿
Pinot Noir-Blanc: *Fruity, crisp, fairly dry* ♥

RUTHERFORD RANCH CELLARS *Napa 1975* From vineyards in the hills west of St. Helena, it makes 1,000 cases of Zinfandel and 1,200 of Cabernet Sauvignon. First vintages have been exceptional.

Zinfandel: *Ripe varietal, big, rich, and tannic* ✿/✿✿
Cabernet Sauvignon: *Complex aroma and flavors, tannic* ✿

RUTHERFORD VINTNERS *Napa 1977* This compact winery with its 30 acres represents working retirement for former Louis Martini employee Bernard Skoda. Cabernet Sauvignon, Johannisberg Riesling, and Pinot Noir come from the adjacent vineyard; a sweet muscat is made from Fresno grapes. The first series of varietals was inauspicious. 1978 Riesling offered encouragement for the future. Production is at 10,000 cases with plans to double.

ST. CLEMENT VINEYARDS *Napa 1975* Small winery producing high-quality wines to date. Sales will double (to 5,000 cases) in early 1980s. A small amount of Sauvignon Blanc will be added.

Cabernet Sauvignon: *Good varietal, oaky, fairly tannic style* ✿
Chardonnay: *Oaky, fat style with good varietal fruit* ✿/✿✿

ST. FRANCIS VINEYARDS *Sonoma 1979* New winery in Kenwood surrounded by 100 acres of vineyards containing 5 cool-climate varieties. Its grapes are also sold to other Sonoma Valley wineries. Current production amounts to 5,000 cases.

ST. HELENA WINE COMPANY *Napa 1978* Early output of 1,800 cases is expected to increase gradually to 5,000 in the near term. First wines, barrel-aged Cabernet Sauvignon and Merlot, were eye-opening successes. Sauvignon Blanc will complete the line.

SANFORD & BENEDICT VINEYARDS *Santa Barbara 1970* 5,000-case producer emphasizing barrel-fermented Chardonnay and Pinot Noir, both grown in its 110-acre vineyard. Other varietals include Cabernet Sauvignon, Merlot, and Johannisberg Riesling. Variable-quality performance to date. Maximum production will be 10,000 cases.

Chardonnay: *Ripe varietal, oily, round, oaky* 🍷/❀
Pinot Noir: *Complex, medium-bodied, soft, tannic* ❀

SAN MARTIN WINERY *Santa Clara 1908* Dramatically improved quality has been registered recently by this 250,000-case winery, once a funky roadside outfit. White wines represent close to 75% of the current total. Most are average to slightly above in quality and are made in a fresh, fruity, simple style for immediate consumption. An Amador Zinfandel heads the red wine roster. Almost all other varietals come from purchased Central Coast grapes. This winery was instrumental in the production of soft, low-alcohol table wines and occasionally offers a limited amount of late harvest Riesling with Botrytis. Very reasonable prices.

🌢 **Chardonnay:** *Grassy varietal fruit, simple, balanced, light oak* 🍷
🌢 **Chenin Blanc:** *Fruity, lively, spritzy, medium sweet* 🍷/❀
🌢 **Fumé Blanc:** *Herbaceous, round, fruity, light oak* 🍷/❀
Johannisberg Riesling: *Fragrant, citrusy, tart, slightly sweet* 🍷
Zinfandel: *Spicy, ripe flavors, woody, sharp* 🍷/❀

SANTA BARBARA WINERY *Santa Barbara 1962* Jug wine bottler that has added a 42-acre vineyard operation and its own line of varietals. Production at 35,000 cases. Erratic results to date.

SANTA CRUZ CELLARS (BARGETTO WINERY) Line of inexpensive, fair-quality jug wines.

SANTA CRUZ MOUNTAIN VINEYARD *Santa Cruz 1975* A Pinot Noir specialist with 12 acres planted on mountainous terrain quickly learned that it is unwise to make only Pinot Noir. Pinot Noir now represents one-third of the winery's 3,000-case production. The rest is divided between Cabernet Sauvignon and Petite Sirah, both from purchased grapes.

Pinot Noir: *Aromatic, complex, rich, tannic* ✿/✿✿✿

SANTA YNEZ VALLEY WINERY *Santa Barbara 1976* About 7,000 cases are made in a refurbished dairy barn with grapes coming from the adjacent 130-acre vineyard. Quality to date is mixed; highest for white and Blanc de Noir wines.

Sauvignon Blanc: *Strong varietal, good fruit flavor, hot* ✿

SARAH'S VINEYARD *Santa Clara 1978* One of the first new, small, quality-minded wineries in the Hecker Pass area. It has 7 acres planted to Chardonnay. Its first few vintages from purchased grapes included a good-quality Chardonnay (Edna Valley) and a rich late harvest Zinfandel (Dry Creek). Petite Sirah and Grenache fill out the varietal line of this 3,000-case winery.

V. SATTUI WINERY *Napa 1975* This small (3,000-case) winery is attached to a tourist-oriented gift store and gourmet shop, both of which seem to command higher priority than wine production. The assorted wines come from different regions and bulk purchases. The quality, at best, is average.

SAUSAL WINERY *Sonoma 1973* Primarily growers (owning 150 acres in the Alexander Valley) who wanted to make only bulk wine originally. By 1975 they decided to bottle some of their own, offering red varietals. Other wineries, notably Joseph Phelps, have produced excellent Zinfandel from Sausal grapes. Sausal's first Zinfandels were long-aged and about average in quality. The winery's capacity is 30,000 cases.

Zinfandel: *Mature, medium full-bodied, slightly woody* ❦

SCHRAMSBERG VINEYARDS *Napa 1966* Only Methode Champenoise sparkling wines, possibly the finest produced in California, are offered by this hillside winery reoccupying the 19th-century vineyard site and aging caves. The winery owns 40 acres of vineyards (split between Chardonnay and Pinot Noir), but purchases most grapes that go into its 25,000 cases. The best-selling Blanc de Blancs, primarily Chardonnay with a little Pinot Blanc, is aged 2 years on the yeast *(en tirage).* Blanc de Noir, about two-thirds Pinot Noir and one-third Chardonnay, is kept *en tirage* for over 4 years. Cuvée de Pinot and the dessert-styled Crémant represent 25% of the winery's output.

Blanc de Blancs: *Crisp, fruity, slightly yeasty:* ❀/❀❀
Blanc de Noir: *Crisp, slightest hint of sweetness, aged yeasty champagne nose, deep and complex in best years* ❀/❀❀❀
Crémant: *Sweet, floral, inviting* ❀/❀❀
Cuvée de Pinot: *Pinkish color, somewhat fat style* ♈/❀

SEBASTIANI VINEYARDS *Sonoma 1889* Though enjoying a rustic image, this family-run winery has expanded enormously and now sells close to 4 million cases per year. Once known for its hearty red wines, it offers a full range of wines, including dessert wines, champagnes, and vermouth under its label. It owns 400 acres in Sonoma but buys grapes and ready-made wines from throughout California. Most of its varietals are vintage-dated with either Northern California or North Coast as appellations. The reds approach average quality; the white vintaged varietals are often poor quality. Sebastiani also produces nonvintage varietals and generics with California Mountain as an appellation, and these, while representing a high percentage of its production, are no bargain in today's market. A series of long-aged, vintage-dated red wines are offered under the Proprietor's Reserve banner, with the Burgundy and Barbera typifying the style and quality once associated with Sebastiani.

Barbera: *Berryish, mature, tart* ♈/❀
Mountain Burgundy: *Rough, coarse, heavy* ♈
Mountain Chablis: *Thin, medium sweet* ♈
Chardonnay: *Artificial, flat, dry* ☾/♈
Chenin Blanc: *Dull, flat, sweet* ☾/♈
Zinfandel: *Berryish, sometimes raisined; full-bodied* ♈

SEQUOIA CELLARS *Yolo 1977* 400-case production of this part-time effort is split among Amador County Zinfandel and Cabernet Sauvignon, Alexander Valley Gewurztraminer and locally grown Carnelian.

ROBERT SETRAKIAN VINEYARDS (GROWERS WINERY) Though viewed as the company's top line, its table wines are no better or worse than those under the Growers label. However Setrakian Brandy is of good quality, and the Solera Ports and Sherries are of average quality.

CHARLES F. SHAW VINEYARD *Napa 1979* After purchasing an established 35-acre vineyard north of St. Helena, Shaw built a 5,000-case winery. The winery offers Napa Gamay, made by carbonic maceration, and Napa Valley Zinfandel, traditionally fermented and oak-aged. The Napa Gamay, aged briefly in large oak casks, is made in a light, fruity style.

SHENANDOAH VINEYARDS *Amador 1977* Developing a 30-acre vineyard planted to Barbera, Cabernet, Sauvignon Blanc, and Zinfandel, its first vintages were made from purchased grapes. The quality of the white varietals is uneven. Cabernet is the most successful first release. Production is set for 4,000 cases at maximum when vineyards mature.

SHERRILL CELLARS *San Mateo 1973* Settled into a new winery in 1979 and committed itself to buying only Central Coast grapes for its limited production line of varietals, totaling 4,000 cases annually. More successful with Petite Sirah and Zinfandel. 7 acres planted to Chardonnay.

SHOWN & SONS WINERY *Napa 1979* A fairly well-known grower, with 75 acres in Rutherford, built a winery along the Silverado Trail. About 15,000 cases were made in 1979, predominantly Cabernet Sauvignon and small amounts of Johannisberg Riesling.

SIERRA VISTA WINERY *El Dorado 1977* This winery makes 2,000 cases from its 12 acres and purchased grapes. It offers Fumé Blanc, Zinfandel, Chardonnay, and Cabernet. It has a few acres of French Syrah planted.

SILVER OAK CELLAR *Napa 1972* Using grapes from the Alexander Valley, this Cabernet-only winery makes 5,000 cases per year. Each vintage is aged 4 years prior to release. Prices increase while quality does not.

Cabernet Sauvignon: *Herbaceous, oaky, simple* ♥

SIMI WINERY *Sonoma 1867* A historic winery that has changed ownership and direction several times since the late 1960s. Its present owner, Schieffelin, trimmed the line to 9 varietals and, though eliminating popular generics, has increased annual production to the 100,000-case mark. It was among the first to offer both Cabernet and Pinot Noir Rosé wines in a spritzy, slightly sweet style. Some current varietals may carry Sonoma or North Coast appellations, but its current desire is to use only Alexander Valley as a place-name for all varietals. Most wines are of average quality. The reds are released when fully mature and ready for enjoyment.

Cabernet Sauvignon: *Varietal fruity character, medium-bodied* ♥/❀
Chardonnay: *Fruity, light oak, usually balanced* ♥
Chenin Blanc: *Fruity, floral, round, slightly sweet* ♥
Gewurztraminer: *Spicy, sometimes complex, slightly sweet* ♥/❀❀
Zinfandel: *Berrylike, light oak and tannin* ♥/❀

SMITH-MADRONE VINEYARDS *Napa 1977* Quality-oriented winery atop Spring Mountain producing 2,000 cases. 38 acres of vineyards favor Cabernet Sauvignon and Chardonnay with lesser amounts of Johannisberg Riesling and Pinot Noir.

Chardonnay: *Fruity, good acid, oaky* ❀
Johannisberg Riesling: *Slightly sweet, good acid balance, fresh fruity taste* ❀

SMOTHERS *Santa Cruz 1977* A winery built on the historic Vine Hill property (lately used by Ridge and Bargetto for Chardonnay, Riesling). Owner Dick Smothers is now planting grapes at brother Tom's property in Glen Ellen, Sonoma Valley, and will probably move the winery operations there. Interestingly, comedian Pat Paulsen's vineyard (excellent Sauvignon Blanc made by Chateau St. Jean) adjoins the new Smothers brothers' vineyard. Initial success with whites at the Santa Cruz property has been followed by less success with reds.

SOMMELIER WINERY *Santa Clara 1976* This winery makes 3,000 cases per year of red varietals from different regions. The first releases were big and dark, but often poor in quality. Grapes are purchased from many sources.

SONOMA VINEYARDS *Sonoma 1971* Evolved from the Windsor Tiburon Vintners mail-order business. After a shaky beginning due to too-rapid expansion, it has recently settled down. The winery owns or manages 2,600 acres and offers a wide variety of table wines and a small quantity of champagne by the *méthode champenoise.* The more interesting table wines carry Sonoma County appellations or specific vineyard designations. Those with Northern California appellations are often made from purchased wines or grapes. The overall quality is inconsistent, but vineyard-designated Chardonnays have improved. 3 blended table wines introduced in 1979 brought the annual production to 500,000 cases.

Cabernet Sauvignon: *Light varietal, thin, tannic* ♟; *"Alexander's Crown": Ripe, harsh, tannic variable* ♟/❀
Chardonnay: *Vague varietal, clean, crisp* ♟; *the estate-bottled version has more fruit, body, and oak, and after 1976 is* ♟/❀; *"River West": intensely fruity, crisp, oaky* ❀/❀❀
Chenin Blanc: *Varies from fruity to bland, thin to heavy, and slightly sweet to medium sweet* ♟
Pinot Noir: *Medium varietal, spicy, supple, oaky* ♟/❀
Zinfandel: *Varietal fruit, simple, some wood* ♟; *Estate-bottled: ripe berry flavors, oaky* ♟/❀

SOTOYOME WINERY *Sonoma 1974* This small (2,000-case) winery makes 3 red varietals from 8 acres. The first 2 vintages were generally poor wines. The 1976s, sold to Wolfgang, were only marginally improved.

SOUVERAIN CELLARS *Sonoma 1973* This Geyserville winery was built by Pillsbury and is now owned by a limited partnership of 240 growers. They bought the label, but there is no historical link to the early Souverain in Napa. The winery is large and continues to make wines for numerous private labels. Its own wines sport the North Coast appellation. Total cases made number close to 350,000. Recent vintages of red varietals offer good value. The whites are average quality.

ᵩ **Cabernet Sauvignon:** *Fruity varietal, moderate intensity, oaky* ♟/❀
Chardonnay: *Grassy varietal, simple, light oak* ♟
Chenin Blanc: *Always dry style; sometimes low in fruit* ♟/◌
ᵩ **Colombard Blanc:** *Fruity, light, spritzy, slightly sweet* ♟
Fumé Blanc: *Light, understated, firm, dry* ♟
Zinfandel: *Low varietal, simple, fruity* ♟

SPRING MOUNTAIN VINEYARDS *Napa 1968* Among the first to define a dry, relatively complex style of Sauvignon Blanc, it also made many fine Chardonnays and several good Cabernet Sauvignons. Now drawing from its 125-acre vineyard, it has become less consistent in quality. Recent Sauvignon Blancs and Chardonnays are weak. The prices are above average. Production has reached the 20,000-case level. Recently added a Pinot Noir.

Cabernet Sauvignon: *Tight, hard wines, medium tannins* ♟/❀❀

Chardonnay: *Medium intense, balanced, stylish, ages well* ♥/❀❀ *through 1975; thereafter* ♥
Sauvignon Blanc: *Once superb, recently somewhat flawed* ♥

STAGS' LEAP VINEYARD *Napa 1972* A historic winery with 100 acres in the Stag's Leap area, best known for its Petite Sirah. All wines were made elsewhere until 1979, when winery restoration was completed. It also offers a dry, sometimes dull, Chenin Blanc and a heavy Pinot Noir, and has plans to add a Cabernet Sauvignon as it builds toward 10,000-case production.

Petite Sirah: *Ripe, tannic, oaky* ❀

STAG'S LEAP WINE CELLARS *Napa 1972* Cabernet Sauvignon in a supple, refined style is a major success. The 45-acre vineyard is planted to Cabernet and Merlot, and the top-quality varietals bear Stag's Leap Vineyard as an appellation. Wines with Napa Valley appellation are made from purchased grapes and include an attractive Chardonnay and a Johannisberg Riesling. Half of the 15,000-case production is Cabernet. Hawk Crest is a second label.

Cabernet Sauvignon: *Complex, ripe varietal, moderate tannins* ❀/❀❀❀
Chardonnay: *Refined varietal, subtle, light oak* ♥/❀
Johannisberg Riesling: *Delicate varietal, fruity, slightly sweet* ♥/❀

P. & M. STAIGER *Santa Cruz 1973* Small winery producing several hundred cases a year of unfiltered and unfined wines. Varieties include Zinfandel and Chardonnay. The wines are not free of winemaking problems.

ROBERT STEMMLER WINERY *Sonoma 1978* This new winery in Dry Creek has 4 acres of Chardonnay, but purchases most grapes. The first 2 Chardonnays, made elsewhere, were weak. Maximum production will be 5,000 cases. Cabernet Sauvignon and Fumé Blanc are also offered.

STERLING VINEYARDS *Napa 1967* This tourist-alluring winery, majestically perched on a hilltop, was acquired by Coca-Cola of Atlanta in 1977. The line was trimmed to 4 varietals (Cabernet, Merlot, Chardonnay, and Sauvignon Blanc) and total production reduced to 60,000 cases. Through 1979, however, it made a Chenin Blanc and a Cabernet Blanc. Newly acquired 100-acre hillside vineyard and a new winemaking team promise continuation of high-quality standards.

Cabernet Sauvignon: *Ripe varietal, full, flavorful* ♥/❀
Cabernet Reserve: *Big rich varietal, ripe, tannic, oaky* ❀/❀❀
Chardonnay: *Good varietal, rich, oaky* ❀❀/❀❀❀
Merlot: *Complex, herbal, full, warm* ❀
Sauvignon Blanc: *Varietal, oaky* ♥/❀❀

STEVENOT VINEYARDS *Calaveras 1978* From 15 acres of its own and grapes bought from El Dorado County, this winery is making 4,000 cases. First Chenin Blanc was good. Other varietals are Cabernet and Zinfandel.

STONE CREEK VINEYARDS Private label owned by a San Francisco–based distributor covering 50,000 cases of inexpensive, drinkable North Coast wines. "Bottled at Geyserville" on the label confirms rumored Souverain origins.

STONEGATE WINERY *Napa 1973* An 8,000-case winery with an unpredictable performance record. It has a 35-acre vineyard adjacent to the Calistoga-based winery and a small parcel established in the mountain area west of the winery. Many wines have suffered from mustiness or an unpleasant chemical character. Cabernet Sauvignon and Sauvignon Blanc are its 2 most popular varietals but also typical in terms of quality.

Cabernet Sauvignon: *Varietal, rich, sometimes earthy* ♥
Chenin Blanc: *Sometimes fruity, sometimes off* ♉/♥
Sauvignon Blanc: *Firm, low varietal, hot, often off character* ♥

STONERIDGE *Amador 1975* From 3.5 acres and grapes from a leased Zinfandel vineyard, this winery makes under 1,000 cases total. Production is predominantly Zinfandel, but includes Blanc de Noirs and late harvest styles.

STONY HILL WINERY *Napa 1953* Small producer (2,000–3,000 cases), located in hills above Napa Valley floor and founded by the late Fred McCrea, a man of incredible energy and vision. Wines of exceptional quality are sold to the lucky few on its mailing list. One of the first great, small wineries to develop after Prohibition.

Chardonnay: *Intense, fruity, often with high acid, little oak, ages well* ❀/❀❀
Gewurztraminer: *Dry, good acid, elegant, spicy* ❀
Johannisberg Riesling: *Slightly sweet, good balance, sometimes intense varietal* ❀/❀❀

STONY RIDGE WINERY *Alameda 1976* Present owners restored the old Ruby Hill Winery and leased the adjacent 120-acre vineyard. Annual 35,000-case output consists of a wide array of wines carrying different appellations and vintages. In early years, red wines have evinced fewer flaws than the whites.

STORY VINEYARDS *Amador 1973* After making wines as a hobby from his 30 acres of Zinfandel and Mission grapes, Story opened a winery and now produces about 3,500 cases for sale. Production consists predominantly of Zinfandel, but includes a tiny amount of Mission.

RODNEY D. STRONG Another label from the Sonoma/Windsor Vineyards company. Named after the winemaker, this one seems aimed at direct-mail customers and selected retail outlets. The first offerings, Sonoma County Cabernet, Chardonnay, Pinot Noir, and Brut Champagne, mostly sounded better in writing than they tasted in the glass. Prices are not low.

Pinot Noir: *Ripe, very tannic, needs age* 🍷/🏵

SUMMIT WINES (GEYSER PEAK WINERY) Large (over 500,000-case) line of low-priced generics. A few varietals are packaged in the bag-in-a box wine dispenser. The white generics are bland and medium sweet; the reds are dull and pruney.

SUNRISE WINERY *Santa Cruz 1976* Just getting on track after a fire in 1978 and poor wines made in its first vintages. Recent Pinot Noir showed promise. Makes 2,500 cases, all from purchased grapes.

SUTTER HOME WINERY *Napa 1960* This winery dates back to 1874 and the brand name to 1904, but the present owners didn't assume control until 1960. It made its first Amador Zinfandel in 1968 and a White Zinfandel in 1972; together these account for 54,000 cases. It also offers a medium sweet Muscat Amabile (8,000 cases), and recently added an El Dorado Zinfandel (10,000 cases) made in a fruity, slightly sweet style. From 1968–1973, the Amador Zinfandels were ripe, powerful, and tannic, consistent 🏵. Recent vintages have been less intense and also less consistent in quality.

Muscat Amabile: *Varietally assertive, simple, medium sweet* 🍷
Zinfandel: *Amador is ripe, slightly tannic, sometimes lacking balanced flavors* 🍷/🏵*; El Dorado is fruity, uncomplex, early-maturing* 🍷

JOSEPH SWAN VINEYARDS *Sonoma 1969* Small (less than 2,000-case) winery specializing in superb Zinfandel with minuscule amounts of Pinot Noir and Chardonnay. Wine is sold by mailing list to fans of big-styled wines.

Zinfandel: *Ripe, full-bodied, tannic, intense* ❁/❁❁❁

SYCAMORE CREEK VINEYARDS *Santa Clara 1976* Some old Carignane and Zinfandel vines are included in this Hecker Pass area winery's 13 acres. Other grapes are purchased from Central Coast growers. Production is in the range of 3,000–5,000 cases.

Petite Sirah: *Light, fruity, rich, easy drinking* ❁
Zinfandel: *Fruity, direct, pleasant* ❦/❁

TAYLOR CALIFORNIA CELLARS Combining the well-known Taylor name of New York with California, Coca-Cola of Atlanta launched a line of generics—Burgundy, Chablis, Rhine, and Rosé--in late 1978 by means of an ad campaign. The blends were assembled by the winemaker at the Monterey Vineyard. Aimed at both national and international markets, the line grew to 4 million cases by 1980. First generics were clean, fresh, and generally better than their major competition at the low-priced end of the market. Several "California" varietals have been added, all nonvintage wines.

THOMAS VINEYARDS (FILIPPI VINTAGE COMPANY) Historic winery claimed to be the state's oldest and now used as a sales and tasting room in Cucamonga. Wines under this label are sold only from the tasting room.

TREFETHEN VINEYARDS *Napa 1973* The owners have completely replanted 600 acres to wine varieties in their vineyard adjacent to the winery located north of Napa. Production of table wines has increased slowly to 40,000 cases, although most of their grapes are sold to Chandon, Schramsberg, and several small wineries in the Napa Valley. 4 varietals are produced by Trefethen, plus 2 popular blended wines under the Eshcol logo. Chardonnay is the most successful varietal.

Cabernet Sauvignon: *Ripe, tannic, woody* ❦
Chardonnay: *Crisp, spicy, fairly full, balanced* ❁
Johannisberg Riesling: *Light varietal, fruity, fairly dry* ❦

TRENTADUE WINERY *Sonoma 1969* Primarily a grower whose grapes from the 200-acre vineyard go to Ridge (Geyserville Zinfandel) and many other wineries. Of the 12,000 cases made under its own label, only a heavy Zinfandel and a

Cabernet attract occasional interest. White wines are generally of poor quality.

TRINITY VINE Owned by a San Francisco importer, this label includes a typical range of varietal wines, all with North Coast appellations. Bottled at Souverain, the wines are generally simple; the reds offer direct varietal character, while the whites are thin. About 20,000 cases are being offered.

TULOCAY WINERY *Napa 1975* Small producer (1,200 cases) specializing in Pinot Noir—mostly from vineyards adjoining the winery near the city of Napa. Wine follows oak-aged, un-fined style. Cabernet Sauvignon and Zinfandel are in limited quantities. Sales are primarily to mailing list.

Cabernet Sauvignon: *Good fruit, tannic* ❁
Pinot Noir: *Ripe-tasting, medium body and tannins* ❦/❁

TWIN OAKS About 25,000 cases of jug-quality wine called Burgundy, Chablis, and Rosé, marketed by a San Francisco–based distributor.

TYLAND VINEYARDS *Mendocino 1979* From a 250-acre vineyard started in 1971, the winery made 7,000 cases. Most grapes are sold. Major varietals are Chardonnay and Gamay Beaujolais, aged in American oak. Production goal is 14,000 cases.

E. VACHE & CIE (BROOKSIDE CELLARS) A new line of medium-priced, vintage-dated, varietal wines being distributed outside of Brookside tasting rooms. The first released were fair to poor in quality.

VALLEY OF THE MOON *Sonoma 1944* This winery is best known for its jug generics popular in many California restaurants because of their low prices. An effort to make a few varietals from the 200 acres is underway, leaving a wide margin for improvement. Most of its 90,000-case production is in the jug end of the spectrum. Reds have had fewer problems than the whites.

VEEDERCREST VINEYARDS *Alameda 1972* Temporarily located in the Bay Area until a facility is built in Napa or Sonoma. By then, a 100-acre vineyard on Mount Veeder planted to Cabernet Sauvignon and other reds will be in production. For now, grapes are purchased, and labels identify the grower, vineyard, and other specifics. Most successful with whites, particularly Johannisberg Riesling and Gewurztraminer in the late harvest style. The reds tend to be fruity and simple. Current production of 12,000 cases will grow to 20,000. Prices range from average to high.

Cabernet Sauvignon: *Fruity varietal, simple, pleasant* ♥/❀

Chardonnay: *Fruity, light oak, inconsistent* ♥

Johannisberg Riesling: *Lush fruit, rich flavors, sweet* ♥/❀❀

Merlot: *Herbal, varietal, soft, supple, some oak* ♥/❀

VEGA VINEYARDS *Santa Barbara 1978* Small (1,800-case) winery producing Johannisberg Riesling and Gewurztraminer from its own vineyards and Cabernet Sauvignon from the nearby Santa Ynez Valley.

VENTANA VINEYARDS *Monterey 1978* A large (300-acre) vineyard and a 15,000-case winery located in Soledad. First releases of limited production varietals were of above-average quality with Chardonnay, Pinot Noir, and Sauvignon Blanc topping the list. Ventana Vineyards appears on labels of many wineries buying its grapes.

Chardonnay: *Varietal, medium-bodied, oaked* ❀

VENTANA WINERY *Alameda 1976* The old name for the winery now called Fenestra. Change made in order to avoid confusion with Ventana Vineyards.

CONRAD VIANO WINERY *Contra Costa 1946* Small winery north of Oakland. The heavy-handed style offered seems out of step with improvements in California winemaking.

VILLA ARMANDO *Alameda 1903* Medium-sized (400,000-case capacity) jug wine producer selling mainly at the winery and in the old ethnic neighborhoods of the New York area. The wines tend to be sweetish, often cooked-tasting products of little charm.

VILLA MT. EDEN *Napa 1974* Well-financed winery specializing in Cabernet, Chardonnay, and Pinot Noir, all made from vineyards planted in 1973. Chenin Blanc and Gamay are part of the 8,000-case total, but they come from old vineyards acquired with the estate. The winery style is decidedly toward ripe grapes and heavy oak character. The prices are slightly ahead of quality.

Cabernet Sauvignon: *Ripe varietal, very oaky, tannic* ♥/❀❀

Chardonnay: *Ripe, rich, yet overoaked* ♥/❀

VIN MARK (MARKHAM WINERY) Second label used for wines not considered up to the quality of the first label.

VINA VISTA VINEYARDS *Sonoma 1971* This small winery (4,000 cases) began by buying wines and now buys grapes from Sonoma growers. Petite Sirah and Zinfandel head the varietal line offered primarily through a mailing list.

VINTNERS RESERVE A wine distributor's private label that lasted one round, but failed to answer the bell for the second. Death was announced in late 1979. No mourners appeared.

VOSE VINEYARDS *Napa 1978* Located on Mount Veeder, Vose planted 100 acres of Cabernet, Chardonnay, and Zinfandel in 1973 with plans to double the acreage in the next few years. Production is 8,000 cases, most of which consisted of a slightly sweet Zinfandel Blanc de Noir given the proprietary name of Zinblanca.

WEIBEL CHAMPAGNE CELLARS *Alameda 1939* 2 production facilities—an aging plant near Fremont (Alameda County) and a new winery in Mendocino County—produce a full array of table wines, champagnes, and dessert wines. Much of the winery's 500,000-case capacity is devoted to private label bottlings of bulk process champagne for wine merchants and restaurants. The winery's transfer process champagnes are often pleasant, but table wines under the Weibel label have shown very poorly over the last decade. New vintage-dated varietals with specific appellations brought slight improvement in younger wines; aged reds showed no change.

Brut Champagne: *Slightly sweet, floral, very bubbly* ♛
Gamay Beaujolais: *Earthy, tea-like flavors, light fruit* ♛/◑
Green Hungarian: *Sweet, insipid stuff, surpassed in quality by most jug wines* ♛/◑

WENTE BROS. *Alameda 1883* Large (600,000-case) family-owned winery with long-standing, highly deserved reputation for white wines; reds have been less well received. Substantial vineyard holdings (1,400 acres) in Alameda and Monterey counties. Winemaking style for whites stresses cold fermentation in stainless steel to achieve very fruity wines. The winery's late harvest Rieslings of 1969 and 1972 were trend setters of the style in California. The 1973 Riesling Auslese was a classic ✿✿✿. Prices are always reasonable.

Blanc de Blancs: *Chenin Blanc–based, medium sweet, fruity* ♛/✿
Chardonnay: *Dry, fruity, crisp, medium-bodied, no oak style* ♛/✿; *lately less attractive*

Grey Riesling: *Dry, good acid, vinous, well suited for use with fish* ♟

Johannisberg Riesling: *Slightly sweet, fruity, some grapefruity notes in floral, varietal style* ♟/❀

MARK WEST VINEYARDS *Sonoma 1976* A family-owned winery located in a cool, sometimes fog-prone region above the Russian River Valley. The 62-acre vineyard is planted to early-maturing wine varieties. The wines offered over the first few vintages have been uneven in quality. About 7,000 cases were produced in 1979, almost half of the expected 15,000-case maximum target. Only the medium sweet Gewurztraminer has performed consistently well to date.

WILLOW CREEK CELLARS If the place name is Geyserville and the fine print reads "a Robert Haas Selection," the wine under this label, whether varietal or generic, was purchased by an East Coast distributor from Souverain Cellars. The prices are low. The quality varies from average to mediocre.

WILLOW CREEK VINEYARDS *Humboldt 1976* Tiny (200-case) winery has 2.5 acres and buys grapes from Sonoma. 7 varietals are sold to neighbors and through a mailing list. No connection to Willow Creek Cellars.

WINDSOR VINEYARDS (SONOMA VINEYARDS) Originally a humble mail-order business known as Tiburon Vintners. Its success led to creation of Sonoma Vineyards, leaving this label to be reworked as a direct sales line. Sold through a large mailing list (California only), at the winery, or in winery-owned retail outlets, the wines are usually inexpensive and cover a variety of types. Most are of ho-hum quality; sometimes a quality item of limited production is made available. Sales are over 200,000 cases.

WINE AND THE PEOPLE *Alameda 1970* Started as a supplier for home wine- and beer-makers. Now produces limited quantities (under 4,000 cases) of table wines and port from same grapes that it sells to home winemakers. Wines are usually made in full-bodied rich style. Berkeley Wine Company is a second label.

Merlot (Winery Lake): *Supple yet firm, rich good depth in best years* ♟/❀❀❀

Zinfandel (Sonoma): *Nice berryish character, fairly tannic* ♟/❀

WINEMASTERS A label belonging to the Guild cooperative wineries, the third largest in the U.S. when all its labels (Cresta

Blanca, Cribari, Roma, and Tavola) are combined. Winemasters offers a large line of table, dessert, and sparkling wines, all inexpensive. Most table wines are weak and thin, with a noticeable, slightly cooked Central Valley character.

WINES BY WHEELER *Santa Cruz 1959* Pioneer Santa Cruz Mountains winemaker producing 200 cases of wine annually on part-time basis. Quality has been variable. (Also known as Nicasio Vineyards.)

WITTWER WINERY *Humboldt 1969* Tiny winery (fewer than 400 cases annually) in Eureka run as part-time venture. Produced French Colombard from the outset and then added Cabernet Sauvignon in 1976. Both are from Napa Valley.

WOLFGANG Private label owned by a San Francisco importer. Only wines offered to date are the 1976 red varietals produced at Sotoyome. Its incredibly garish label attracts more attention than the wines.

WOODBURY WINERY *Marin 1979* This label adds another voice to the port wine revival. Its speciality is Vintage Port, and it debuted with a good 1977 released after 2 years of aging. Grapes are purchased from the North Coast regions, and Woodbury's preference is to blend Petite Sirah with Cabernet and Zinfandel. 1979 production was close to 3,000 cases. Optimum is set at 5,000.

WOODSIDE VINEYARDS *San Mateo 1960* Among the earliest home winemakers to go commercial, Woodside has maintained its small size (1,000 cases) and commitment to Chardonnay and Cabernet. Quality has rarely risen above indifferent.

YORK MOUNTAIN WINERY *San Luis Obispo 1882* Historic winery and vineyards now being refurbished. Chardonnay, Cabernet, and Pinot Noir are being planted. Zinfandel continues to set the pace for the moment. 3,000-case output.

Zinfandel: *Ripe flavor, little refinement, light oak and tannin* 🍷

YVERDON VINEYARDS *Napa 1970* A handsome stone winery built by hand. There are 12 acres near the winery and another 80 in the Calistoga area. The early offerings were inconsistent. Some red varietals were made in a fairly full style and succeeded when they were able to avoid an earthy, musty character that occurred all too often. Wine-making ceased in 1974 and 1975. Nothing of consequence has been released from the 1976 vintage onward. Cabernet Sauvignon and Chenin Blanc are the 2 primary varietals in the 5,000-case annual output.

ZACA MESA WINERY *Santa Barbara 1978* A 30,000-case winery supplied by 220 acres owned by or associated with the winery. The 1978 releases were the first made entirely at the new winery. 3 previous vintages offered were made elsewhere and varied widely in quality. Recent bottlings indicate the white varietals are more interesting than the reds.

Johannisberg Riesling: *Floral, citrusy, slightly sweet* ☘/☸
Zinfandel: *Fruity, simple, light tannins* ☘

ZAMPATTI'S CELLARS *Monterey 1978* Located in Carmel and making few hundred cases of *méthode champenoise* champagne. The cuvée is predominantly Pinot Noir purchased from Monterey County. Sales are to neighbors and tourists.

ZD WINES *Napa 1969* Offered a wide range of table wines from various sources and mostly in small lots. Moved from Sonoma to Napa in 1979. The line has been trimmed to Pinot Noir, Chardonnay, and Cabernet Sauvignon. Most of its 6,000 cases are from purchased grapes, plus 4 acres in the Carneros region owned by one of the partners. Some superb wines have been offered, but the overall record has been erratic.

Chardonnay: *Medium intense, tart, oaky* ☘/☸
Pinot Noir: *Spicy, sometimes complex, medium-bodied* ☘/☸

☸☸☸ An exceptional wine, worth a special search.

☸☸ A distinctive wine, likely to be memorable.

☸ A fine example of a given type or style.

☘ A wine of average quality. The accompanying tasting note provides further description.

ŏ Below average. A wine to avoid.

♦ A wine regarded as a "best buy," based on price and quality.

Wineries and Wines
Outside California

ADAMS COUNTY WINERY *Orrtanna, Pennsylvania 1975* Makes 3,000 cases of white hybrid and vinifera varietals. The only red is Foch. Owns 1 acre, so purchases most grapes. Vidal Blanc and occasionally Chardonnay top the list. Also makes Seyval Blanc.

ADELSHEIM VINEYARDS *Willamette Valley, Oregon 1978* This winery has so far produced small lots of Semillon and Merlot from grapes grown at Sagemoor Farms, Washington. Production will hit 5,000 cases when its vineyards mature (19 acres of Chardonnay, Pinot Noir, and White Riesling).

AMITY VINEYARDS *Willamette Valley, Oregon 1976* Small (4,000-case) winery relying mostly on its own 15-acre vineyards. Pinot Noir, Chardonnay, and White Riesling are the primary varietals. It makes a Pinot Noir Nouveau and, on occasion, a barrel-fermented Pinot Noir. Somewhat inconsistent quality over first few vintages.

ASSOCIATED VINTNERS *Redmond, Washington 1962* Run by a group of university professors, it became the first Northwest winery to make good-quality vinifera wines. A new winery was built in 1976 to increase production to 8,000 cases. The partners own 30 acres in the Yakima Valley. Its Gewurztraminer remains the most consistently successful wine; Cabernet and Chardonnay are less dependable.

Gewurztraminer: *Spicy aroma and flavor, firm, dry* ♥/❀

ALEXIS BAILLY VINEYARDS *Hastings, Minnesota 1976* Run part-time by lawyer Bailly, who planted 10 acres to French hybrids in 1973. His reds, Leon Millot and Foch, are dark and flavorful, and the Seyval Blanc is pleasant. Production is about 1,500 cases.

BANHOLZER WINECELLARS *New Carlisle, Indiana 1974* Likely the largest in the state with 72 acres planted—including 25 acres of vinifera—this winery makes about 7,000 cases per year. The French hybrids are blended and sold under proprietary names. Of several vinifera varietals, Cabernet and Chardonnay have attracted attention. Winery went into liquidation in 1980.

BARRY WINE CO. *Conesus, New York 1937* Church-owned winery in the Finger Lakes region using the historic O-Neh-Da Vineyard brand for its dessert and sacramental wines and Barry for its table wines. The emphasis falls on generics and varietal rosés from native American and French hybrid varieties for the often sweet-finished table wines.

BENMARL VINEYARDS *Marlboro, New York 1971* Launched as a cooperative society of wine lovers, this dynamic Hudson River winery is currently producing around 12,000 cases. From the 72 acres planted, it makes varietal French hybrids and vinifera wines. The most successful have been Seyval Blanc, Baco Noir, and occasionally Chardonnay. Blended Marlboro Village wines are consistently good.

BJELLAND VINEYARDS *Umpqua Valley, Oregon 1968* Annual output of 1,500 cases consists of blackberry wine and vinifera varietals. The 2 primary wines being emphasized are Sauvignon Blanc and Semillon.

BOORDY VINEYARDS *Riderwood, Maryland 1942* The owners, Philip and Jocelyn Wagner, began experiments with developing and cultivating French hybrids in 1930. Their success encouraged most wineries east of the Rockies. Today, they make blended table wines in a fresh, youthful style. Production is small. Their influence continues as suppliers of vines to Eastern wineries.

BOSKYDEL VINEYARD *Lake Leelanau, Michigan 1976* Small winery (8,000 cases) founded on mid-1960s plantings that opened up the Grand Traverse region. From an experimental planting of 30 different French hybrids, 6 were chosen and a 20-acre vineyard established. Wines offered are blended generics and varietal hybrids. Best sellers are the De Chaunac Rosé and De Chaunac.

BRIGHT WINE CO. *Niagara Falls, Ontario, Canada 1874* The largest Canadian winery, using 3 facilities and boasting a storage capacity of over 11 million gallons. Bright established French hybrid vineyards in 1946, and about half of its 1,200 acres are planted to hybrids. It has been moderately successful with making Chardonnay and Gewurztraminer from vineyards located close to Lake Ontario. In its large line, the best sellers are Baco Noir, Foch, rosé, and the Du Barry brand of champagnes.*Hartford, Michigan 1933* Now the second largest (around 1-million-gallon capacity) in Michigan, it claims to have been the first to make a Cold Duck and a commercial Baco Noir. It offers numerous types of wine, ranging from hybrid table wines to Charmat champagne. The most interesting wines are the nonvintage Baco Noir, Foch, and Hartford Port.

BROTHERHOOD WINERY *Washingtonville, New York 1839* Possibly the oldest ongoing U.S. winery, it attracts thousands of tourists to its vast aging caves. Offering a large array of table and dessert wines, it enjoys more success with ports and cream sherry. Storage capacity is 500,000 gallons.

BUCKINGHAM VALLEY VINEYARDS *Buckingham, Pennsylvania 1966* A well-regarded French hybrid producer. From its 10-acre vineyard and purchased grapes, it makes 5,000 cases annually.

BUCKS COUNTY VINEYARDS *New Hope, Pennsylvania 1973* Operating a wine museum and winery, the owners offer close to 20,000 cases per year. In addition to several French hybrid varietals, it makes Chardonnay and Johannisberg Riesling. The wines are made from purchased grapes, except for those from its own 4 acres. Inconsistent quality.

BULLY HILL VINEYARDS *Hammondsport, New York 1970* Run by Walter S. Taylor, who left the family wine business after a tiff, it makes close to 25,000 cases of varietal hybrids, regional blends, and small amounts of champagne in the Finger Lakes area. The consistently good wines are the vintage-dated red and white, along with a Seyval Blanc—fruity, light, and dry.

BYRD VINEYARDS *Meyersville, Maryland 1977* After planting 15 acres to vinifera and hybrid varieties, the owners built a winery and made their first wines in 1977. The 2,500-case output is primarily white varietals under the Byrd label. Blended table wines are labeled Church Hill Manor.

CENTURY HOME WINE *Willamette Valley, Oregon 1977* Housed in a historic 1860 structure, the winery makes 1,000 cases of berry and grape wines. It uses its 2 acres of vinifera and also makes Concord and Niagara wines, all for direct sale.

CHALET DEBONNE VINEYARDS *Madison, Ohio 1971* Its 40-acre vineyard is planted to labrusca and French hybrid varieties. 8,000-case production is sold at the winery. The most popular wines are blended labrusca and hybrid wines.

CHÂTEAU GAI WINES *Niagara Falls, Ontario, Canada 1890* Located near Niagara Falls, this 5-million-gallon capacity winery produces a full line. The table wines are primarily from French hybrids. Some red vinifera, notably Pinot Noir and a Cabernet-Merlot blend, have been moderately successful. Its champagnes, particularly Spumante, are popular sellers.

CHÂTEAU GRAND TRAVERS *Traverse City, Michigan 1974* An ultramodern, multimillion dollar winery in the Grand Traverse region that represents a major commitment to vinifera wines. The first varietals—Chardonnay and Johannisberg Riesling—coming from its 45-acre vineyard won several high awards in Michigan. It also offers varietals and generics from purchased grapes. Production is about 12,000 cases.

CHÂTEAU LAGNIAPPE *Cleveland Heights, Ohio 1974* Produces annually about 2,500 cases of blended hybrids, a few hybrid varietals, and about 300 cases of vinifera varietals. Careful winemaking is evident in all wines; the Seyval Blanc and Vidal Blanc are quite successful.

CHÂTEAU LUCIENNE The primary champagne label for the Monarch Wine Co., which, under numerous brands, produces close to 500,000 cases per year. The champagnes are transfer process, made from New York–grown labrusca varieties, and priced inexpensively. Other labels include Chateau Laurent, Pol d'Argent, and Le Premier Cru.

CHATEAU STE. MICHELLE *Woodinville, Washington 1934* Until the 1960s the winery produced fruit and berry wines and dessert and Concord-based wines. Then it established vinifera vineyards in the Yakima Valley and made a major commitment to vinifera wines. It now has around 2,000 acres planted, and its production averages close to 300,000 cases. The parent company, U.S. Tobacco Company, built a handsome winery in a rural suburban area of Seattle, where most of its white wines are produced. Another facility in the Yakima Valley is used for red wines.

Though its early reputation rested on successful Johannisberg Riesling and Grenache Rosé, Ste. Michelle began making good Fumé Blanc in 1977 and occasionally offers good vintages of Gewurztraminer, Chardonnay, and Cabernet Sauvignon. A limited amount of Johannisberg Riesling Ice Wine (exceptional!) debuted in 1980. Annual production could reach 1 million cases by the mid-1980s.

Cabernet Sauvignon: *Medium varietal, variable, oaky* ☘
Fumé Blanc: *Medium varietal, flavorful, balanced, dry* ☘/✿
Grenache Rosé: *Cranberry color and flavors, fruity, medium sweet* ☘/✿
Johannisberg Riesling: *Floral, sometimes austere, sometimes medium sweet with Botrytis complexity* ☘/✿

CHICAMA VINEYARDS *Vineyard Haven, Massachusetts 1971*
Located on Martha's Vineyard, its wines are popular among the vacationing set. There are 35 acres planted to vinifera, and annual production is close to 5,000 cases. The quality record is uneven, and prices are on the high side.

CLINTON VINEYARDS *Clinton Corners, New York 1977* A Seyval Blanc specialist whose first vintage won many awards. About 14 acres are planted to Seyval Blanc in the Hudson Valley region, and 4,500 cases are viewed as the maximum production. A few acres were planted recently to Chardonnay and Johannisberg Riesling.

COLORADO MOUNTAIN VINEYARDS *Golden, Colorado 1978*
After the only Colorado winery folded, the partners in a 20-acre vineyard opened their own winery. It has made Colorado-grown Johannisberg Riesling and Pinot Noir-Blanc. Chardonnay and Gewurztraminer are also planted. Its 3,000-case output is filled out by Napa Valley Cabernet and Zinfandel and by Monterey County Chenin Blanc.

COMMONWEALTH WINERY *Plymouth, Massachusetts 1978*
Small, new winery expecting to make wine from local grapes when they mature; both vinifera and hybrids are planted. For the time being, wines are made from hybrids purchased in neighboring states. Results to date have been clean and pleasant.

COTE DES COLOMBES *Willamette Valley, Oregon 1977* Current production of 1,200 cases is divided among 4 vinifera wines. The winery will gradually expand its 10-acre vineyard to 20 acres; production goal is set at 10,000 cases.

DUPLIN WINE CELLARS *Rose Hill, North Carolina 1975* 9 growers with about 75 acres scattered throughout the county became partners in this winery. 3 varietal wines are offered: Noble, Carlos, and Scuppernong. All are sweet-finished. Total production is about 14,000 cases.

ELK COVE VINEYARDS *Willamette Valley, Oregon 1977* Recent successful releases bode well for this 3,000-case winery. It has 21 acres planted to early-ripening vinifera and purchases Cabernet and Merlot from Washington growers. Maximum production is 5,000 cases, and all wines will eventually be produced from its own acreage.

Chardonnay: *Appley, clean, crisp* ♀/✿
White Riesling: *Flowery, flavorful, slightly sweet* ♀/✿

EYRIE VINEYARD *Willamette Valley, Oregon 1966* A 4,000-case winery emphasizing barrel-fermented Chardonnay and Pinot Noir, both grown in its 20-acre vineyard. It offers small quantities of other varietals (Pinot Gris, Sauvignon Blanc, Muscat Ottonel, and Merlot) regularly. Its 2 main varietals are inconsistent but recent Pinot Noirs have shown improvement.

Pinot Noir: *Medium body, spicy, fruity, varietal* ♀/✿

FENN VALLEY VINEYARDS *Fennsville, Michigan 1973* While offering over 20 different wines, this producer has gained a reputation for solid quality. It has 50 acres planted to hybrids and some vinifera; production totals just over 10,000 cases annually. The most consistent wines are Vidal and Seyval Blanc for whites and de Chaunac and Chancellor for reds. Gewurztraminers have been made from West Coast grapes.

FORGERON VINEYARD *Willamette Valley, Oregon 1977* Located in an untried, cold-climate area west of Eugene, this winery has 17 acres planted to several vinifera and a few French hybrids. The first releases totaled 1,200 cases and included an attractive White Riesling, finished medium sweet to balance an unusually high acidity. Otherwise, the winery is experimental, and its general winemaking ability remains unknown.

DR. KONSTANTIN D. FRANK & SONS *Hammondsport, New York 1962* The winery's legal name, Vinifera Wine Cellars, reveals Frank's preference for vinifera wines. In his 100-acre Finger Lakes vineyard, 70 are planted to commercial varieties, the remainder going to ongoing experiments with new varieties. On occasion, the winery makes exceptional late harvest Johannisberg Rieslings and ripe Chardonnays. Annual production comes close to 6,000 cases.

FRONTENAC VINEYARDS *Paw Paw, Michigan 1933* Offers 40 different wines in every imaginable type made from grapes, fruits, and berries. The grape wines produced by this 500,000-gallon-capacity winery are usually labrusca generics, often sweet-finished.

GLENORA WINE CELLARS *Dundee, New York 1977* A quality-conscious, innovative, and very successful Finger Lakes winery with 250 acres planted. Its major emphasis is on vintage-dated varietals, primarily French hybrids. Small amounts of Chardonnay and Johannisberg Riesling have met with success. Unusual wines include an excellent Cayuga White and a Foch Nouveau. Present 10,000-case production will expand with vineyard maturity. Rapidly gaining a fine reputation.

GOLD SEAL VINEYARDS *Hammondsport, New York 1957* Now owned by Seagram's, this large (over 1.5-million-case) winery in the Finger Lakes region is best known for its bottle-fermented champagnes. They are offered under Gold Seal or Henri Marchant or with the Charles Fournier signature, honoring the firm's long-time winemaker. Fournier Blanc de Blancs may be the state's best champagne. The table wines cover all types, but emphasize blended hybrids and sweet-finished generics, which are labrusca-based. New plantings of about 100 acres of vinifera in the 600-acre vineyard consist of Chardonnay, Johannisberg Riesling, and Pinot Noir.

GOLDEN RAIN TREE WINERY *Wadesville, Indiana 1975* Started by a consortium of growers in southwestern Indiana, this winery makes hybrid wines. Most are blends, with the best given a Director's Choice title. Production is over 10,000 cases. Sales are from the winery or in neighboring states.

GRAND RIVER WINERY *Madison, Ohio 1971* For several years, grapes from the 20-acre vineyard went to other wineries. The winery is now completed, and production capacity is about 7,000 cases. Wines offered include Pinot Noir and blended French hybrids. Chardonnay and Gamay Beaujolais are planted.

GREAT RIVER WINERY *Marlboro, New York 1944* Formerly known as Marlboro Champagne Cellars, the winery now concentrates on French hybrid table wines grown in its 100-acre Hudson River Valley vineyard. It offers 4 varietals and blended red and white table wines. All champagnes are *méthode champenoise* and are marketed under the Marlboro or Chaumont brands.

GREAT WESTERN VINEYARDS *Hammondsport, New York 1860*
Made at the Pleasant Valley Wine Company, the first winery in the Finger Lakes, Great Western is now part of Coca-Cola of Atlanta's wine division. It offers numerous native labrusca and hybrid wines as varietals or blends, a range of widely popular champagnes, and *solera* sherries and ports. The best of the transfer process champagnes is the Brut. Though Great Western's generics are dull and sweet, the better-quality varietal wines are represented by the red hybrids—Baco Noir, De Chaunac, and Chelois. One of many New York wineries making New York–California blends for its generics.

GROSS HIGHLAND WINERY *Absecon, New Jersey 1934* Best known for its Charmat champagnes under Gross Highland and Bernard d'Arcy labels, which together represent close to a third of its 40,000-case output. Also offers a small amount of cream sherry and table wines with a labrusca personality.

HAIGHT VINEYARDS *Litchfield, Connecticut 1978* The state's first winery. It has 15 acres planted to Chardonnay, Johannisberg Riesling, and Foch. Production of the 3 varietals totals 2,000 cases. The first two vintages were well-received.

HAMMONDSPORT WINE CO. *Hammondsport, New York 1840*
This old winery in the Finger Lakes was acquired by the large Canandaigua Wine Co., which uses the name as a label for its champagnes and varietal French hybrids. Made by both the bulk and transfer processes, the champagnes represent close to 200,000 cases per year. The best are of average quality.

HARGRAVE VINEYARD *Cutchogue, New York 1973* With 50 acres of vinifera on Long Island's North Fork, Hargrave has been most consistent with Cabernet Sauvignon and has also made a good vintage or two of Chardonnay and Sauvignon Blanc. Production is about 5,000 cases.

HENRY'S ESTATE *Umpqua Valley, Oregon 1978* 14 acres were planted to early-ripening vinifera varieties in 1972, and the first wines were made in 1979. Both Chardonnay and Pinot Noir are barrel fermented; Gewurztraminer conventionally fermented. Present production is 4,000 cases. Vineyards could expand to 50 acres, and production would increase to 10,000 cases.

HERON HILL VINEYARDS *Hammondsport, New York 1977* 30 acres planted in 1970 in the Finger Lakes district; a 5,000-

case winery completed in 1977. Its 2 vinifera, Chardonnay and Johannisberg Riesling, so far have ranked among New York's best. The dry-finished hybrids and native American varietals have also won awards.

HILLCREST VINEYARD *Roseburg, Oregon 1963* In the Umpqua Valley. One of the state's pioneers with vinifera plantings, beginning in 1961. Most of its current 6,000-case output consists of White Riesling, which represents two-thirds of its 20-acre total. Erratic quality to date.

HINZERLING VINEYARDS *Prosser, Washington 1971* Planted 17 acres in the Yakima Valley to vinifera in 1971 and 1972, and produced its first wines in 1976. It has since added 5 acres and is currently making 4,000 cases per year. During the first vintages it produced some attractive late harvest Gewurztraminer and Johannisberg Riesling bottlings. Its Chardonnays and Cabernets have not attracted as much attention.

Johannisberg Riesling: *Fruity, citrusy, medium sweet* ♥/✿

HONEYWOOD WINERY *Salem, Oregon 1934* The state's oldest operating winery offers a line of fruit and berry wines. It also makes Concord wines and added a White Riesling in 1979.

HUDSON VALLEY WINES *Highland, New York 1907* Old-timer turning out an array of generic wines, mostly sweet-finished, labrusca-flavored. It has 200 acres and is directing attention toward a hybrid varietal program, led by Foch and Chelois. Also sells about 5,000 cases of champagne.

HUMBUG WINERY *Umpqua Valley, Oregon 1978* Tiny (600-case) winery offering 3 vinifera varietals made from its 3-acre vineyard.

IMPERATOR The primary label used by a large (2.5 million-gallon capacity) company, Robin Fils & Cie, out of New York. Production of its inexpensive bottle-fermented champagne is close to 500,000 cases.

INNISKILLIN WINES *Niagara-on-the-Lake, Ontario, Canada 1975* This new winery, finished in 1979, is located on the Niagara peninsula. Built mostly underground, it can produce 40,000 cases today; 100,000 cases eventually. There are 50 acres planted to French hybrids and some vinifera varieties. Purchased grapes are used for blended wines. Foch is its most successful varietal wine.

JEFFERSON STATE (VALLEY VIEW VINEYARDS) A label used for varietals made from grapes grown at Mount Lassen Vineyards in California. Cabernet and Gewurztraminer have appeared to date.

JOHNSON ESTATE *Westfield, New York 1962* This winery offers a range of varietals and generics from French hybrids and native American grapes. Seyval Blanc and Chancellor Noir are the better hybrids; a Dry Delaware is the most popular wine. Production is over 10,000 cases per year. Vineyards total 135 acres located near Lake Erie.

JONICOLE VINEYARDS *Umpqua Valley, Oregon 1973* From its own 5-acre vineyard and purchased grapes, this small-scale (2,500-case) winery offers Cabernet Sauvignon and other vinifera varietals. The present facility was completed in time for the 1976 crush.

KNUDSEN-ERATH WINERY *Willamette Valley, Oregon 1967* Current production of 12,000 cases consists of several vinifera varietals, headed by Chardonnay, Pinot Noir, and White Riesling. About half of its production comes from the partners' 90-acre vineyards. Chardonnay is its most consistent wine. Plans call for experimenting with champagne.

Chardonnay: *Citrusy, subtle varietal and oak flavors, crisp* ♀/✿

LEELANAU WINE CELLARS *Traverse City, Michigan 1975* A modern, well-designed winery making fruit and berry wines and a growing line of hybrids and viniferas in the Grand Traverse region. It has about 20 acres of hybrids and 10 of vinifera, with plans for another 45 vinifera acres in a few years. First wines, from purchased hybrids and Washington State vinifera, were uneven in quality. Winery could grow to 40,000 cases annually.

LEONETTI CELLARS *Walla Walla, Washington 1977* A little (200-case) winery with 3 acres planted primarily to Cabernet Sauvignon.

MARKKO VINEYARD *Conneaut, Ohio 1968* From 10 acres planted in 1968, it makes a little over 1,000 cases annually. 2 varieties are offered—Chardonnay and Johannisberg Riesling—both in a dry style with some oak aging. The quality from this northeastern Ohio winery has been uneven. Cabernet will be added.

MAZZA VINEYARDS *North East, Pennsylvania 1972* Offering a line of hybrid and vinifera table wines, bottle-fermented champagnes, and a Catawba Rosé. Most of the 10,000-case output is made from purchased grapes. Also makes fruit and berry wines.

MEIER'S WINE CELLARS *Cincinnati, Ohio 1895* A large (2.5-million-gallon capacity) winery best known for its inexpensive champagnes and dessert wines. Close to 100,000 cases of Charmat champagne are produced, and port and sherry sales are close to that mark. Labrusca grapes are used for the line of table wines, but French hybrids are increasing in Meier's vineyards located on Isle St. George. Vinifera varieties were established in 1977. Best item remains the cream sherry.

MEREDYTH VINEYARD *Middleburg, Virginia 1975* A family-run, small (7,000-case) winery. Its 35-acre vineyard is planted predominantly to hybrids, led by Maréchal Foch and Seyval Blanc. From a test plot it made Virginia's first Johannisberg Riesling in 1978.

MOGEN DAVID WINES *Chicago, Illinois 1932* The largest producer of kosher, sweet Concord wines in the United States. It is owned by Coca-Cola of New York and has vineyards in several states; the largest acreage is in New York, where both French hybrids and vinifera varieties have been planted. A trio of Mogen David Light wines, blends of labrusca and California wines, has been added.

MON AMI CHAMPAGNE Used by Ohio's Catawba Island Wine Co. for its line of bottle-fermented champagnes. Makes around 5,000 cases of champagne from labrusca and French hybrid grapes. Average-quality reputation.

MONTBRAY WINE CELLARS *Westminster, Maryland 1966* After offering the first U.S. Seyval Blanc in 1966, this quality-minded, small (2,000-case) winery scored other firsts. It made Maryland's first Johannisberg Riesling, Chardonnay, and Cabernet and, in 1974, a rare ice wine. The 20 acres are mostly hybrids. Vinifera plantings are being increased.

MOUNT ELISE VINEYARDS *Bingen, Washington 1975* Formerly known as Bingen Wine Cellars, this winery has 24 acres of vinifera varieties planted on a mountainous site overlooking the Columbia River Gorge. Current production is close to 4,000 cases.

MOUNT HOPE WINERY *Cornwall, Pennsylvania 1980* A new small winery located on a historic 87-acre estate. 10 acres of French hybrids were planted in 1980. The initial 5 wines were produced off-site from purchased grapes.

MOUNT PLEASANT VINEYARDS *Augusta, Missouri 1968* A leader of the state's wine revival. Makes table wines from both French hybrids and American varieties. The best are the Seyval Blanc and a Missouri Riesling. 3 blended wines carry the *Emigre* proprietary name. Production is currently at 10,000 cases.

NEHALEM BAY WINE CO. *Nehalem, Oregon 1974* Using a converted cheese factory, the winery began by producing fruit and berry wines. Today, about half of the 4,000-case total consists of vinifera varietals. Virtually all of the wines are sold at the winery, located in the Tillamook cheese area.

NISSLEY VINEYARDS *Bainbridge, Pennsylvania 1976* Using a century-old barn as the winery, the owners produce close to 8,000 cases annually. Their 27 acres are planted to French hybrids. The best wines to date are the De Chaunac and Aurora.

OAK KNOLL WINERY *Willamette Valley, Oregon 1970* Known first for its numerous fruit and berry wines, it began making vinifera table wines in 1975. About 5,000 cases of vinifera varietals are produced each year, all from purchased grapes. It is still best known for fruit and berry wines.

OLIVER WINE CO. *Bloomington, Indiana 1972* One of the first small Indiana wineries, it now makes over 10,000 cases. The vineyards, planted to French hybrids, have been expanded to 40 acres. The biggest seller from the tasting room is a Camelot Mead.

PEACEFUL BEND VINEYARDS *Steelville, Missouri 1972* Tiny, family-run winery making small amounts of blended hybrid wines. Each is of good quality.

PENN-SHORE VINEYARDS *North East, Pennsylvania 1969* Most of the 20,000-case output consists of labrusca-flavored wines. New plantings in the 125-acre vineyards have been to Seyval Blanc, Chardonnay, and Johannisberg Riesling. It produces about 5,000 cases of champagnes and has recently offered a *méthode champenoise* Seyval Blanc. Catawba wines are Penn-Shore's best sellers.

PIEDMONT WINERY *Middleburg, Virginia 1978* 300 cases were made in 1978, including the state's first Chardonnay. Plans call for varietal vinifera and hybrids grown in a 15-acre vineyard. Near-term production will hit 2,000 cases.

PONZI VINEYARDS *Willamette Valley, Oregon 1970* From 10 acres of vinifera planted in 1970, it currently offers 4,000 cases per year. The most consistent quality has been with its White Riesling.

POSSUM TROT VINEYARDS *Unionville, Indiana 1978* Tiny (400-case) winery making French hybrid wines. 6 acres are planted to Foch and Ravat, both made as varietals.

PRESQUE ISLE WINE CELLARS *North East, Pennsylvania 1964* A small (2,000-case) winery whose founders were active in launching the state's wine industry. They have 20 acres, 16 of hybrids and 4 of vinifera, and have made small lots of palatable Chardonnay and Cabernet. The winery sells grapes and winemaking equipment to home winemakers.

PRESTON WINE CELLARS *Yakima Valley, Washington 1976* A quality-minded winery that is the second largest (30,000 cases) in the Pacific Northwest. It has 200 acres of vinifera varieties planted; 80% of the total consists of white grapes. Recently it has won awards for both Chardonnay and Fumé Blanc. Other major varietals include Chenin Blanc, Johannisberg Riesling, Merlot, and Muscat Blanc. The winery capacity today is 60,000 cases.

Chardonnay: *Fruity, balanced, firm, crisp* 🍷/❀
Fumé Blanc: *Spicy, floral, firm, some depth and oak* 🍷/❀

RENAULT WINERY *Egg Harbor City, New Jersey 1864* The state's oldest winery. With a storage capacity of 500,000 gallons, it offers a vast assortment of table wines, champagnes, and vermouth. The winery attracts thousands of tourists.

REUTER'S HILL VINEYARD *Willamette Valley, Oregon 1883* Historic site renamed by owners, who acquired the Charles Coury Vineyard in 1978. Erratic quality continued, however. Production is close to 12,000 cases, with Chardonnay, White Riesling, and Pinot Noir-Blanc emphasized. Ceased operation in 1980.

ROSATI WINERY *St. James, Missouri 1934* Offers 11 different wines consisting of Concord-based generics and a few French hybrid varietals. Uses Rosati for its transfer method champagne and Sparkling Burgundy; Ashby Vineyards for table wines. Annual 20,000-case output.

ST. JAMES WINERY *St. James, Missouri 1970* A new, relatively modern broad-line winery. The 22-acre vineyard is planted to native American varieties and French hybrids. Most popular wines are sweet generics and Pink Champagne. Production at 20,000 cases.

ST. JULIEN WINE CO. *Paw Paw, Michigan 1921* A large (1.5-million-gallon capacity) winery that offers a vast array of wines and attracts many tourists. The Charmat process champagnes, under the Chateau St. Julien label, are among the state's award winners. Table wines enjoying some success are those under the Friars trademark.

STE. CHAPELLE VINEYARDS *Caldwell, Idaho 1976* Located 25 miles northwest of Boise, this modern winery, completed in 1979, has a capacity of 50,000 cases. It currently makes 17,000 cases of vinifera varietals from its own 90-acre vineyard and from local growers. Close to half of its output is in Johannisberg Riesling, which has been of surprisingly good quality since the beginning. The other varietals offered have met with some success.

Johannisberg Riesling: *Flowery, fruity flavors, medium sweet* ♥/✿

SAKONNET VINEYARDS *Little Compton, Rhode Island 1975* From 35 acres planted to 12 varieties, the winery makes varietal hybrids and limited amounts of vinifera wines. Production is over 4,000 cases, half of its future maximum. Aurora and Vidal Blanc share honors as best wines.

SALISHAN VINEYARDS *La Center, Washington 1976* Its first 4 small crushes occurred elsewhere until the winery was built in 1980. Pinot Noir is the predominant vinifera grape in its 12-acre vineyard.

SOKOL BLOSSER VINEYARDS *Willamette Valley, Oregon 1977* Began by establishing a 40-acre vinifera vineyard in 1971 and crushed its first vintage in 1977. With a 25,000-case capacity its handsome winery is already Oregon's largest. 10 varietals are offered, but the major emphasis falls on Chardonnay, White Riesling, and Pinot Noir. Several of its first releases won awards in regional competition.

Sauvignon Blanc: *Grassy, refined fruity flavors, crisp* ♥/✿

STONE HILL WINE CO. *Hermann, Missouri 1965* The second largest U.S. winery in 1900. Now owns 40 acres planted mostly to native American grapes. The nonvintage generics and champagne rank among the state's best efforts. Production, including fruit and berry wines, is close to 9,000 cases.

SWISS VALLEY VINEYARDS *Vevay, Indiana 1974* Tiny (500-case) winery. Its 3 acres of French hybrids were sufficent to revive winemaking in historically important Switzerland County.

TABOR HILL VINEYARD *Buchanan, Michigan 1970* After experimenting with 45 varieties, the winery settled on several French hybrids, Johannisberg Riesling, and Chardonnay. Greatest success has been with white varietals—Seyval Blanc, Vidal Blanc, and Johannisberg Riesling—with the latter 2 occasionally made in a late harvest style. Baco Noir is the best red. Blended generics account for a large part of the 36,000-case output. New owners appeared in 1979 to steady a shaky financial situation created by overexpansion.

TAYLOR WINE CO. *Hammondsport, New York 1880* The seventh largest U.S. winery (33-million-gallon capacity). It was acquired in 1977 by Coca-Cola of Atlanta. Owns 1,200 acres in the Finger Lakes area, planted to hybrids and native American varieties. Best known for its inexpensive, bottle-fermented champagnes and its Lake Country blended table wines. Under the Taylor label the table wines are mostly sweet-finished generics.

TEDESCHI VINEYARD *Maui, Hawaii 1977* A 20-acre vineyard was planted primarily to Carnelian on the basis of successful trials. Since the first vinifera varietal will not appear until 1982, the winemaker is making a dry pineapple wine and plans a sparkling pineapple wine.

THOMPSON WINERY *Monee, Illinois 1964* From 30-acre vineyard it produces bottle-fermented champagnes sold under the Père Marquette and Père Hennepin labels. Production is just under 5,000 cases, including blended table wines.

TUALATIN VINEYARDS *Willamette Valley, Oregon 1973* The first few vintages offered were made from Washington- and Idaho-grown vinifera grapes, but the winery is now using grapes from its own 70-acre vineyard, established in 1973. Current production of 12,000 cases is about half of its projected maximum output. To date, most of the varietals have been early-maturing whites. The winery emphasizes both White Riesling and Gewurztraminer, which have varied widely in quality through 1979.

White Riesling: *Perfumed and spicy at best, medium sweet* ♥/✿
Muscat of Alexandria: *Fragrant, sometimes fresh, sometimes flat* ♥

VALLEY VIEW VINEYARDS *Jacksonville, Oregon 1976* Located in a historic gold mining region, this winery has 26 acres of vinifera. It crushed in its own facility in 1978, after its first 2 vintages were made elsewhere. Cabernet and Chardonnay are the dominant varieties; others are planted for experimental purposes. Current production is 6,000 cases.

VENDRAMINO VINEYARDS *Paw Paw, Michigan 1976* A supplier of home winemaking equipment planted 10 acres to French hybrids in 1973 and now makes about 2,000 cases annually. The best wines are the blended table wines—red and white. In the works are varietal Aurora and Seyval Blanc.

MANFRED VIERTHALER WINERY *Pierce, Washington 1976* Its 20 acres represent the only commercial vineyards in the Puget Sound area. First vintages were made from purchased grapes. When its vineyards mature, the winery plans to emphasize Johannisberg Riesling and Müller-Thurgau varietals. Quality to date has been spotty.

VILLA MEDEO VINEYARDS *Madison, Indiana 1974* Produces around 2,500 cases of blended hybrid table wines and native American varietals. The hybrids are grown in the winery's 11-acre vineyard.

WARNER VINEYARDS *Paw Paw, Michigan 1939* The state's biggest winery, having 2 facilities and a combined capacity of 3 million gallons. Among its large line the best items are the *solera*-aged sherries and ports and bottle-fermented champagnes. The table wines offered are ordinary at best. Recent experiments with vinifera varieties suggest future improvement is possible. The winery's 225-acre vineyard is planted mostly to French hybrids.

WHITE MOUNTAIN VINEYARDS *Laconia, New Hampshire 1969* 25 acres planted to cold-tolerant French hybrids. The early vintages were blended with California wines. The first home-grown varietal appeared in 1975. Capable of making about 10,000 cases annually.

WIDMER'S WINE CELLARS *Naples, New York 1888* This large (4-million-gallon capacity) winery in the Finger Lakes region is owned by the R. T. French Co. of mustard fame. Its large line of wines carry New York State and American appellations. The finest are the Solera Sherries, both the Pale Dry and Cream, and a Special Selection Port. Whereas most table wines are sweet-finished generics, Widmer has succeeded with both a dry Cayuga White and

Moore's Diamond. Charmat-process champagnes total close to 20,000 cases annually. Lake Niagara is used as a proprietary name on champagnes and generic table wines.

WIEDERKEHR WINE CELLARS *Altus, Arkansas 1880* Located in the northwestern part of the state, this large (1.8-million-gallon capacity) winery owns 575 acres of vineyards planted mainly to labrusca and French hybrids. It offers a wide range of table, dessert, and sparkling wines. Several popular table wines carry proprietary names, and its Dry Cocktail Sherry heads the dessert wine sales. Its ambitious efforts with vinifera varietals, notably Johannisberg Riesling and Chardonnay, have yet to produce wines beyond the neutral, simple level. Best known today for inexpensive champagnes.

THE WINERY RUSHING *Merigold, Mississippi 1977* The first "ole Miss" winery since Prohibition now has 30 acres planted to muscadine grapes. Grapes from North Carolina were used for first products—blended table wines. This modern winery has a capacity for 15,000 cases annually.

WOLLERSHEIM WINERY *Prairie du Sac, Wisconsin 1976* An old property, founded in 1857, was purchased in 1973. 20 acres were planted to French hybrids and a few to Chardonnay and Johannisberg Riesling. Vinifera grapes have experienced problems, but good wines have been made from Seyval Blanc and Foch.

Wine Language

ACETIC All wines contain acetic acid—vinegar. Usually the amount is quite small, being less than 0.06% and ranging as low as 0.03%. When table wines reach 0.07% or above, tasters begin to notice a sweet, slightly sour and vinegary smell and taste in the wine. Such wines are acetic and are also said to have ascescence. At low levels, ascescence often enhances the attractiveness of a well-made wine. At higher levels (over 0.10%), the acetic qualities can become the dominant character of the wine and are considered a major fault. A related substance, ethyl acetate, contributes the smell associated with the presence of acetic acid.

ACIDIC Describes wines whose total acid is so high that they taste tart or sour and have a sharp feel in the mouth.

ACIDITY Labels mentioning acidity express it in terms of total acid, a measure of the several most common acids. These are tartaric, malic, lactic, and citric. The acidity of balanced dry table wine falls in the range between 0.6% and 0.75% of the wine's volume. However, for sweet wines, 0.70% total acidity or less is considered low because the wine usually tastes flat or unbalanced. For balance, generally, the sweeter the wine, the higher the acidity should be. It is legal in California to correct deficient acidity by adding malic, tartaric, or citric acid to achieve a balanced wine.

AFTERTASTE The taste left in the mouth after the wine is swallowed. Both the character and the length of the aftertaste should be described. Finish is a related term.

ALCOHOL BY VOLUME Wineries are required by law to state the alcohol level on their labels—usually expressed as a numerical percentage of the volume. For table wines the law allows a 1.5% variation in either direction from the stated percentage as long as the alcohol does not exceed 14%. An alternative taken by a few producers is to describe the wine as a table wine or light wine, omitting the percentage notation. By definition, sherry ranges from 17%–20% alcohol by volume; other dessert wines fall into the 18–21% range.

ANGULAR The combination of hard, often tart-edged flavors and tactile impressions given by many young dry wines. Angular wines are the opposite of round, soft, or supple.

APERITIF A legal classification for wines having not less than 15% alcohol by volume; vermouth is the best example. However, current fashion also uses the term generically to describe any wine likely to be enjoyed before a meal, regardless of alcohol level.

APPLEY This term often carries additional modifiers. "Ripe apples" suggests a full, fruity, open smell characteristic of some Chardonnays. "Fresh apple" aromas are occasionally associated with Rieslings, whereas "green apple" aromas come from wines made from barely ripe or underripe grapes. And, should you encounter a wine with the aromas of "stale apples," you are probably smelling a flawed wine exhibiting the first stages of oxidation.

AROMA Traditionally defined as the smell that wine acquires from the grapes and from fermentation. Now, more commonly means the wine's smell, including changes that occurred in the bottle. One assesses the intensity of aroma and also describes its character with virtually any adjective that fits, ranging, for example, from appley to raisiny and from fresh to tired. Bouquet has a similar meaning in common usage.

ASCESCENCE The sweet and sour, sometimes vinegary smell and taste that, along with a sharp feeling in the mouth, mark the presence of acetic acid and ethyl acetate.

ASTRINGENT Many red wines and a few whites have a rough, harsh, puckery feel in the mouth, usually from tannin. When the harshness stands out, the wine is astringent. Tannic astringency is reduced with age, but sometimes a wine will fail to outlive the tannin.

AUSTERE Used to describe wines, usually dry, relatively hard, and high in acid, that lack depth and roundness. Young

Cabernet Sauvignon and Chardonnay are often austere when grown in cool climates or harvested early. Such wines may soften somewhat with age.

BALANCE A wine has balance when its elements are harmonious—no one part dominates. Acid balances against sweetness; fruit balances against oak and tannin; alcohol balances against acid and flavor. Wine not in balance may be acidic, cloying, flat, or harsh, among other things.

BARREL FERMENTED The practice of fermenting wine in small casks (usually 55-gallon oak barrels) instead of in large tanks. Advocates believe that it contributes better harmony between the oak and the wine and increases body. Its liabilities are that more labor is required and greater risks involved. It is being used increasingly with California Chardonnay and for a few of the dry Sauvignon Blancs, Pinot Blancs, and Chenin Blancs.

BERRYLIKE The expected aroma and taste of Zinfandel. Berrylike is equated with the ripe, sweet, fruity qualities of blackberries, raspberries, cranberries, and cherries. Other red grapes may also produce wines with berrylike character.

BIG A wine, either red or white, possessing rich, full flavors and fairly full body. Big red wines are usually tannic. Big whites often are high in alcohol and glycerine.

BITTER 1 of the 4 basic tastes (along with sour, salty, and sweet). Some grapes—notably Gewurztraminer and muscat—often have noticeable bitterness in their flavors. Another major source of bitterness is tannin. If the bitter quality dominates the wine's flavor or aftertaste, it is considered a fault. In sweet wines a trace of bitterness may complement the flavors and make the wine more enjoyable.

BODY The tactile impression of weight or fullness on the palate usually experienced from a combination of glycerine, alcohol, and sugar.

BOTRYTIS CINEREA A mold or fungus that attacks grapes under certain climatic conditions. Botrytis requires high humidity and/or some moisture. When it commences just before the grapes reach maturity, it causes them to shrivel, concentrating both sugar and acid. It is beneficial and highly desirable for some white varieties, especially Johannisberg Riesling. The resulting wines are uniquely aromatic and flavored, sweet and luscious, if the Botrytis is widespread.

Lacking official definition, wines said to have Botrytis vary both in flavor intensity and in sweetness.

BOTTLE FERMENTED Generally indicates the champagne was not produced by the bulk process. It could apply to either the *méthode champenoise* or the transfer process. However, since producers following the former method usually say so on their labels, champagne bearing this description is more likely made by the transfer method.

BOTTLED BY When it appears by itself without the "produced" or "made," the indication is that the named winery played a very minor role in the wine's production. The wine could have been purchased ready-made and simply bottled; or it could have been made under contract by another winery only to be transfered, aged, and then bottled by the designated producer.

BOUQUET Technically, that part of a wine's smell that develops after it is put in the bottle. Since most of the smell develops before bottling and bouquet comes mostly with years of cellar aging, the term aroma is almost always more appropriate when discussing a wine's smell.

BRAWNY Wines that are full of muscles and low on elegance. The term is used mainly for younger reds with high tannin and alcohol levels—thus referring both to body and to texture. Petite Sirahs with Napa, Sonoma, and Mendocino appellations are more likely than not to be brawny. Most reds from Amador are brawny.

BREED Used for the loveliest, most harmonious, and refined wines, those whose charms reach classical expectations of varietal character, balance, and structure. The term is usually reserved for wines from the best varieties and is rarely associated with common grapes like French Colombard or Ruby Cabernet.

BRIARY Like the thicket of thorns from which the wine term is derived, a briary wine gives a prickly, aggressive tactile impression on the palate not unlike flecks of black pepper. The term is most often applied to young, dry red wines with noticeable tannin and alcohol.

BRILLIANT The appearance of very clear wines: absolutely no visible suspended or particulate matter in evidence. Brilliant wines are often the product of heavy filtration, a process that may remove the flavor along with the solids. See also Clear, Unfiltered, Cloudy, and Hazy.

BRIX Name of a system used by American winemakers to measure the sugar content of grapes, must, and wine. On labels Brix normally refers to the degree of ripeness (meaning the sugar level at harvest) and occasionally is used to indicate the sugar in the finished wine. For most table wines the usual range at the harvest is 20° to 25° Brix. By multiplying the stated Brix at harvest by .55, one obtains the approximate alcohol by volume possible if the wine were fermented to dryness.

BROWNING The normal tints of young table wines contain no brown. Browning is a sure sign that wine is beginning to age. Wines with good depth and character can be quite enjoyable even though a good deal of browning shows. For lesser wines the onset of browning usually signals the downside of the hill.

BRUT An exclusive champagne modifier widely used to designate a relatively dry-finished wine, often the driest champagne made by the producer. In the absence of a legal definition, *brut* does not guarantee, however, that the champagne will be dry. Wineries in the United States use the term as they see fit.

BULK PROCESS A speedy, large-volume, and inexpensive method of making champagnes. The secondary fermentation that provides the bubbles takes place in a large, closed container, as opposed to a bottle. Wineries have the option of putting either "bulk process" or "Charmat" (a synonymous term) on their labels.

CANDYLIKE Modern technology enables winemakers to capture the perfumed fresh fruit aromas and flavors of the grape. This candylike fruitiness can be attractive in wines intended for early consumption, such as *nouveau*-style wines and slightly sweet whites and rosés. It is out of place in longer-aging reds and in the better white varieties.

CARBONIC MACERATION A technical procedure in which grapes are placed whole into a fermenter. Their weight breaks the skins, beginning an intracellular fermentation. The resulting wines (usually red) are intensely fruity, light-bodied, and meant for early consumption. Some wines labeled *"nouveau"* are made this way. Occasionally a winery may blend some carbonic maceration wine with conventionally fermented wine for added fruitiness and freshness.

CASK # Sometimes attached to very special wines; sometimes used as a gimmick. It is meant to imply that the wine spent its entire cellar life in one cask and that it was produced in small amounts. Neither condition need be met for the term to be used.

CELLARED BY Technically means the wine was not produced at the winery where it was bottled. Usually indicates that the wine was purchased from someone else and aged or cellar treated by the bottling winery, but there is no minimum time requirement for aging. This lack of precision makes "cellared by" highly suspect, even though it occasionally appears on wines that received long aging and personal attention from the bottling winery.

CHARMAT Same as the bulk process of champagne making. The second fermentation occurs in large tanks, not individual bottles. It is a large-volume method involving fewer hand procedures. Since the champagne can be made quickly and the costs are lower, it is the usual method for all inexpensive champagnes. Many wineries prefer this label term since it sounds better than "bulk process."

CHEWY Rich, heavy, tannic wines are said to be chewy because, figuratively, one could not swallow them without chewing first.

CITRUSY A wine with aroma and flavor constituents reminiscent of citrus fruits. Such wines need not be high in acid since citrusy refers to taste sensations that go beyond the basic qualities of sour, sweet, salty, and bitter. Many white wines from colder climates, especially Monterey County, have a citrusy quality that recalls grapefruit.

CLASSIC An overworked word that is meaningless in the context of a label.

CLONE A group of vines originating from a single, individual plant whose descendants are propagated asexually, usually by means of cuttings or grafts. A clone is selected for its special viticultural and wine merits (productivity, adaptability to particular growing conditions, and wine quality). Clonal selection studies have improved California Chardonnay and could lead to improved Pinot Noir.

CLOSED-IN Wines that are presently low in intensity, but high in concentrated, correct character, and that are expected to develop greater intensity with age.

CLOUDY An obvious lack of clarity in wines is undesirable. With the exception of old wines not decanted properly, cloudy wines are usually the result of winemaking error. They are caused by a variety of unwanted occurrences, such as protein instability, yeast spoilage, and refermentation in the bottle. Cloudy wines usually taste unpleasant.

CLOYING When the sweetness annoys by dominating flavors and aftertaste, a wine is said to be cloying. Such excessively sugary wines lack the balance provided by acid, alcohol, bitterness, or intense flavor.

COLD STABILIZATION A clarification technique involving lowering the temperature to 32° F. for 1 to 3 weeks. The cold encourages the tartrates and other insoluble solids to precipitate, rendering the wine clear. The tartrates cast by the wine are actually tasteless and harmless and are removed for appearance only.

COMPLEX A wine of beauty and balance harmoniously combining many aroma and flavor elements is considered complex. This is the elusive quality that separates a great wine from a very good one.

COOPERAGE Those who build wooden barrels are called coopers. In present usage cooperage refers to any container for holding or aging wine. Collectively, it covers containers of all sizes and of all materials, from oak to stainless steel.

CRACKLING A wine with less effervescence than champagne, but with sufficient amounts of carbon dioxide in solution to remain bubbly after being poured into glasses. If produced by the bulk process, the labels must so state. If the label reads only "crackling," its bubbles were likely added by artificial carbonation during bottling. Taxed at a lower rate than champagnes, crackling wines are normally low-priced.

CREAM Loosely used term for a style of sherry that is very sweet and is intended for enjoyment with desserts.

CROSS A grape created by mating 2 members of the same vine species. For example, the mating of 2 *Vitis vinifera* grapes, Cabernet Sauvignon and Carignane, produced Ruby Cabernet. Other notable crosses are Emerald Riesling, Flora, and Carnelian.

CRUSH Popularly used in the United States for the harvest season or the vintage. It also refers more specifically to the breaking (or crushing) of grape skins, which begins the winemaking process.

CUVÉE Commonly used in the United States to identify a specific batch or lot of wine (as in Cuvée 8). Seen on both champagnes and table wines as a substitute for a vintage date.

DECANTING Procedure by which wine is poured slowly and carefully from the bottle into another container before serving. The purpose is to leave the sediment behind. Many old red wines and a few young ones made with a minimum of clarification tend to throw a deposit or sediment in the bottle.

DELICATE Any wine of light to medium-light body and of lower-intensity flavors can be described as delicate. The term is usually, but not always, applied to attractive wines.

DEMI-SEC For reasons now forgotten, the language of champagne relating to sweetness is misleading when interpreted literally. Although this word means half-dry, *demi-sec* champagnes are usually slightly sweet to medium sweet. The term is occasionally applied also to still wines.

DEPTH A wine with flavors of good intensity that seem to fill the mouth from front to back. It is a characteristic that one should expect of most premium wines, save for youthful, lighter-bodied whites. See also Lingering.

DESSERT WINE A term with 2 meanings. The first is a legal classification of wines whose alcohol content is at least 17% by volume, but not higher than 24% by volume, and whose higher alcohol was obtained by adding either brandy or neutral spirits. Such wines are also known legally as fortified wines. The second use is general, covering sweet and very sweet wines of any alcohol level that are customarily enjoyed with dessert or by themselves after a meal.

DIRTY This term covers a multitude of vinous sins. All of the foul, rank smells that can show up in wine—from the musty cachet of unclean barrels to the cabbage and garlic odors of undesirable fermentation by-products—render a wine dirty.

DOSAGE In bottle-fermented champagne, the yeast sediment collected is eventually removed. Along with it a little wine is lost. To replace the wine and to adjust the sweetness level of the final product, winemakers add a dosage, usually a mixture of sweet syrup and wine.

DRY A wine with no perceptible taste of sugar in its makeup. Wines fermented to dryness have 0.2% residual sugar or less. Most wine tasters begin to perceive the presence of sugar at levels of 0.5% to 0.7%. For our purposes, we use

dry for any wine with residual sugar up to 0.5%. The term is used more loosely on wine labels.

DUMB   A young wine with undeveloped aromas and flavors is often called dumb because it seems unable to speak. Closed-in is a similar term. Both words are reserved for wines expected to improve.

EARTHY   Wine tasters use this term to cover characteristics that range from the pleasant, rich earthiness of loamy topsoil to the unpleasant, rotting-grass earthiness of the compost heap. Earth may be dirt, but an earthy wine is not necessarily dirty.

ELEGANT   Wines of grace, balance, and beauty are called elegant. The term is applied more often to white wines than to reds, although a few medium-bodied Cabernet Sauvignons of breed and complexity may also be called elegant.

ESSENCE   Used for a time by wineries to describe a late harvest, sweet red wine. It appeared on several Zinfandels made from grapes picked at 35° Brix or higher.

ESTATE BOTTLED   Once used by producers for those wines made from vineyards that they owned and could see from the winery. More recently, its definition has been stretched beyond recognition. Currently, no regulations govern its use in this country. The government has proposed to tighten its definition and restrict its application after 1983.

ETHYL ACETATE   The sweet, vinegary smell that often accompanies acetic acid is ethyl acetate. It exists to some degree in all wines and can complement other elements in the aroma and taste, especially those of sweet, rich wines. In most wines, however, noticeable ethyl acetate is considered a flaw.

EXTRA DRY   A common champagne term not to be taken literally. Most champagnes so labeled are sweet.

FAT   The combination of medium to full body and slightly low acid gives wine a fat impression on the palate. The wine feels and tastes a bit more obvious and often lacks a touch of elegance. In fuller-flavored wines the fat quality is highly prized by some tasters. A fat, oily Riesling would be less so, unless made in a late harvest style.

FERMENTATION   A complex chemical reaction by which yeasts through their enzymes transform the grapes' sugar into equal parts of alcohol and carbon dioxide. The process generates heat, so most winemakers control the temperature nowadays by circulating cooling agents within the jackets of their stainless steel fermentation tanks.

FIELD BLEND This was once a widespread practice in California. Vineyards were planted to several different varieties, and the grapes were harvested together to produce a single wine. Thus, the wine was blended in the field. A few such vineyards, mainly of red varieties, remain in California.

FIELD CRUSHING Generally used in concert with mechanical harvesters. The grapes are picked and immediately crushed in the vineyards or field, the fresh juice must being ultimately transfered to the winery for fermentation. The advantages are that the juice avoids oxidation and, since blanket of carbon dioxide surrounds it, the juice will no ferment too early. Still experimental and somewhat controversial with regard to wine quality.

FILTERED A mechanical process of removing yeast cells and other particles from wine after fermentation. Sometimes used before fermentation to clarify press juice. Most wines (except those labeled unfiltered) are filtered for both clarity and stability.

FINED Technique of clarifying wine by introducing various agents. The most common fining agents are bentonite (powdered clay) and gelatin; the most traditional is egg whites. Such agents precipitate to the bottom of the tank or barrel, carrying suspended particles with them.

FINISH The tactile and flavor impressions left in the mouth when wine is swallowed. The tactile sensations of the finish may be hot, harsh, tannic, smooth, or soft and lingering, short, or nonexistent.

FLAT Caused by lack of balance or lack of flavor. Flat means the absence of vigor and liveliness and is caused by very low acidity. Flat flavors are insipid or old.

FLOR A specific yeast that imbues *flor* or *fino* sherries from Spain with their unique aroma and flavor. This *flor* yeast (Saccharomyces fermentati) does not occur naturally in the United States or in other wine regions outside Spain. However, several Canadian and California researchers have developed a *flor* yeast culture that can be introduced to the would-be sherry and imparts a similar character. The technique is called the submerged *flor* or cultured *flor* process.

FLORAL (also Flowery) Literally the characteristic aromas of flowers. Floral is employed without modifier to describe pleasant, often delicate aromas found in white wines. In particular, Johannisberg Riesling often displays such attributes, as do Chenin Blanc, Muscat, and Gewurztraminer to a lesser degree. Very few red wines are floral.

FORTIFIED A wine whose alcohol content has been increased by the addition of brandy or neutral spirits. In the United States sherries are fortified to a minimum of 17% alcohol by volume; other fortified wines have an 18% alcohol minimum. Dessert wine is a synonymous term when used to describe a wine that has been fortified.

FOXY Poorly chosen word traditionally used to describe the unique musky and grapey characters of many native American labrusca varieties and many French-American hybrids.

FREE-RUN JUICE The juice that flows freely after the grape skins are crushed and before the stems and pulp are pressed for the remaining yield. About 60–70% of the total juice yield is free-run; it is generally smoother, less bitter, and less tannic than press wine. A few special bottling wines are fermented entirely from free-run. However, most winemakers choose to blend the two in some proportion.

FRESH The lively, youthful, uncomplicated qualities sought in lighter reds, rosés, and most whites. Such wines are usually fruity and clean and have ample acidity.

FRUITY The distinctive aroma and taste of fruit, found mostly in young wines. A fruity wine usually has intensity, freshness, and distinctive character; for example, it is berrylike, appley, or herbaceous. Young wines lacking fruitiness, especially whites, are often sweetened to fill the holes in their flavor profiles.

GASSY Said of table wines containing carbonation (gas) usually from unwanted fermentation in the bottle. The term spritzy also describes carbonation in wine, but does not carry the negative connotation of gassy.

GENERIC WINE Any wine whose name is part of a general category or type, as opposed both to varietal wines (which are derived from a grape variety such as Cabernet Sauvignon) and to specially coined proprietary names (Masson's Rubion, Phelps's Insignia). The best-known generic designations are those with European place-names (Burgundy, Chablis, Chianti, Champagne, and Rhine) as well as the type categories (Blanc de Blancs, Blanc de Noir, Claret, Rosé, Sherry, and Table Wine).

GLYCERINE This by-product of fermentation is found to some extent in all wines. It is most noticeable in higher-alcohol and late harvest wines, in which high levels of glycerine give the wine a slippery, smooth tactile impression and contribute fullness to the wine's body. Glycerine has a sweet taste on the tip of the tongue.

GRAPEFRUITY Cold-climate white wines often exhibit a distinct grapefruity character. Such wines also may contain floral qualities that blend nicely with the more citrusy grapefruit notes. The young white wines of Monterey County frequently possess this intriguing, fresh quality.

GRAPEY Simple flavors and aromas more like fresh table grapes than fine wine. Many of the native American varieties and French-American hybrids produce grapey wines.

GRASSY A light fresh grassiness can enhance some wines (especially Sauvignon Blanc). However, the more grassy a wine is, the more likely it is to be unappealing. In the extreme, grassiness can take over a wine and render it unattractive.

GREEN Wines made from unripe fruit have a green taste. The flavors are usually monochromatic, somewhat sour and angular, and often grassy. The color green (light tints in a straw/pale yellow color) is not unusual in many young white wines, especially Johannisberg Riesling, and does not necessarily signal a green wine.

GROWN, PRODUCED, AND BOTTLED BY Used by a few producers to declare explicitly that they performed all functions, from growing the grapes to bottling the wine. Much more precise and reliable than "estate bottled."

HARD Tactile firmness taken one step further by high acidity or tannin yields a hard wine. The quality is appropriate in young red wines suitable for aging and can also enhance dry white wines that are served with shellfish.

HARSH Highly astringent wines, often relatively high in alcohol, may give this nasty, rough tactile sensation. With age, some of the nastiness goes away, but the relevant question is whether the wine is worth the wait. Rough and hard are related terms.

HAZY Wines with moderate amounts of visible particulate matter. If you see a slight haze in wine, especially if it carries the words unfined or unfiltered, there is probably no cause for alarm. But if the wine is so hazy that the suspended matter causes it to lose clarity, it may be flawed.

HEARTY Generally used to describe the full, warm qualities found in red wines with high alcohol, especially those made in straightforward styles such as the heavier red jugs, some Zinfandel, and Petite Sirahs.

HERBACEOUS Literally, the taste and smells of herbs (undefined as to species). Herbaceous is often said to be a varietal character of Cabernet Sauvignon and, to a lesser extent, of Merlot and Sauvignon Blanc.

HOT Wines high in alcohol that tend to burn or prickle the palate and nose are called hot. This character is accepted in dessert offerings like port, sherry, and late harvest Zinfandel. It is noticeable but less appreciated in Cabernet Sauvignon and Chardonnay and actually undesirable in light, fruity wines like Johannisberg Riesling.

HYBRIDS Varieties developed by geneticists through crossing (and often recrossing) grapes from 2 or more different species. Full-scale efforts began in the search for resistance to the phylloxera disease. Grapes resulting from the cross-pollination experiments of vinifera with a native American variety became known as French hybrids or as French-American hybrids. Those hybrids presently cultivated in the United States were chosen for their ability to survive cold winters and to yield balanced wines in short growing seasons. Among the best known hybrids are Baco Noir, De Chaunac, Foch, Seyval Blanc, and Vidal Blanc.

JAMMY, JAMLIKE The combination of ripe, concentrated fruitiness and the natural grapey or berrylike character of certain red varieties yields wines that have jamlike aromas and flavors. Zinfandel from Amador County is frequently jammy.

JUG WINES Inexpensive wines generally sold in large containers. The term originates in the tradition of consumers' bringing their own containers, jug bottles, to wineries for their purchases. Most wines so described are generics, but a few varietals also appear in jug containers. Jug wine quality describes wines low in character and palatable at best.

LABRUSCA Shorthand for the native American grape species, *Vitis labrusca,* whose wines have a heavy, grapey character of the sort typified by Concord grape juice.

LATE HARVEST On labels, a signal that the wine was made from grapes picked at a higher Brix than normal. The term describes the condition of the fruit, not the calendar date. It is possible, though not requisite, that the high sugar levels were achieved through the influence of Botrytis cinerea. The general implication for late harvest white wines is that the wine is finished sweet to some degree; for red wines it means they may be either high in alcohol or finished sweet. Most late harvest wines are enjoyed after the main course as unfortified dessert wines.

LEAFY Some wines, including attractive wines, exhibit a slightly herbaceous, vegetative quality analogous to the smell of leaves. When a wine is leafy, it is not necessarily flawed and may actually be more interesting if the leafy quality adds a note of complexity.

LEES The sediment falling to the bottom of a wine container. When mentioned on labels, it usually refers to the sediment precipitated during fermentation, most of which consists of dead yeast cells. Wine is normally removed from the lees as soon as possible, since they often contribute inappropriate and unappealing odors and flavors.

LEMONY White wine with fairly high acid often takes on a lemony quality. Such wines are not necessarily tart or sour; the acid may be balanced by intense flavors or sweetness.

LIMITED BOTTLING In the absence of legal definition, this high-sounding phrase is used on bottlings that run the gamut from small lots of special wine to every drop of the designated wine that the producer has to offer.

LINGERING Both flavor and tactile impressions may remain in the mouth after the wine is swallowed. When the aftertaste or finish remains in the mouth for more than a few seconds, it is said to be lingering. One would hope that the character is also clean, balanced, and attractive.

LIVELY Wines that are fruity and fresh in character, usually with ample acidity, are called lively because of their vigor. Such wines may occasionally be spritzy and usually are relatively low in sweetness and alcohol. The term is applied more often to white wines, but sometimes to reds.

LOT # Used in several different ways. The most legitimate is to differentiate wines of the same type from the same vintage that were bottled at different times. It also can suggest that the wine is a blend of 2 or more different vintages or different growing regions. A very few use it to indicate that the same wine was aged in different kinds of barrels. However, the term has no legal definition and, therefore, means as little or as much as the winery wishes it to mean.

LUSH Wines with the soft, viscous tactile impression created by high levels of residual sugar (usually in the sweet and very sweet ranges) are called lush.

MADE AND BOTTLED BY Though sounding the same as "produced and bottled by," this term has an entirely different meaning. The only requirement is that the named producer fermented a minimum of 10% of the wine in the bottle. That is hardly an intimate personal involvement with the wine.

MADERIZED This term originates in the brownish color and slightly sweet, slightly appley, sometimes nutty character found in the wines of Madeira. However, it is not intended as a compliment when used in conjunction with table wines. Maderized wines have been exposed to air and have lost their freshness. Sherrified is a similar term, but oxidized is the most common synonym.

MALOLACTIC FERMENTATION A secondary fermentation occuring in some wines, this natural process converts malic acid into softer lactic acid and carbon dioxide, thus reducing the wine's total acidity. It is also accompanied by fairly unpleasant odors that blow off as the gas escapes into the air. If it is not complete before bottling, the gas and undesirable odors remain trapped in the wine, usually spoiling its appeal. Malolactic fermentation is said to add complexity as well as softness to red wines, but, with the exception of high-acid Chardonnay, is considered undesirable in whites.

MATCHSTICK An unpleasant smell coming from high levels of sulfur dioxide (widely used chemical preservative); similar to the smell of burnt matches. A cardboard or chemically grassy note often comes across as well. Fairly common in newly bottled white wines. It should dissipate with airing.

MEDIUM SWEET We use medium sweet to describe wines with residual sugar levels in the range of 1.5–2.9%. Such wines are perceptibly sweet to the taste, yet are not so sweet as to be limited to use with dessert. However, wines labeled medium sweet may be much sweeter than our range, because there is no industry agreement on how the term should be applied. See also Sweet.

MÉTHODE CHAMPENOISE The most labor-intensive and costly way to make champagne. Once the wine is placed in the bottle to begin its second fermentation, it never leaves that bottle until it is poured into a glass for drinking. When expertly done, the champagne achieves a persistent effervescence of extremely tiny bubbles. It is the only permitted method for all French champagnes. On U.S. labels, producers normally state that their wine was made by the *méthode champenoise* and often add "fermented in this bottle." If the label reads "fermented in the bottle" or "bottle fermented," chances are that the wines were made by the transfer process.

MOUNTAIN Labels carrying this term are often attached to wines of lowly jug wine quality. Most come from grapes grown in the flattest and hottest areas of California, where the mountains are seen only on clear days.

MOUTH-FILLING Wines with intense round flavors, often in combination with glycerine or slightly low acidity. They seem to have character and tactile presence everywhere in the mouth.

MUSCATTY The character of muscat grapes shows up from time to time in the wines of other varieties—most notably Flora and Gewurztraminer. (See Muscat Blanc for a more complete description of muscatty character.)

MUST The unfermented juice of grapes produced by crushing or pressing.

MUSTY A wine with dank, moldy, or mildewy smells, the result of being stored in improperly cleaned tanks and barrels, being made from moldy grapes, or victimized by a poor cork.

NATURAL A champagne term indicating that the wine is either totally dry or the driest made by the producer. Variants occasionally seen are *naturel, natur,* and *au naturel.* The term lacks strict definition.

NOSE The character of a wine ascertained through the olefactory senses is called its nose. This can also be called the aroma and includes the bouquet.

NOUVEAU A style of light, fruity, youthful red wine often presented as harbinger of the new vintage. In the United States some are produced by carbonic maceration, and others are simply bottled as soon as possible. *Nuevo* and *premier* are synonyms. All indicate a wine that is best when young.

NUTTY Table wines exposed to air will often take on a nutty smell similar to some sherries. The wine is usually oxidized and, thus, flawed.

OAKY Having aroma or taste elements contributed by the oak barrels or casks in which the wine was aged. Both vanillin, which comes from the oak itself, and toasty or roasted qualities, derived from the char contributed by the open flame used to heat the staves during barrel-making, are common characteristics of oaky wines.

OFF-DRY On our scale of describing and measuring sweetness in wine, we equate off-dry with slightly sweet and mean that the residual sugar in the wine is barely perceptible (0.6–1.4% residual sugar). In wine-labeling the term has no agreed-on definition and is used by wineries indiscriminately to indicate levels of sweetness from slight to overbearing. (See Sweet for a more complete discussion.)

OILY The fat, round, slightly slippery tactile impression on the palate created by the combination of high glycerine and slightly low acid. It is a characteristic found and enjoyed in many of the best Chardonnays and also in other big wines, as well as in sweet, late harvest wines.

OVERRIPE Grapes left on the vine beyond normal maturity develop a concentrated, often dried-out, sometimes raisiny character. Zinfandel can yield very attractive overripe tasting wines; Chardonnay and Cabernet are generally not enhanced by overripe qualities.

OXIDIZED Wine exposed too long to air takes on a brownish color, loses its freshness, and often begins to smell and taste like sherry or old apples. Oxidized wines are also called Maderized or sherrified.

PERFUMED The strong, usually sweet and floral aromas of some white wines, notably Johannisberg Riesling, Gewurztraminer, and Muscat.

PH A chemical measurement (hydrogen ions in solution) used by wineries—along with grape ripeness and acid levels—

as a possible determinant of grape and wine quality. pH in general affects a wine's color, taste, textural feel on the palate, and long-term stability. The desirable pH range for table wines is 2.9–3.5. For most dessert wines a range of 3.4–3.8 is normal.

PHYLLOXERA A vine disease brought about by tiny aphids or root lice that attack *Vitis vinifera* roots. It was widespread in both Europe and California during the late 19th century. Eventually, growers discovered a solution, which entailed grafting vinifera onto Native American root stocks that were naturally resistant to phylloxera. Most vines today are grafted, except in the new vineyards of California's Central and South coasts and the Pacific Northwest.

POMACE The mass of grape skins, seeds, and stems left after a wine has been pressed.

PONDEROUS Wines that are full in body and low in acid or tannin are ponderous. They have weight on the palate, but nothing to give them balance and structure.

POWERFUL Wines high in alcohol (and tannin for reds), often with big flavors, are said to have power. Brawny is a similar concept. The term is applied most often to red wines, but may also be useful to describe big, dry white wines.

PRESS WINE Juice extracted under pressure after pressing for white wines and after fermenting for reds. It is the opposite of free-run juice. Press wine has more flavor and aroma, deeper color, and often more tannins—all resulting from longer contact with grape skins. Wineries usually handle it separately and later blend all or part back into the free-run and bottle what is left under second labels, using generic or proprietary names; some may sell it off in bulk to other producers.

PRIVATE RESERVE This high-minded phrase may once have had meaning for special, long-aged wines. Lacking external regulation, it is now used inconsistently. It should apply to wines deemed worthy of special attention. Often it does, but not often enough to serve as a reliable guide.

PRODUCED AND BOTTLED BY Indicates that the named winery crushed, fermented, and bottled at least 75% of the wine in the bottle. Quite different from the similar-sounding "made and bottled by."

PROPRIETOR'S RESERVE A variant of "private reserve."

PRUNEY Very overripe, dried-out grapes give a pruney, pungent quality that is undesirable in fine wines.

PUCKERY Used to describe wines high in tannin, which tend to dry out the mouth and cause one's teeth and cheeks to feel as though they were stuck together.

RACKING The most traditional way of clarifying a wine: transfering it from one container to another, leaving the precipitated matter behind. This labor-intensive practice has been augmented (and often replaced) by filtration, fining, and centrifugation.

RAISINY Somewhat rich, almost caramel, concentrated, dried-grape taste. Some wines, such as Late Harvest Zinfandel and port, can be pleasant with a little raisiny character, but most other wines are not. Some wines made from Central Valley–grown grapes taste raisiny because the excessive heat of the area dries out the grapes even as they are ripening on the vine.

REFINED Said of wines that are in balance, have distinct varietal character, and are not brawny nor out of proportion. The term is almost always used in a highly favorable context with varieties that tend to be powerful.

REGIONS I–V A classification of grape-growing regions according to the amount of heat to which the vines are exposed during the growing season. Its basis is the "degree day" system, using 50° F. as the base line. (There is almost no shoot growth below 50° F.) The mean temperature above 50° F. each day during the period of vine growth is multiplied by the number of days in the period, giving the total of degree days.

Using the degree-day system California is divided into five climatic categories. Region I is the coolest (fewer than 2,500 degree days) and is comparable to European areas where Johannisberg Riesling and Gewurztraminer thrive. Region II is warmer (2,501–3,000 degree days) and is comparable to Bordeaux. Region III (3,001–3,500) is comparable to the Rhone region in France and to Tuscany in Italy. Region IV (3,501–4,000) compares with the Midi of France, and Region V (4,000+) experiences conditions comparable to Mediterranean growing areas.

RESIDUAL SUGAR A statement of the unfermented grape sugar in a finished wine expressed either as the percentage by volume or the percentage by weight. Thus, residual sugar either of 2.6% or of 2.6 gm/100 ml is exactly the same. Such information helps determine how the wine should be enjoyed and is most often found on sweet-finished white wines. For a detailed breakdown, see Sweet.

RICH Wines with generous, full, pleasant flavors, usually sweet and round in nature, are described as rich. In dry wines, richness may be supplied by high alcohol and glycerine, by complex flavors, and by vanilla, oaky character. Decidedly sweet wines are also described as rich when the sweetness is backed up by fruity, often ripe flavors.

RIPE The desirable elements within each grape's own special varietal character come out when the grapes reach optimum maturity in the vineyard. Ripe-tasting wine usually has round flavors, tends toward being rich, and is more sweetly fruity than other wines possessing the same levels of scientifically measurable sweetness.

ROTTEN EGG The smell of hydrogen sulfide (H_2S) in wine, a flaw that ranges from mildly bothersome at low levels to malevolent at very high levels.

ROUGH The grainy, somewhat puckery tactile sensation of young, tannic red wines. A related term, astringent, refers to more noticeable levels of harsh tannins.

ROUND Used to describe both flavors and tactile sensations. In both contexts, round connotes completeness, the absence of angularity or any dominating characteristic. Round flavors are balanced and tend toward richness and ripeness. On the palate, round wines usually are slightly low in acid, often have glycerine or residual sugar to fill in the angles or cover any roughness, and are low in tannin.

SEC Literally means dry. However, tradition is that a champagne labeled *sec* is either medium sweet or—more likely —sweet.

SELECT Implies that the wine has special qualities. Lacking legal definition and consistent application, it most often means nothing.

SELECT HARVEST Absolutely inconsistent usage and, therefore, meaningless.

SELECTED LATE HARVEST Seen on white wines, primarily Johannisberg Rieslings, but lacking consistent usage. A few producers use it to indicate that the grapes were riper and the wine finished sweeter than a late harvest style. However, the phrase has different meanings from winery to winery.

SHARP The slightly biting tactile sensation of excess acidity, or high acetic acid, and the accompanying bite in the taste.

SHERRIFIED When table wines are exposed to air over long periods, they become oxidized. One of the signs of oxidation is a nutty aroma and taste reminiscent of sherry. Maderized is a comparable term.

SIMPLE Wines with very straightforward character—immediately accessible with no nuances or complex notes. Most of the world's wines are simple when compared to the highly praised château and estate bottlings, yet can be delightful if clean, fruity, and fairly well balanced.

SLIGHTLY SWEET Most appropriately used to describe the levels of sweetness lying just above the threshold of perception (in the range of 0.6–1.4% sugar). Off-dry is a similar term. See Sweet.

SOFT Describes wines low in acid or tannin (sometimes both) that are, therefore, not firm and hard on the palate. Also, for wines with reduced alcohol levels and less of the consequent hot impact of higher alcohol.

SOLERA A blending system used for both sherries and ports. A *solera* consists of barrels stacked in tiers with the oldest wine on the bottom tier and the youngest on top. As wine is drawn from the oldest barrel for bottling, younger wine from each tier is moved forward a stage. The objective is to blend for uniformity and consistency. About 10 California wineries and several in New York and Michigan maintain *soleras*.

SOUR When wine is so high in acid that it is out of balance, it tastes sour or very tart.

SPICY Somewhat pungent, often attractive aromas and flavors suggestive of cloves, cinnamon, anise, caraway, and similar substances. The most typically spicy grape is Gewurztraminer; other varieties that may show lesser degrees of spiciness are Zinfandel and Chardonnay.

SPRITZY Wines with fairly modest degrees of pinpoint carbonation are described as spritzy. In slightly sweet and medium sweet white wines, a little spritz can give a lively impression that enhances the wine's balance. Most dry wines are not enhanced by spritziness.

STALE Wines that have lost their fresh, youthful qualities and have taken on dull, tired, sometimes stagnant qualities—often from being stored too long at the winery in large containers before bottling. Tanky is a related term.

STRUCTURE A wine's structure is determined by the interplay of those elements that create tactile impressions in the mouth: acid, tannin, glycerine, alcohol, body. It is a term that needs a modifier like firm, sturdy, or weak to be meaningful.

SUPPLE Used most often to describe the tactile impression of red wines possessing general amiability and underlying softness in spite of fairly firm structure, ample acid, and noticeable tannin. Young, hard wines are often allowed to age until they achieve more agreeable, supple qualities.

SWEET One of the 4 basic tastes perceived by the tongue, as opposed to the hundreds of flavors that we actually experience with our olefactory senses. The presence of sugar (or occasionally of glycerine) is required to taste sweetness, according to the wine scientist.

A few wine writers, ourselves included, have attempted to define sweetness levels in terms that can be applied consistently. The gradations of sweetness appearing in *Connoisseurs' Guide to California Wine* and adopted in this book are:

Less than 0.5% residual sugar	Dry
0.6–1.4% residual sugar	Slightly Sweet
1.5–2.9% residual sugar	Medium Sweet
3.0–5.9% residual sugar	Sweet
More than 5.9% residual sugar	Very Sweet

The scents of intense fruitiness, of ripe or overripe grapes, and of vanilla oakiness often seem to be sweet, especially when found in conjunction with each other. For that reason, when we use sweet to describe a wine's aroma, we add other descriptive terms to indicate the probable source of the sweet scents. The sweet taste of wine may be similarly modified when describing a nonsugary sweetness. Varying levels of acid, alcohol, and tannin and the inherent bitterness of some grape varieties balance against sugar and affect the level of sweetness that is perceived in wine.

TANKY The tired, somewhat dank qualities that show up in wines aged too long in large tanks.

TANNIN The puckery substance in red wines and a few whites is tannin. It is derived primarily from grape skins, grape seeds and stems, and the barrels in which wine is aged. Brawny, young red wines usually have substantial tannin that requires years of cellar aging to soften. Tannin serves as a natural preservative that helps the wine develop, but must be kept in balance with depth and potential. Excessively tannic wines can remain tannic long after the flavors have peaked. Tannin can dry out the aftertaste and can taste bitter if not kept in balance. Astringent is a related term.

TART The sharp taste of acidity in wine is described as tart or sour.

THIN Wines lacking body and depth are known as thin. Such wines tend to feel and taste watery. The French describe such wines as meager—a very apt word.

TIGHT Young wines with angular flavors and a hard tactile impression in the mouth. Closed-in and dumb are related terms.

TOPPING Winery practice of adding wine to barrels and tanks to replace what was lost by evaporation. It minimizes contact with air and, thus, oxidation.

TRANSFER PROCESS A modern method of making bottle-fermented champagne. At the end of its second fermentation, the wine is poured out of the bottle into pressurized tanks where it is filtered to remove the sediment prior to being rebottled. Such champagnes may be labeled "bottled fermented" or "transfer process," often accompanied by "fermented in the bottle."

UNDERRIPE When grapes fail to reach maturity on the vine, their wines usually lack round flavors and tactile impression. Typically, their varietal character remains undeveloped, they possess high acidity, and they display green flavors.

UNFILTERED Indicates that the wine achieved its state of clarification and stabilization without being filtered. However, this does not mean that other cellar treatments, such as fining, centrifugation, and cold-stabilization were necessarily also avoided.

UNFINED Seen on many Cabernets and Zinfandels to suggest the wine received minimal treatment. It means the wine was not fined, though it could well have been filtered or clarified by other methods.

VARIETAL A wine named after the predominant grape variety in its composition. Current regulations, enacted in the 1930s, require a wine to have only 51% of a given grape in its makeup to qualify as a varietal. This antiquated ruling is now under deserved attack, and in 1983 the limit will probably be raised to 75%. The varietal system took hold in California in the 1960s, and today most of the finest wines produced are varietals.

VARIETAL CHARACTER The unique combination of smells, tastes, and tactile impressions typically offered by a grape when ripened to maturity. The most highly prized wine grapes have distinctive and attractive varietal character. Lesser grapes have less distinct varietal character. And some grapes, including such familiar names as Green Hungarian and Grey Riesling, have virtually no uniquely identifiable character. In Zinfandel the berrylike taste is the typical varietal character; in Cabernet it is black currants; and in Chardonnay it is a round, oily texture and generous, round, fruity flavors. Breed is a related concept.

VEGETAL The smell and taste of some wines contain elements reminiscent of plants and vegetables. In Cabernet Sauvignon a small amount of this vegetal quality is said to be part of varietal character. However, when the vegetal element takes over the wine or when it shows up in wines in which it does not belong, those wines are considered to be flawed. Wine scientists have been able to identify the chemical constituent that makes wines smell like asparagus and bell peppers, but are not sure why it occurs more often in Central Coast vineyards than in others.

VERY SWEET In our system of differentiation, wines that possess 6.0% or more residual sugar are described as very sweet. Their obvious, inescapable sweetness leads generally to enjoyment with dessert or by themselves after the meal. Some of California's most exciting (and expensive) wines fall into this category, including late harvest Rieslings and Gewurztraminers.

VINOUS Literally meaning winelike, vinous is usually applied to dull wines lacking enough character to be described in more vivid terms. Vinous, and its noun, vinosity, are used with relatively clean wines.

VINTAGE DATE To give a wine a vintage date, the winery must have made at least 95% of the wine from grapes harvested in the stated calendar year. Such dates provide useful information about a wine's freshness or its aging requirements. However, a vintage-dated wine is not necessarily a "vintage" wine, even though most high-quality wines carry vintage dates.

VINTED BY A pleasant sounding but meaningless phrase that may be used on wine labels even when the named winery had no more involvement with the wine than purchasing it in bulk from another winery and bottling it upon arrival.

VITICULTURAL AREA A new concept intended to define and tighten appellations of origin for areas that are defined neither by the boundaries of a single state nor by a county or combination of counties. The key elements are specific boundaries, geographic features, and national recognition of the place-names. The regulations allow appellations currently in use to continue until January 1, 1981. At least 75% of the wine's volume must be derived from grapes grown within the designated region or county.

VITIS LABRUSCA A species of wild grape vine believed to be native to North America. Few of the grapes used to make wine are pure labrusca because most have been accidentally cross-pollinated with other species, including vinifera. All labrusca-type wines share, to varying degrees, a characteristic aroma and flavor traditionally and inexplicably described as foxy. This is another way of saying that they smell like Concord grape juice and have a strong grapey personality. The best-known wine varieties are Concord, Catawba, Delaware, and Niagara.

VITIS VINIFERA The species of grape vine responsible for the world's best wines. It probably originated in the Mediterranean basin and subsequently was cultivated throughout Europe. Today, the species is often referred to as the Old World or European vine. The vinifera (wine-bearer) family may have close to 5,000 members, but fewer than 100 are considered important as wine grapes. As a family, vinifera vines require sufficient heat to bring the grapes to ripeness and are not at all hardy to freezing winter spells. They are also vulnerable to numerous parasites and to many fungus diseases. Vinifera vines also interbreed easily and do not breed true when propagated from seeds.

Freezing winter temperatures have stymied their cultivation in many parts of the United States; high summer humidity encouraging various molds has eliminated their cultivation in many Southern states as well. With its mild, rainy winter and long, dry, warm summer,

California offers a climate generally favorable to vinifera vines. Parts of Washington, Oregon, Michigan, and New York and several mid-Atlantic states have also been successful in cultivating the European vine.

VOLATILE Aromas that come out of the glass aggressively, almost fiercely. They are usually caused by high levels of volatile acidity and alcohol or by chemical faults.

VOLATILE ACID The smell of ethyl acetate and the palate sharpness of acetic acid (they almost always occur simultaneously) is often referenced collectively as volatile acid or volatile acidity. Occasionally wine labels will tell the level of volatile acidity (VA) in the wine. In general, the lower, the better. The threshold at which most tasters notice VA in wine is just under 0.1%—more than most wines contain. The legal limit of volatile acidity is just over 0.1%.

WEIGHTY Wines with a heavy, full-bodied sense of presence on the palate.

WOODY The smell or taste of the wooden containers in which wines are aged—usually strongest for wines aged in new barrels. The aromas and flavors of some wines are substantially benefited by the extra dimension garnered from the wood. However, wines that stay too long in the barrel become excessively woody and lose their interest. Oaky is a closely related term.

Touring

A visit to California's wine country can begin anywhere within its borders, for virtually every large city is within range of some vintner. Flourishing vineyards dot the landscape in most parts of the state and encompass over 1,000 square miles—an area larger than the entire state of Rhode Island. Although some are more obvious about it than others, most premium wineries love to have visitors. In the continuing boom-and-bust history of the wine industry, they have never been able to take their customers for granted. In fact, you can probably count on your fingers the number of wineries complacent about their position in the market over the next couple of years. The tasting room, therefore, becomes a valuable means of promoting the winery's reputation and output.

Casual dress is appropriate for visiting wineries. In the North and Central Coast areas during summer, you can usually expect morning temperatures in the sixties and overcast skies until 10 or 11 a.m. The mid-afternoons are warm. Occasionally a summer hot spell will take temperatures over 100° for a few days, but that is unusual; and evenings are generally cool. The humidity stays low all year.

Spring and the fall harvest season are filled with beautiful days, some of them cool. In winter it is important to wear warm shoes (thick soles are best) because winery floors are often cold and damp. Rain is concentrated in the months between November and March, but an occasional shower

comes in April. From May through September, expect no
more than a freak rainstorm.

We have divided our discussion of touring into six main
segments by geography. This was done to facilitate a more
compact look at the options. If you live in San Jose and
have never visited a winery, you need look no further than
your doorstep. If you are in San Francisco, your choices are
wider, but some decisions must be made. Napa's concentration of well-known wineries is hard to top. But do not
overlook the charms of the Sonoma Valley if you want a
relaxing, easy day, and the Redwood Highway's winery
area approaches Napa in beauty and touring facilities. The
choices south of San Francisco, although fewer and farther
between, stretch all the way to Southern California. Each
of the areas has its own unique set of virtues, and it is up
to you to match them with your interests.

NAPA VALLEY Napa's five dozen establishments cover every
premium winemaking and marketing style and approach.
Full-line, million-gallon wineries exist side by side with
tiny "boutique" properties. Champagne makers share
the land with Burgundians and seekers of the "California Lafite." For every venerable Inglenook and Charles
Krug, there are two, three, four fledgling Clos du Vals,
Stag's Leaps, and Phelpses. Here are our impressions
of the pluses and minuses of Napa's major taste-and-tour
wineries.

Visiting the Major Wineries The comparative tastings
made by *Connoisseurs' Guide* often find Inglenook or
Krug, Mondavi or Beaulieu wines rating on a par with and
often surpassing the offerings from less-established vintners. Clearly, large size, diversity, and "Fortune 500" corporate ownership have not disqualified the major wineries
as producers of fine wines and as solid objects of interest
for visitors.

Beringer Vineyards Beringer's Rhine House is perhaps
the most impressive example of European architecture in
the wine country. Its richly decorative style and stained
glass make it an attraction in itself; a tour here is as much
for a view of the facilities as for a look at winemaking.

Inside the winery's limestone caves, beautifully crafted wood barrels date back to the earliest days of the Napa Valley's vinous history. At tour's end, in a wood-paneled room in the Rhine House, the tour group is allowed to sample several wines. Beringer presents an air of civility missing to some extent at other taste-and-tour wineries.

Beaulieu Vineyards The visitor center is something of a shrine to the grape. The magnificent vineyard photography lining the walls is in itself easily worth the stop. So, for that matter, is the fifteen-minute film-and-slide extravaganza devoted to the grape-growing side of winemaking. While you examine the photography or wait for a tour to begin, Beaulieu will quietly ply you with a glass or two of their wine choices for that day. Tours are quite informative, especially when combined with the movie.

Christian Brothers The Christian Brothers' St. Helena wine-aging facility (no winemaking here) is an alternative to visiting Beringer. Greystone, as it is called, also offers a glimpse of limestone caves. Their tour is lengthy, but not always as informative as we like. In addition, Brother Timothy's much heralded corkscrew collection is on display. The tasting portion is conducted at tour's end.

If you are looking for a ride off the valley floor, Christian Brothers also offers taste and tour at their winemaking facility, Mont La Salle. You will need a map to get there. In fact, getting there is the prime reason for taking the trip. The tour is informative and fairly comprehensive, but no more so than others in the valley.

Inglenook Vineyards The pleasures of dropping in at Inglenook are familiar to the frequent Napa Valley visitor. On a crowded Saturday afternoon, when cars line the highway bumper to bumper and the parking lots are filled at Mondavi, Christian Brothers, and Beringer, the scene at Inglenook retains a degree of calm.

The probable reason is that Inglenook tours rate among the least attractive in the Napa Valley. Winemaking activities are not carried out at the visitor facility, so the short walk-around becomes a history lesson and another look at cask and tank aging in a dark room. Nevertheless, the main Inglenook building, erected circa 1880, is worth seeing, and the intimate half-mile drive through the vineyards—from Highway 29 to Inglenook's front door—is pleasant enough.

You will not be disappointed by tastings at Inglenook. The setting is a museumlike gallery just inside the winery's main door, and tasting is available whether or not you take the tour.

Hanns Kornell One of Napa's three champagne-only houses. The plant, an old winery converted by proprietor Kornell in 1958 to his special purposes, is anything but spectacular. The tour, however, is of value not for the plant but for what goes on within it. Tour guides, sometimes members of the Kornell family, lead visitors through a step-by-step explanation of how the classic and expensive *méthode champenoise* champagnes are produced. On weekdays the whole dramatic disgorging process is on display. Tasting generally occurs at the end of the tour.

Charles Krug Winery Virtually across the street from Beringer and Christian Brothers, the Charles Krug Winery is another of the Napa Valley's historic sites. Krug offers a generally informative, comprehensive, and helpful tour much like those of Christian Brothers and Martini. The rambling length is required to explain Krug's methods and to show off the winemaking and storage facilities. Tasting is available at tour's end, although persistence may enable you to slip into the tasting room without going through the tour. However, tour groups have priority. Typically, three lower-priced wines are offered. Compared to Mondavi's ultramodern set-up (see below), a visit to Krug offers a view of a more traditional winemaking approach.

Louis M. Martini Winery This winery is as unpretentious as any in the valley. The plant, office, and visitor facilities are totally functional. So is the tour and the attitude toward visitors. If there is a saving grace about visiting Martini, it lies in the availability of wine to taste. All of its regular wines are poured at a long bar by generally knowledgeable hosts. The glasses are fairly small, to be sure, but interested, serious tasters can sample their way through a number of Martini wines. We frequently take a quick swing through the Martini tasting room when we are buying wines just to check their latest offerings. Incidentally, no other winery offers a broader and more reasonably priced collection of aged wines.

Robert Mondavi Winery We often suggest that first-time visitors to the Napa Valley take the Robert Mondavi tour. It is one of the few tours that starts with the vines. We find the tour informative, well planned, and able to present a good view of how a modern winery operates. The better guides at Mondavi can answer specific questions about the uses of the winery's sophisticated equipment. (Not all tour leaders here—or anywhere—are as knowledgeable as they might be.) Be sure to press your guide about Mondavi's choice of stainless steel versus wood fermentation and aging, about their use of the centrifuge to clarify some wines and not others, and about changes in styles of their wines.

Wine tasting at Mondavi, however, is *not* one of our favorite experiences. It is provided only at the end of a tour and is generally not available unless you take the tour. Your tour group is ushered into a cubicle of a room for the pouring of three wines. While you stand around elbow to elbow, the tour guide passes among the group, filling glasses and explaining the wine.

Still, if you want to see how a modern, full-line winery operates and to learn a little in the process, a stop at Mondavi rates very high.

Sterling Vineyards "Stark, monastic, and lonely" or "rich and alive"—it all depends on one's point of view. From our perspective, Sterling's rugged, starkly modernistic architecture is a thing of beauty made doubly exciting by the premium winery within its confines. It is almost a model winery. But, in our opinion, Sterling is a place to be visited only by those with a basic understanding of what winemaking is all about. (Tours at one or two other wineries should suffice as preparation.) At Sterling the walk-around is strictly a do-it-yourself operation, from viewing galleries with signboards explaining what is unfolding before you. Sterling's hilltop location is accessible only by tramway from the winery's valley-floor parking lot. A fee is charged —a practice that some find annoying. However, it restricts the visitor flow to manageable numbers, thereby making Sterling an excellent choice on those crowded summer and harvest weekends.

After Beringer . . . What? When you have had your fill of the bigger wineries, there are still 50 or more establishments in and around the valley. Some are more accessible than others, but each has its virtues for dyed-in-the-wool fans. A couple seem to bring us back frequently.

Sutter Home Winery This is a frequent stop on our travels. Its recent fame is based not on a Napa Valley wine, but on Amador County Zinfandel, now the major item in the Sutter Home line. On many weekends you may find winemaker Bob Trinchero or another family member pouring tastes behind the bar.

Pope Valley Winery If you want to try something different in a Napa Valley winery, venture off the valley floor to the Pope Valley Winery. It is a genuine, down-home treat. You will need a map to find it and a healthy respect for old-time winemaking. This is a winery in a barn with tasting on the premises. Pope Valley is in the beginning of a new era under owner-manager Jim Devitt, who is quite willing to talk about his plans, the unique problems and successes of his winery, and most other things vinous.

Franciscan Vineyards A spacious tasting room and a tour-optional attitude make this an inviting way to conclude a day in Napa Valley. Several wines are offered.

By Appointment Only Many of Napa's smaller establishments are working wineries with limited production operated by a very few people. They have no visitor centers, tour guides, audio-visual aids or oak-paneled, wall-to-wall-carpeted tasting rooms. When a visitor arrives and engages the attention of owner, winemaker, or cellarman (sometimes one person is all three), the actual operation of the winery stops. For that reason, most unannounced calls result in an "I'm sorry. We're in the middle of bottling (or pumping, fixing, cleaning, racking, filtering). I won't be able to see you."

The solution, of course, is a prearranged visit. The requirements are simple enough: an honest, knowledgeable interest in the small winery you care to visit. Familiarity with its wines, history, ownership, and objectives is also important. A letter to the winery is the first step. With luck, you will get a favorable response. After all, winery owners are just like everybody else: They enjoy meeting their friends. Among our favorites in this category are Chateau Montelena (the setting is beautiful), Rutherford Hill, Joseph Phelps (one of Napa's most elegant newer wineries), and Burgess Cellars (a lovely view of the valley from the hills above the Silverado Trail).

SONOMA VALLEY Sonoma Valley houses eleven wineries. Only one of these, Sebastiani, has achieved the general distribution and size of Napa's larger concerns. For this reason alone, a visit to the rustic Sonoma Valley is a much more relaxed, almost casual affair. The flow of visitors is smaller and the strings of tourist buses, so common in the Napa Valley, less bothersome.

Sebastiani Vineyards Sebastiani offers the only genuine taste-and-tour opportunity in the Sonoma Valley. Wood carvings are not new to the wine business, but no West Coast winery has so formidable a collection of new carvings as Sebastiani.

An outdoor perch for tour groups overlooks the grape-receiving area. The tours come and go, but true aficionados are welcome to stay on during harvest times to watch the winery weigh in and inspect ton after ton of freshly harvested grapes. Sebastiani is also a good tasting stop (no tour necessary), since their wood-paneled tasting room offers a fairly complete line to sample.

Buena Vista Winery An ideal alternate to Sebastiani from the standpoint of historic interest is Buena Vista Winery. Within its hoary walls, you can practically feel the presence of the fabled Agoston Haraszthy. The informal tour is, in fact, no tour at all, but a series of pictures and drawings attached to walls and barrels. They depict scenes going back some hundred years to the founding of Buena Vista by Haraszthy and of the California wine industry. We consider it one of the highlights for any visitor to the Sonoma Valley.

Buena Vista also possesses the most elaborate picnic

grounds in the wine country. Towering eucalyptus and formal plantings provide travelers with refreshing relief from the day's heat. Wine and sandwiches (from the Sonoma Cheese Co.) are on sale inside the winery's slightly dingy limestone-cave tasting room. Buena Vista's picnic grounds are well used even on weekdays, so we recommend an early arrival.

Hacienda Wine Cellars This is one of the most idyllic stops anywhere in the region and is rarely crowded. Lolling under the trees at Hacienda with a bottle of Claire de Lune Chardonnay suits perfectly our predilections for a day in the country. Just right for relaxing and feeling yourself a part of the wine country.

Grand Cru Vineyards A visit often brings you face to face with one of the principals, Al Ferrara, who runs the place, or with Bob Magnani, who makes the wine. The deck of their A-frame tasting facility and office sits on a knoll overlooking the valley. You can picnic there or retreat to the picnic tables under nearby trees when the sun gets too hot.

Kenwood Vineyards Up Highway 12 from Grand Cru is the inviting Kenwood winery. This is one of the wine country's most relaxed places. You can get all the conversation you would ever need and an opportunity to taste some of winemaker Bob Kozlowski's latest creations. Just drive up to the barn and walk inside: There is the winery and tasting room. Then, glass in hand, walk back out the door and enjoy the sun, vineyards, and tree-lined vistas. You will find most of the wines available for tasting, the tour nonexistent, and the people friendly.

Chateau St. Jean Not much further up the road is Chateau St. Jean, new and spectacularly successful. Tasting occurs in the stately villa that dominates the sloping hillside. The tasting room is tiny, and few of the top wines are poured. The grounds are attractive, and picnic tables are available.

NORTHERN SONOMA If you miss the Napa turnoff while heading north on Highway 101, do not despair. Simply continue another 40 miles to the Alexander, Dry Creek, and Russian River valleys. Many wineries there welcome visitors, and this includes one of the most visited of all California wineries, Italian Swiss Colony. Here also are four of the most handsome, visitor-oriented wineries in existence: Sonoma Vineyards, Simi Winery, Korbel, and Souverain.

Souverain Nestled into the hills near Highway 101, Souverain's stunning winery was inspired by old Sonoma County hop kilns. You will find it a rich architectural experience throughout. Besides architecture and marvelous scenic views, there is an art show, a restaurant, an elegant picnic site, and an informative winery tour. Adjacent to the dining room, a terrace surrounding a large fountain has been set aside for picnicking. No blanket-on-the-grass operation here. The winery provides chairs and tables and awnings. For picnics without hardships, this is your best choice.

Sonoma Vineyards The other spectacular, relatively new winery building in this area belongs to Sonoma Vineyards. In the midst of a cluster of purely functional buildings is a structure in the shape of a cross. Each of the four wings contains the various types of vessels used in winemaking. In the middle of the building is the heart of the operation, containing pumps and filters and centrifuges and all the apparatus of modern winemaking. Floating on a platform above all of this unromantic hardware is a tasting room comfortably provided with tables and chairs and viewing decks from which the winery's operations can be watched at your leisure. A formal tour is available.

Simi Winery This thoroughly modern winemaking operation is housed in a huge stone building of the historic Montepulciano Winery (parts of which date back to 1876). The tour is particularly informative. The guides have organized a master reference work containing all there is to know about Simi, and they are able to respond to most any question. Tasting is independent of touring, and most Simi wines are available to taste. A pleasant area has been set aside for picnicking.

Korbel Winery This winery receives a lot of visitors each year—for good reason. We have tagged along on the Korbel tour and regard it as the best place to see champagne making. Across from the winery, a nicely finished, one-story California ranch-style tasting room offers tastes of Korbel's wide range of wines.

Italian Swiss Colony It may not be historically accurate to say that Italian Swiss Colony was a tourist facility before it was a winery, but its many owners have always taken advantage of the area's substantial tourist traffic. This popular rest stop along Highway 101 sees close to 400,000 visitors each year. The grounds are well landscaped, and there is a large grassy area for picnicking. Visitors sometimes line up to take photographs of their children, whose smiling faces appear above boards painted with Swiss costumes. If this does not suit your taste, avoid this winery completely.

Dry Creek Vineyards You can meet the president of the winery, the winemaker, and the national sales director—simultaneously—by stopping at Dry Creek and introducing yourself to David Stare. Dry Creek Vineyards is the same kind of "bare basics" premium winemaking setup you can see only by appointment in the Napa Valley, but no appointment is needed here. The winery is surrounded by its own young grape vines. Most wines can be tasted.

MENDOCINO COUNTY Because Mendocino County is 120 miles from San Francisco, its wineries have not seen many visitors. Weibel is betting all this will change and has invested a considerable sum in a rather slick visitors' center—shaped like an upside-down champagne glass—at their new Ukiah winery.

Parducci Wine Cellars Capital has gone into equipment, a building for case goods and bottling, new vineyards, and a handsome new tasting room and giftshop. One of the pleasures we find in visiting this winery is in talking with John Parducci and Joe Montessori, who seem to share responsibility as winemakers.

Fetzer Vineyards An operation that began as a home-winemaking venture, Fetzer has now grown to a fairly large scale. Tours are by appointment only; tasting is available in nearby Hopland at the winery's sales room.

LIVERMORE VALLEY

Concannon Vineyards Concannon has recently catapulted itself into contemporary winemaking techniques through a large investment in new equipment. Yet the winery retains its homeyness. The tour proceeds from a discussion of how the family got into winemaking to an inspection of the vines; finally it leads past the bottling line to an informal tasting in the shipping area. Concannon is a fine blend of winery tradition and contemporary wine-making.

Wente Bros. This family-run operation is much larger than Concannon. Its tours, given only on weekdays, are a good opportunity to see contemporary winemaking techniques. The tasting room is independent of the tour and open daily. Most of the line is available. The winery is surrounded by 800 acres of vineyards.

CENTRAL COAST

Mirassou Vineyards Set alone in the eastern foothills of the Santa Clara Valley, Mirassou enjoys a country setting and is surrounded by new vineyards. The tasting room was converted from a concrete fermentation tank and a fire-place was added, so the room is cool on hot summer days and warmed by a real log fire in the winter. All of the regular line is available for tasting. Periodically the tasting room is used to test consumer response to new wines. Mirassou also gives a good tour.

Paul Masson Vineyards Paul Masson's modern pink and cream-colored facility in Saratoga can be visited only on weekdays and should be toured only if you can tolerate being processed like the thousands of bottles that are run through each of their multiple bottling lines. Since no wine is made at this plant, the tour's best feature is a demonstration of the transfer method of champagne mak-ing. The many wines of Paul Masson are also available for tasting.

Bargetto Winery This winery always seems like an anom-aly to us. It is in the town of Soquel, and there is not a sign of vine around. But Bargetto has achieved a particularly nice ambience in its tasting room. Just about everything is available for tasting. The tour is interesting and offers a unique opportunity to see fruit wine being made.

Ridge Vineyards Considering its limited visiting hours, the difficulty of reaching the site, and the lack of a tour, Ridge hardly appears to have a visitor's program. Open only on Saturdays for most of the year, this winery offers its fans the opportunity to talk with Dave Bennion or Paul Draper about winemaking and to pick up odd lots and limited-quantity wines that never reach retailers. The site is marvelous for a picnic.

Monterey Vineyard Nicely designed tours take visitors throughout the winery, an architecturally impressive structure in Gonzales. The guides will point out the many special touches that winemaker Dick Peterson has designed into the facility. Wine tasting is an integral part of the visit.

Firestone Vineyard Located on a bluff overlooking vineyards and mountains, this modern Santa Ynez Valley winery is well set up to welcome visitors. The compact, cathedral-like building allows an easy view of Firestone's equipment and winemaking. Tasting takes place in a gem of a room with views both inside and outside of the winery.

REFERENCES Many guide books and winery commentaries are available to help you get the most out of touring the wine country. In our opinion, the following are the most useful.

Sunset's California Wine Country This 9-by-12-inch softcover book from Sunset is the most widely distributed touring guide. Updated several times since its original publication, the work has recently undergone a total revision. It is the best general-purpose touring guide available.

Wines of America Leon Adams' excellent book is not a touring guide nor a substitute for one. It is highly recommended because Adams has assembled an authoritative biographical compendium of United States wineries, past and present. A thorough look at the pertinent chapters is a great primer for enhancing the pleasure of your trip before heading out to visit vintners.

Vintage Image Wine Tours At $5.95 each for editions on the Napa Valley, Sonoma-Mendocino, and the Central Coast, these books give generalized background information and specific touring guidance, including advice on restaurants, lodgings, and side attractions.

California's Wine Wonderland In 30 pages this free pamphlet provides basic maps and visiting information for most wineries in California. Write to the *Wine Institute*, 165 Post Street, San Francisco, California 94108. This is well worth the stamp.

Largest U.S. Wine Producers Offering Branded Table Wines

(In California, Except as Noted) Producers and Brands	Storage Capacity in Gallons (000s)
E. & J. GALLO Gallo, André, Paisano	253,000
HEUBLEIN Beaulieu, Inglenook, Colony	113,000
GUILD Cresta Blanca, Winemasters, Cribari	59,000
NATIONAL DISTILLERS Almadén, C. Le Franc, Le Domaine	39,800
COCA-COLA OF NEW YORK Franzia, Mogen David, Tribuno	39,700
LA MONT M. La Mont, Mtn. Gold, Mtn. Peak	36,000
COCA-COLA OF ATLANTA Sterling, Monterey, Taylor, Great Western	34,300
SIERRA Philip Posson Sherry	30,000
JFJ BRONCO JFJ Bronco, CC Vineyards	29,600
JOSEPH E. SEAGRAM Paul Masson	29,500
MONT LA SALLE Christian Brothers	29,500
A. PERELLI-MINETTI Perelli-Minetti, Guasti, Ambassador	20,000
CA GROWERS Setrakian, Growers, Le Blanc	19,200
DELICATO Delicato	16,000
GIUMARRA Giumarra, Breckenridge	12,500
BEATRICE FOODS Assumption Abbey, Brookside	8,000
ROBERT MONDAVI Robert Mondavi	7,300
SEBASTIANI, Sebastiani	6,000
EAST-SIDE Conti-Royale, Royal Host	5,900
R. J. FRENCH *New York* Widmer, Moussec	4,000
LODI Chateau Vin	3,700
NORTON SIMON San Martin	3,600
PAPAGNI Papagni, Yerba Buena	3,600
CHARLES KRUG Charles Krug, C. K. Mondavi	3,500
SONOMA Sonoma, Windsor, Tiburon	3,400
GOLD SEAL *New York* Gold Seal, Henri Marchant	3,000
WARNER *Michigan* Cask, Warner, Pol Pereaux	3,000
WENTE Wente Bros.	2,800
LOUIS MARTINI Louis Martini	2,600
CUCAMONGA CA Bonded Winery #1, Pierre Biane	2,500
MARTINI & PRATI Fountain Grove, Martini & Prati	2,500
PARAMOUNT DISTILLERS *Ohio* Meier's	2,500
NESTLÉ, INC. Beringer, Los Hermanos	2,500
J. SCHLITZ BREWING Geyser Peak, Summit	2,500
SOUVERAIN Souverain	2,400
MIRASSOU Mirassou	2,300
U.S. TOBACCO *Washington* Chateau Ste. Michelle	2,000
BARENGO Barengo	1,900
WEIBEL Weibel, Leland Stanford	1,800
WIEDERKEHR *Arkansas* Wiederkehr, Granata	1,800
ST. JULIAN *Michigan* Chateau St. Julian, Continental	1,500
SCOTTO FAMILY Villa Armando	1,400
MARKHAM Markham, Vinmark	1,300
FETZER Fetzer, Bel Arbres	1,200
VILLA BIANCHI Villa Bianchi	1,200
PARDUCCI Parducci	1,100
BRONTE *Michigan* Bronte, Jean Doreau, Award	1,000
FOPPIANO Foppiano	1,000
F. KORBEL Korbel	1,000

		Alameda	Amador	Mendocino	Monterey	Na
Barbera	1960	12	0	0	0	
	1980	14	5	22	153	
Cabernet Sauvignon	1960	4	0	0	0	4
	1980	39	49	926	4,242	5,4
Chardonnay	1960	95	0	40	6	
	1980	139	0	743	3,108	3,7
Chenin Blanc	1960	6	0	0	19	2
	1980	151	0	437	3,160	1,9
French Colombard	1960	75	0	219	0	3
	1980	66	0	1,068	505	4
Gamay Beaujolais	1960	26	0	1	0	
	1980	36	0	697	1,005	4
Gewurztraminer	1960	0	0	0	0	
	1980	7	0	216	979	5
Grey Riesling	1960	79	0	20	0	
	1980	354	0	174	647	3
Johannisberg Riesling	1960	20	0	0	0	
	1980	28	0	354	2,797	1,4
Merlot	1960	0	0	0	0	
	1980	2	6	104	673	7
Muscat Blanc	1960	6	6	0	0	
	1980	30	5	0	134	
Napa Gamay	1960	14	0	24	0	
	1980	71	0	111	1,089	1,1
Petite Sirah	1960	86	0	155	0	1,7
	1980	105	0	568	2,385	8
Pinot Blanc	1960	45	0	0	15	
	1980	75	0	32	975	
Pinot Noir	1960	29	0	17	3	
	1980	76	0	369	2,137	2,
Sauvignon Blanc	1960	67	0	23	0	2
	1980	159	37	322	1,129	1,2
Semillon	1960	550	0	2	0	2
	1980	298	1	18	644	
Sylvaner	1960	15	0	10	0	
	1980	58	0	26	676	
Zinfandel	1960	358	404	1,062	0	9
	1980	74	839	1,330	2,774	2,
All Other Grapes	1960	1,304	163	3,530	4	3,9
	1980	205	93	2,587	2,420	1,6
Totals	1960	2,791	573	5,103	47	9,
	1980	1,987	1,035	10,104	31,632	25,3

nia Vintages

chart summarizes information presented and
more detail on pages 23 through 29. The five
d are those whose aging characteristics and
ty levels vary the most according by vintage

| '68 | '69 | '70 | '71 | '7 |

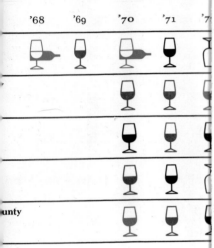

unty

Good to great year

Average to slightly
above average year

Below average year

Virtual loss

California (by County), 1960, 1980 (as of January 1)

San Benito	San Luis Obispo	Santa Barbara	Santa Clara	Sonoma	Central Valley	All Others	Totals
0	0	0	16	38	37	78	229
0	47	0	0	88	19,690	418	20,446
75	0	0	26	84	0	11	615
545	963	1,422	187	4,812	2,391	2,598	23,592
43	0	0	10	16	9	6	295
975	611	1,497	53	4,034	768	311	15,956
59	0	0	10	54	0	0	402
102	424	283	36	725	18,792	1,578	27,685
0	0	0	162	341	578	7	1,700
0	34	0	125	1,147	31,860	508	35,800
20	0	0	0	0	0	0	61
505	60	405	85	799	130	128	4,339
52	0	0	0	23	0	0	117
262	79	312	5	985	23	23	3,396
0	0	0	0	0	40	2	164
61	90	0	10	123	320	164	2,271
58	0	0	0	20	0	0	201
327	185	1,842	31	1,456	105	996	9,565
0	0	0	0	0	0	0	2
0	37	302	0	600	113	212	2,778
40	0	0	0	0	42	12	106
0	40	18	25	68	685	40	1,183
0	0	0	35	31	0	31	630
0	91	24	1	417	949	1,419	5,347
0	0	0	203	1,493	581	174	4,440
0	112	63	103	1,155	6,537	1,272	13,168
145	0	0	69	40	0	0	336
170	0	30	56	158	44	61	1,792
142	0	0	40	105	0	26	531
764	96	793	94	2,755	58	106	9,789
25	0	0	34	261	73	28	788
15	474	247	7	728	1,108	732	6,235
9	0	0	95	155	244	0	1,276
24	23	4	64	127	1,411	15	2,754
127	0	0	177	78	34	23	596
122	20	137	28	56	171	4	1,410
158	472	0	469	3,964	7,380	8,300	23,516
204	927	75	125	4,405	12,747	4,258	29,884
771	22	0	1,880	3,896	45,100	19,838	80,484
538	122	21	620	2,577	97,117	7,314	115,291
1,684	494	0	3,226	10,599	54,118	28,536	116,489
4,614	4,435	7,475	1,655	27,215	195,019	22,157	332,681

Shipments of California Wine to All Markets, 1938–1979

(In Thousands of Gallons by Types of Wine)

Year	Table Wines	Fortified Wines	Sparkling	Total
1938	16,299	38,591	89	54,979
1940	19,350	56,146	177	75,673
1945	20,537	59,821	552	80,910
1950	22,650	96,960	423	120,033
1955	26,440	90,770	789	118,000
1960	35,989	91,751	1,706	129,355
1961	38,639	94,270	1,931	143,840
1962	39,770	85,914	1,972	127,656
1963	43,820	88,323	2,151	134,294
1964	48,719	92,025	2,740	143,483
1965	52,657	87,461	3,216	143,334
1966	55,230	85,619	3,857	144,706
1967	61,590	82,603	4,779	148,972
1968	71,038	79,619	6,034	156,690
1969	87,581	75,900	8,906	172,386
1970	111,084	70,469	14,563	196,116
1971	138,043	70,938	16,694	225,657
1972	155,294	67,100	15,696	238,090
1973	164,338	63,273	15,010	242,622
1974	177,249	57,312	14,556	249,116
1975	197,173	59,915	15,439	272,527
1976	200,758	55,358	15,909	272,025
1977	216,162	53,655	17,954	287,771
1978	230,460	49,272	18,843	298,575
1979	250,892	43,397	19,881	314,170

Grape Production and Number of Bonded Wineries, by State

State	Tons Crushed (ooos)* 1969	Tons Crushed (ooos)* 1979	Bonded Wineries† 1969	Bonded Wineries† 1979
California	1,985	2,576	236	406
New York	118	162	41	48
Washington	68	102	12	15
Michigan	35	56	11	18
Pennsylvania	23	54	4	26
Ohio	8	12	27	40
Arkansas	10	8	10	10
North Carolina	2	4	4	4
Georgia/South Carolina	5	4	6	6
Missouri	4	4	17	20
Other States	1	1	64	136
Total United States	2,259	2,983	432	729

*Grapes crushed for all purposes. From 50% to 96% of the grapes crushed in Michigan, Pennsylvania, New York, and Washington are used for fruit juice and jelly, not for wine. †Bonded wineries in other states in 1978: Colorado 1; Connecticut 3; Florida 4; Hawaii 1; Idaho 2; Illinois 5; Iowa 14; Kentucky 2; Louisiana 1; Indiana 9; Maine 1; Maryland 7; Massachusetts 3; Minnesota 2; Mississippi 2; New Hampshire 1; New Jersey 15; New Mexico 4; Oklahoma 3; Oregon 31; Rhode Island 3; Texas 4; Vermont 1; Virginia 9; and Wisconsin 8.

Califor

This vintag
discussed i
wines cove
general qua
in Californi

**Cabernet
Sauvignon**

Chardonn

Pinot Noir

Zinfandel

**Amador C
Zinfandel**

California Vintages

This vintage chart summarizes information presented and discussed in detail on pages 23 through 29. The five wines covered are those whose aging characteristics and general quality levels vary the most according by vintage in California.

	'68	'69	'70	'71	'72
Cabernet Sauvignon					
Chardonnay					
Pinot Noir					
Zinfandel					
Amador County Zinfandel					

Good to great year

Average to slightly above average year

Below average year

Virtual loss